MasterLife Together

A DISCIPLESHIP EXPERIENCE FOR SMALL GROUPS

MATT & ALLISON WILLIS

Lifeway Press®
Brentwood, Tennessee

ISBN: 978-1-0877-7176-2
Item number: 005839199

Dewey decimal classification: 248.4
Subject heading: DISCIPLESHIP / DISCIPLESHIP TRAINING / CHRISTIAN LIFE

To order additional copies of this resource, write to Lifeway Resources Customer Service; 200 Powell Place, Suite 100; Brentwood, TN 37027; fax 615-251-5933; call toll free 800-458-2772; order online at *lifeway.com;* email *orderentry@lifeway.com.*

Printed in the United States of America

Adult Ministry Publishing • Lifeway Resources • 200 Powell Place, Suite 100 • Brentwood, TN 37027

Contents

ABOUT THE AUTHORS

Matt and Allison Willis met each other in college on an international mission trip. Serving the Lord together began their relationship and has continued to be its foundation and deepest joy for the last twenty years. They currently serve at Calvary Baptist Church in Winston-Salem, North Carolina, where Matt is the Associate Pastor of Missions and Evangelism. They previously served as International Mission Board missionaries for seven years in South Asia with their three children, who are now fourteen, thirteen, and eleven years old. Matt coauthored *Learning to Soar: How to Grow Through Transitions and Trials* (NavPress, 2009) with his granddad Avery Willis. Matt has a master's of divinity from Southwestern Baptist Theological Seminary. Allison authored a simplified version of *Be Transformed: Discovering Biblical Solutions to Life's Problems* (SCOPE Ministries International, 2016), which she helped translate into South Asian languages and used to train women overseas. Allison is a registered dietitian with a master's degree in dietetics and has also served as a nutrition counselor. Matt and Allison enjoy spending time outdoors, playing games, and laughing together.

PREFACE

The best resources are not created in a vacuum, but rather as a result of a practical need. This is how my granddad Avery Willis developed the curriculum that came to be known as *MasterLife* (Lifeway, 1980). He served as a missionary in Indonesia during an unprecedented time when two million people came to faith in Christ, and he needed a way to comprehensively disciple a multitude of new believers.

Although admittedly on smaller scale, this new content was birthed in a similar way. As we were discipling groups through *MasterLife*, we saw the need for a version more conducive to a new generation. Concurrently, we were reading the biography written about my granddad's life (*I Aim to Be That Man*, by Sherrie Willis Brown, 2018), which allowed us to be retroactively rediscipled by him.

This is what Granddad said in 1983 about his vision for *MasterLife*: "I'll tell you what I'm looking for. I'm looking for an army of two hundred thousand to three hundred thousand people who are ready to go anywhere, anytime, and do anything the Lord says to do—whether they're lay people or clergy—people who are disciples."

The Lord pressed upon our hearts that Granddad's vision was ours to steward. God showed us how He had been preparing us, even from childhood. We took a leap of faith and reached out to Lifeway. Every subsequent step was met with favor, not because of any merit of our own, but because God was the One who conceived the vision and carried it to completion.

Every day we wrote, we were on our knees begging Him to do the work. A jar of beans we got at my Grandmom's funeral sat on our desk as a reminder that God equips those He calls. God called Avery and Shirley to go to seminary, but they couldn't afford it. They went anyway. Poor church members gave him pounds of beans in lieu of money for preaching revival services. Every time Shirley was about to prepare them because they had nothing left to eat, God would provide something else through their ministry around town. They never had to eat the beans. Granddad kept them where he could see them for the rest of his life as a reminder of the faithfulness of God.

The Lord brought Granddad to heaven during our first term as missionaries, and Grandmom joined him in 2018. We will never forget Granddad's smile or how he managed to be both humble and fiercely competitive at the same time. And we will never forget Grandmom's fervor for Bible study and prayer or her love for the game "42."

In preparation for writing this content, the Lord led us to read through the Gospels again to explore the way Jesus followed His Father with His entire being—His spirit, soul (mind, will, emotions), and body—and how He did not go it alone. We came away more passionate than ever to make disciples who are all His together. We together crafted the outline and edited each other's writing, somehow managing to do it without marriage counseling! Matt was the primary writer for weeks 2, 10, and 11, and Allison was the primary writer for the rest of the weeks.

We echo Granddad's desire that this resource will catalyze wholehearted disciples who will go anywhere, anytime, and do anything the Lord says to do. And may the Lord find us faithful to do just that in our own lives for the rest of our days.

INTRODUCTION

My 10-inch candlestick would not stand up straight in its 1-inch holder. It kept leaning.

First I tried tape. Then I tried glue. I even tried chewed-up gum. All to no avail.

Finally, it dawned on me: the candle itself was my solution. All I needed to do was light it, hold it upside down over the holder's opening, let it drip a pool of melted wax inside, stick the candle back in, and voilà. My candle was securely straight.

All I needed was right there—I just didn't know it.

God's Word says He has given you everything you need for life and godliness (2 Peter 1:3). Do you ever wonder why it doesn't feel that way?

Does your relationship with God feel disconnected from the rest of your life—like it doesn't overlap with much of your daily reality? Do you love Jesus but find that much of your real life is untouched by Him as Master? Do you feel like God is contained in a compartment inside you, and its door is shut more often than it is open? Have you ever thought, "Is this all there is to the Christian life?" Do you desire to follow Him more fully but know that in reality you are just a part-time Christian? Do you ever feel like you were made for more?

What's missing in your life's puzzle? God says He hasn't withheld any of the pieces from you. Is it possible that you just haven't fit them together yet? Or could you be withholding from Him a piece of you?

We understand that feeling of unsettledness. Moving overseas to serve God in one of the toughest places in the world with our little kids stripped us to our core. And not all at once, but one painful layer at a time over the next seven years we lived there. Then God jolted us back to the States (or so it felt), and we were confronted with our own brokenness. Thus began an intimate healing journey with the Lord that informed this content and continues to this day.

More than a Bible study focused on knowing, this is a transformative discipleship journey focused on being and doing. If you fully engage in it, you will experience God and His people in a way you never have before.

Over the next twelve weeks, you will grasp who you really are and what you are made to do. You will discover what it looks like to follow Jesus with your whole spirit, soul, and body. You will explore the connection between your relationships and your mission. You will find anchors to keep you grounded in God's love. And you will learn rhythms to keep your walk with Him fresh.

More than anything you can do for God, He just wants you—*all* of you. This discipleship experience is your invitation.

GETTING STARTED

FINDING A GROUP

This discipleship experience was created for seekers and/or believers to experience together as a small group. If you have purchased this workbook individually and do not have a group, contact someone at your church or another local church to see if you can start a new group or join an existing one. While individuals can benefit from going through this workbook alone, the experience will be much more transformative if done with a small group as it was designed.

FINDING A RHYTHM

You can expect to spend fifteen to thirty minutes each day, five days a week, investing in this experience. Optional day 6 and 7 passages are provided in case you are already in the habit of meeting with God every day, or would like to begin this habit (which we highly recommend!). The foundation of this discipleship experience involves you spending time with God reflectively in His Word—so you will need a Bible and a journal or notebook in addition to this workbook. We encourage you to have a designated space to have your conversation with the Lord—which we describe in the next section. If possible, have this conversation with Him in the morning. Most of us need a dose of caffeine each morning to get our bodies going. How much more do we need to hear from God every morning before we engage with anyone or anything else?

DAILY CONVERSATIONS WITH GOD

In your journal or notebook, draw a vertical line down the middle of the page, forming two columns. Write *God* at the top of the left column, and *Me* at the top of the right column. Write the date at the left side, along with the passage that you will find at the top of each day's lesson. See the example to the right.

Begin each day by reading the assigned passage (listed at the top of the page under the title of each day). Write what God says to you from His Word in the left column, and then write your response to what He says (in essence, your prayer to Him) in the right column. If you aren't sure what He is saying to you, don't worry—listening to His voice gets easier with practice. Just write something you learned or that stood out to you from the passage, noting the verse number.

GOD	ME
10/1 Luke 5	
v.10 – Don't be afraid. I want to bring other people to Me through your life.	*I will follow You and learn how I can grow as Your witness.*
10/2 Luke 6	
v.12 – When will you spend an hour or more with Me in prayer?	*Lord, I will gladly spend an hour with You in prayer this Saturday.*

READING & EXERCISES

After having your daily conversation with God, read the day's content and complete the questions and/or experiences included. One of the experiences you will have each week is memorizing God's Word. For your convenience, verse cards that can be cut out are included at the back of this workbook. At the end of this discipleship experience, you will have memorized twelve verses that will help you follow Jesus more closely.

GROUP SESSIONS

You will meet with your group each week for about one and a half hours to discuss the lesson you completed individually the week prior. You will need to bring this workbook and your journal or notebook to group sessions. The format of group sessions will be the same each week and will include prayer, reviewing the verse you memorized, sharing highlights from your conversations with God, discussing the questions you answered throughout the week, and sharing how you plan to apply what you've learned. You will also preview the next week's lesson together.

Section One

YOUR RELATIONSHIP WITH GOD

Week One

BEING ALL HIS

"Love the Lord your God with all your heart and with all your soul and with all your mind and with all your strength."

MARK 12:30

In this very moment, the God who created you is actively loving you. You are not simply a human being. You are a human being loved by God. His love for you has nothing to do with what you have or haven't done. God is loving you right now because of who He is. God is love (1 John 4:16).

God created you to experience His love and belong to Him. Scripture teaches that you are His masterpiece (Ephesians 2:10). He has engraved you on the palms of His hands (Isaiah 49:16). Your life matters because you matter to the Master.

God's immeasurable love for you is the truest thing about you. You are fully known and fully loved by God. This is your true identity. Satan will relentlessly attack it, just as he first attacked Jesus's identity after He spent forty days in the wilderness. Satan repeatedly said, "If you are the Son of God" prove your identity by doing: Make the stones bread. Throw yourself down. Bow down to me (see Matthew 4:1-11).

Satan will likewise tempt you to prove your identity by what you do for God. He will convince you that you must achieve the relationship you've already received. Jesus didn't give in to the temptation to prove Himself. He rebuked Satan with truth from God's Word and commanded him to flee. Jesus wants you to mimic Him by rooting your identity in the love of God. Only these roots will lead to abundant life in Him.

God's love for you steadily flows and He desires that you soak it up as a personal, experiential reality every single day. The abundance of His love allows you to further love and accept yourself. You are only able to love the Lord with all your heart, soul, mind, and strength and love your neighbor as yourself (Mark 12:30,31b) because God first loved you (1 John 4:19).

The quality of the love you give God directly relates to the quantity of love you've received from Him.

God's love is the foundation of the gospel, so it must be the foundation of your relationship with Him. God's love needs to be received and basked in regularly. The quality of your obedience and the extent of your surrender to Him depend on it.

It is possible to halfheartedly follow God and not love Him. But be assured that you can't truly love Him and not follow Him.

If you're like me, being loved can feel uncomfortable and vulnerable. I am better at giving love than receiving it. But God took the initiative and first loved us, so you and I must receive His love empty-handed, over and over again.

Everything you have you received from God, so what can you even give Him that He doesn't already have? The answer is both simple and radical: all of you. He doesn't want your acts of service, your money, or your time as much as He wants you. All of you—your heart, soul, mind, and strength, as the verse you will memorize this week highlights.

Each week of this journey, you will look at one aspect of the diagram to the right, which will help you conceptualize what it is to be all His. Get ready to explore the God who created you and to figure out how to be an all-in, fully alive participant in His unfolding story.

PRAYER

Father, I thank You for loving me even in this very moment. This week, show me all the ways You are actively pursuing me with Your love. Lord, drive out my fear, and give me the desire to belong fully to You. Show me how to surrender my whole being to You, and give my group and me the courage to do so as we journey together. In Jesus's name, amen.

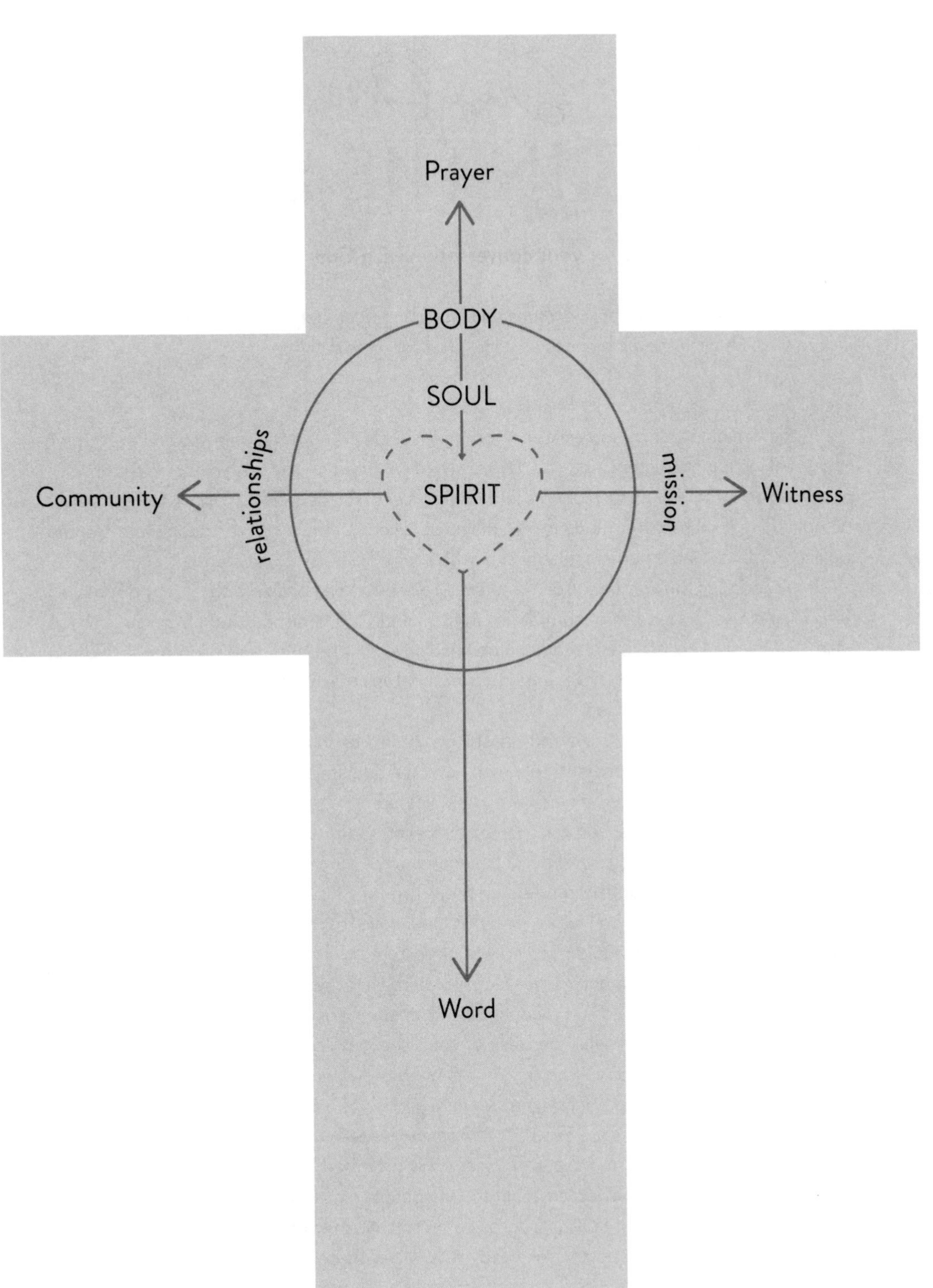
Prayer
BODY
SOUL
SPIRIT
relationships
Community
mission
Witness
Word

Day One
BEING IN HIS STORY

Today's passage for your conversation with God: Romans 11:33-36

Begin today by reading the above passage and journaling what God says to you and what you say back to God. Refer to the instructions on pages 8-9 for more details.

Like all good stories, God's story begins at the beginning.

In the beginning, only God existed. Nothing else. He created the universe and everything in by speaking it into existence day by day for five days. Then on the sixth day of creation God made man and woman and fashioned them "in His likeness" (Genesis 1:26). Human beings are the only thing God has ever made in His image and likeness. He loved the people He created and lived in peace and a perfect relationship with them in a beautiful garden.

Life continued this way until Adam and Eve broke their relationship with God by disobeying Him. Their sin separated them from their Creator, and God banished them from the garden. Adam and Eve had children, and their children had children who later had children—all of these children and all people since have shared a sinful nature that turns their hearts toward their own desires and away from God.

But God's love never ceased and He still desired to be in a relationship with the people He created. So He made a promise to a man named Abraham to give him many descendants through which all the peoples on earth would be blessed.

Abraham believed God, and because of his belief, God restored their relationship. God kept His promise to Abraham, and his descendants were numerous. Some of them followed God, but most of them wanted to rule over their own lives just like Adam and Eve had done. They did evil and suffered its consequences. But God's love for them never stopped, so He sent spokesmen to tell the people He made how to be restored to Him.

One spokesman was named Isaiah. He told them that their evil was sin against God but God would send them a Savior who would take all of their sins on Himself. Isaiah taught this Savior would be beaten and killed because of their sins but promised them that God would raise Him back to life. Through the Savior, Abraham's descendants could be restored to a relationship with God. After hearing this message, Abraham's people began expectantly waiting for this promised Savior—and they waited and waited.

God kept His promise. Years later, He sent this promised Savior—His Son, Jesus. Many people did not recognize who Jesus was, but many people did. Jesus traveled around teaching and performing miracles and healings. Jesus came so that they could have everlasting peace with God. While some believed and followed, many violently opposed Him and convinced the government to have Him executed. Just as God had said through Isaiah, Jesus was beaten and killed—He was broken to end brokenness for all who follow Him. Three days later, God raised Him back to life in victory over sin and death!

Jesus appeared to His followers, proving that He was alive again, and gave them a mission. "But you will receive power when the Holy Spirit comes on you; and you will be my witnesses . . . to the ends of the earth," Jesus said (Acts 1:8). He sent His followers into the world to make disciples of all nations, baptizing them in the name of the Father and of the Son and of the Holy Spirit, and teaching them to obey everything He had commanded them.

The day finally came when Jesus returned to heaven. He ascended into the clouds as His disciples watched. Two angels appeared and told them Jesus would one day come back the same way He left.

From that moment on, Jesus's followers began expectantly waiting for Him to return as they went about the work He had entrusted to them—being His witnesses and making disciples to the ends of earth. The disciples made disciples, and their disciples made disciples who later made more disciples. One day, one of them witnessed to you. You were chosen by a God who loves you and given the same mission as all the disciples who came before.

And this takes us right up to the present moment in His story. Seems like a good spot to pause.

How have the experiences of your life led you to participate in God's love story? Write your thoughts and feelings below.

Spend a few minutes speaking to God and asking Him to show you the specfic ways He wants you to be involved in His story. Record your thoughts below.

Today's passage summarizes some truths about God and His story. Fill in the blanks for Romans 11:36:

"For ______Him and ________Him and ______ Him are all things."

Practice this week's memory verse by saying it and/or writing it a few times:

"Love the Lord your God with all your heart and with all your soul and with all your mind and with all your strength."

MARK 12:30

Day Two
GOD'S BEING

Today's passage for your conversation with God: Colossians 1:15-23

Read the above passage, then journal your conversation with God. Continue this pattern each day throughout this discipleship experience.

The Author of history is a God whose love you can trust.

Jesus was with God in the beginning (John 1). This is clear in Genesis 1:26 where God said, "Let *us* make man in *our* image, in *our* likeness" (italics mine). In His very being, God the Father exists in a supernatural three-in-one relationship with Jesus and the Holy Spirit (Matthew 3:16-17). This relationship is known as the Trinity and is inherent to God's being. Since before time began God has been in relationship with Himself. And since you were created to reflect God's image, you were created to be a part of this eternal relationship with God.

Love is also essential to God's being. In fact, the Bible tells us that God Himself is love (1 John 4:16). The relationship in the Trinity is a loving relationship. God loves and delights in Jesus (Isaiah 42:1). It shouldn't come as a surprise that God created you to experience His love and delight.

You saw in today's passage that Jesus is the exact likeness of the unseen God—the visible representation of the invisible. The fullness of the Deity lives in bodily form in Jesus (Colossians 2:9), who said, "I and the Father are one" (John 10:30). Jesus is fully human and fully God, and Jesus saw God as Father and taught His disciples to as well. Jesus and the Father have eternally existed in a perfect relationship.

The word *father* can evoke a wide range of emotions. The ones you feel are probably rooted in your relationship with your earthly father. Earthly fathers can be attentive and affectionate or they can be aloof, accusing, or even abusive. Even the best earthly fathers are far from perfect.

Describe who your earthly father is/was to you.

Envision the most wonderful earthly father you can imagine. Describe him here.

No matter what kind of earthly father you have had, your heavenly Father wants to refine or redeem your experience of father. David tells us a lot about our Father God in Psalm 103: He is compassionate, gracious, righteous, and sovereign. He heals, redeems, satisfies, renews, and forgives. He is full of loving-kindness.

You can better understand the character and heart of your Father God by studying the life of Jesus, who said, "The one who has seen me has seen the Father" (John 14:9). You can best see Jesus through reading the Gospels—Matthew, Mark, Luke, and John—where you will hear the most important words Jesus spoke and discover the most important events in His life. But don't miss out on the richness of what's written between the lines. Notice His nature, His being—His personality, His emotions, His desires. The way He pursues conversation and relationships. The way He spends His time. There is much more to a person than what he or she says and does, and Jesus is no exception.

Jesus has a body, soul, and spirit just like you do. In Luke 2:52, you read that as a child, Jesus "grew in wisdom [soul] and stature [body], and in favor with God [spirit] and man." Before going to the cross, Jesus told His closest friends, "My soul is overwhelmed with sorrow to the point of death" (Matthew 26:38). Before His death, you can again see these distinct parts of His being as He says from His soul, "It is finished," and then bowed His head (body) and gave up His spirit (John 19:30).

Jesus gave His spirit, soul, and body to His Father (Luke 23:46). But He didn't stop there. Jesus entrusted and released His earthly relationships to God. In His last recorded prayer, Jesus told His Father, "I have brought you glory on earth by finishing the work you gave me to do" (John 17:4). The task God entrusted to Jesus became His mission.

Jesus fully gave His spirit, soul, body, relationships, and mission to glorify His Father. He desires that you do the same.

Practice this week's memory verse by saying it and/or writing it a few times:

"Love the Lord your God with all your heart and with all your soul and with all your mind and with all your strength."
MARK 12:30

Day Three
RECEIVING GOD

Today's passage for your conversation with God: John 13:3-17

The God who created you by and for His love has a gift for you—He is reaching out to give you Himself. The catch is that to accept the gift, you have to receive all of it. It's all or nothing. God is a generous giver, but you cannot pick and choose the parts of Him you want. God is a whole package; He does not come with options.

Until you receive life, you are spiritually dead because of sin. Your sinful nature has made you dead on arrival, and you need to be brought back to life. Simply put, sin is anything in you that misses the mark of His perfection. Because of Adam and Eve's original sin and the curse it brought, you've needed a new spirit from the time of your conception. Jesus died on a cross to pay the price for your sin. In His resurrection, Jesus offers you the chance to become a new creation through His Holy Spirit living inside of you (2 Corinthians 5:17).

Receiving life from God is what the Bible calls salvation, but salvation is more than just a thing—it's a Person.

Jesus stands before you with His arms stretched wide, but you have to actively receive Him. In fact, you were made to receive. Like a newborn whose needs are met through its parents care, God's love must similarly be received. But as you grow older, receiving love and care from others can be difficult.

As you read in today's passage, Peter found it hard to receive God's love. Days before Jesus's death, Jesus gathered His twelve closest disciples to show them the full extent of His love (John 13:1). While they were being served a feast, Jesus got up and began to wash and then dry each of their feet. Peter was so uncomfortable he initially refused—until Jesus told him, "Unless I wash you, you have no part with me" (v. 8). Jesus did not need or want Peter's help. He wanted Peter to receive the full extent of His love. He wants you to receive it, too.

Receiving God involves opening yourself and embracing Him. You will first need to admit to Him that you are a sinner and need a Savior. Then you must believe Jesus died to save you from your sin and commit to making Him Lord of your life. You must make the decision to turn from the path of sin you have been on and walk on the path of life. The Bible calls this process of turning from sin and toward life in God *repentance*. In taking these steps, you will receive Jesus and His embrace. Then the Holy Spirit will immediately come to reside in you forever and empower you to be a disciple.

I received Jesus when I was nine years old. I remember feeling mixed emotions—comforted at receiving eternal salvation and nervous as I made my choice public.

Somewhere along the way, though, I forgot that the foundation of my relationship with God was receiving His ever-present love. Jesus told His followers, "If you love me, keep my commands" (John 14:15). Somehow, I started reading it backward. I got pretty good at obeying Him—at least in the big things. But I followed Him with my obedience before my love. I had stopped receiving. Giving was more natural and comfortable for me. We also see examples of this in Scripture.

Mary and Martha were sisters who were Jesus's close friends. Martha invited Jesus into her home and got busy preparing a meal to serve Him. Mary, on the other hand, sat at Jesus's feet, just listening to all He said. Martha was angry at Mary for not lifting a finger to help prepare the meal. Jesus responded, "Martha, Martha . . . you are worried and upset about many things, but few things are needed—or indeed only one. Mary has chosen what is better, and it will not be taken away from her" (Luke 10:41-42). Being with Jesus was better than Martha's doing. Receiving Him and all He offers is the one thing you need—especially when giving feels more comfortable.

What do you need to receive from God? Look over what you wrote down and take time to receive it!

Once received, the kingdom of God begins to work itself in our lives like a small amount of yeast kneeded into dough (Luke 13:21). What percent of your life has been thoroughly affected by Him? Mark the spectrum between 0-100%.

0% —————————————————— **100%**

If you have never received God's gift of eternal life with Him through salvation from your sins, do you want to ask Him to save you today? To do so right now (or later), you need to believe Jesus died for your sins and that God raised Him from the dead, then confess with your mouth that Jesus is Lord (Romans 10:9). If you just made this decision to receive God's salvation, write down at least one person you will tell here:

If you are interested in making this most important decision of your life but need some help, ask a follower of Jesus whom you trust, such as your group leader.

Practice this week's memory verse:

"Love the Lord your God with all your heart and with all your soul and with all your mind and with all your strength."

MARK 12:30

Day Four

GIVING YOURSELF

Today's passage for your conversation with God: 1 Corinthians 13

Try to quote Mark 12:30 aloud right now. If you can't, keep practicing until you can:

"Love the Lord your God with all your heart and with all your soul and with all your mind and with all your strength."

Don't you wish loving God was as easy as checking a box? It is no coincidence that the two commands He says are most important cannot be fully accomplished or completed. As long as you are still alive, you have more love to give. Love requires an ongoing investment. It is described in today's passage as "the most excellent" and greatest gift (1 Corinthians 12:31; 13:13).

Have you noticed that our verse this week uses "all" four times? Love is not easy to measure, but the measure Jesus gave was "all." Giving just a part of Himself would not have been perfect love. Loving someone well requires a sacrifice of all of oneself. And that's what God wants from you. No one else can give God what He wants from you.

C.S. Lewis said, "Lose your life and you will save it. Submit to death . . . submit with every fiber of your being, and you will find eternal life. Keep back nothing. Nothing that you have not given away will ever be really yours . . . look for Christ and you will find Him, and with Him everything else thrown in."[1]

I have three children whom I love. I cannot give them my love without also giving them myself. I cannot give a hug that doesn't include my body. If my son Joshua, whose love language is gifts,[2] finds a treasure wrapped in a box in the forest, will he feel loved? Happy—yes. But loved? Probably not. However, if I wrap this same treasure in a box and give it to him, will he feel loved? Absolutely. The difference is me.

To love God requires we give all of ourselves to Him. He made all of you to be His. The Dutch theologian Abraham Kuyper said it well: "There is not a square inch in the whole domain of our human existence over which Christ, who is sovereign over all, does not cry: 'Mine!'"[3]

The title *lord* means someone who has ultimate power, authority, and influence. God is Lord over the entire universe. When you receive Jesus as both your Savior and Lord, you can be sure He stands ready to reign over every aspect of your life.

Jesus has domain over every area of your life whether you acknowledge it or not. How much of yourself are you giving to Jesus right now?

0% ____ **100%**

If you have not made Jesus Lord and Savior of your life, what is holding you back?

Humans are gloriously complex beings. The apostle Paul gives a helpful insight into the parts of our being as he prays for the Thessalonian church, saying, "May God . . . sanctify you *through and through*. May your *whole* spirit, soul and body be kept blameless at the coming of our Lord Jesus Christ" (1 Thessalonians 5:23, italics mine). The concept of humans having a spirit and soul as well as a body has been discussed for many years. While scientists and philosophers will never agree, it is widely recognized that humans are more than just physical bodies.

In the New Testament's original language of Greek, the word that Paul used for spirit, *pneuma*, means "that which gives the body life." The Greek word Paul used for soul is *psyche*—which is the root used in the word *psychology*—and can be defined as the seat of your desires, feelings, affections, and aversions.

How do these words compare to the ones used in this week's memory verse for heart, soul, mind, and strength? The word for soul in Mark 12 is the exact same one Paul used. The Greek word for heart—*kardia*, where we get the word *cardiologist* from—means "inmost part." The word for mind—*dianoia*—means "thoughts," and the word for strength is *ischys* and means "force," "power," or "ability."

In other words, Jesus says in Mark 12:30, "Love the Lord your God with all your inmost being, with all your desires and feelings, with all your thoughts, and with all your ability." And Paul prays that the Thessalonian church will be sanctified through and through so that their spirits, desires and feelings, and tangible bodies will be kept blameless until Christ returns.

Throughout this discipleship experience, we will be processing the diagram on page 15 that will help you conceptualize being all His. Everything inside the circle represents you. The solid circle outline represents your physical body, which houses the three parts of your being. Your soul and spirit are equally important parts of you, but are without a physical boundary, and are thus separated by a dotted heart. Your spirit—your connection to God—is the inmost part of you. Your soul—your mind, will, and emotions—connects your spirit and body. Your relationships and what you spend time doing—or your mission—flow out of your being and further shape who you are.

Rank the three parts of your being in the order you invest in them by writing spirit, soul, and body in the blanks next to the numbers they correspond with. (For example, if you prioritize your relationship with God above everything else, you would write spirit beside number 1.)

1. ____________________ **2.** ____________________ **3.** ____________________

Which do you tend to prioritize most in your life: your relationships or your mission?

Which do you invest in most: your being (your body, soul, and spirit) or your doing (relationships and mission)?

Jesus said, "If you are filled with light, with no dark corners, then your whole life will be radiant, as though a floodlight were filling you with light" (Luke 11:36, NLT).

Describe someone you know or can imagine whose whole life radiantly shines with the love of God.

Write out a prayer, asking God to help you give any dark corners of yourself to Him and for Him to begin illuminating all of you.

Continue to practice this week's memory verse:

"Love the Lord your God with all your heart and with all your soul and with all your mind and with all your strength."
MARK 12:30

Day Five
BEING HIS DISCIPLE

Today's passage for your conversation with God: Luke 9:18-27

The word *disciple* means someone who follows a leader. As you saw in today's passage, Jesus told His disciples that those who follow Him must deny themselves and daily take up their cross. Then He said, "For whoever wants to save his life will lose it, but whoever loses his life for me will save it" (v. 24).

If you had to identify yourself using just one word, what would it be?

Maybe the word you wrote is tied to your family, ethnicity, age, or gender, or maybe it's a word that hints at an interest, passion, or skill of yours. Did you write or did it occur to you to write *disciple*? If not, I hope that by the end of *MasterLife Together* you will.

Following Jesus means relinquishing control of your temporary life in view of your eternal life with God. Dietrich Bonhoeffer aptly said, "When Christ calls a man he bids him come and die."[4] To be clear, your salvation comes by grace through faith and not by your own works (Ephesians 2:8-10). But don't confuse the means with the end: you are saved by grace for the purpose of following Jesus. You weren't saved by good works—but for good works. Your salvation as well as the good works you do both bring Him glory. The idea that after you are saved it's optional whether or not you are a disciple is not biblical. Jesus saved you to be His disciple. It is not possible to truly love Jesus and not be His disciple.

In Luke 7:36-50, we read the story of a woman who loved Jesus. She learned that Jesus was eating at a Pharisee's house nearby, so she followed Him there. She came up behind Him weeping, wetting His feet with her tears. She then used her hair to dry His feet, kissed them, and poured an expensive jar of her own perfume onto them.

This woman, Mary, was described as a sinful woman, but loved Jesus with total abandon. It was not just her expensive perfume that she gave Him but also herself—her tears, her hair, her kisses. Jesus responded by affirming that she had done "a beautiful thing" and that wherever the gospel is preached throughout the world, what she did would be told in memory of her.

Mary loved Jesus, so she followed Him as His disciple. Simon, the man who had invited Jesus to his home, was religious but not a true disciple. Jesus admonished Simon, "Her many sins have been forgiven—as her great love has shown. But whoever has been forgiven little loves little" (Luke 7:47).

CHRISTIAN DISCIPLESHIP is a personal love relationship with Jesus Christ that results in a lifelong journey of obedience. As you follow Christ, He transforms you to be like Him; He changes your values to kingdom values; and He involves you in His mission in your home, church, and world. As His disciple, you will progressively know Him more deeply, obey Him more quickly, reflect Him more accurately, and invite others into His kingdom more regularly.

This doesn't mean you don't have bad days or go through some valleys, but it does mean you are increasingly walking closer with Jesus.

Following Jesus is following a Person. Several years ago, my father-in-law Randy led a mission team to Sonora, Mexico. Sonora is largely desert and on moonless nights, it is can't-see-your-hand-in-front-of-your-face dark. They were driving from one town to another in a caravan of four vehicles along winding, mountainous roads with no guardrails. Driving the second car in the caravan, Randy quickly realized that if he did not stay close to the lead car, he would soon be on his own. When he focused on the leader, however, he did not have to focus on the road. When the lead car slowed, he slowed. When it turned, he turned. He glanced at the road, but his focus was on staying close to the lead vehicle. So it is with Jesus. If you stay close to Him, you can take your eyes off your circumstances, confidently trusting that He is leading you well.

As you follow Jesus, you will become fully alive and experience a deep satisfaction in Him, which will then enable you to bless others to the greatest extent possible. As John Piper has said, "God is most glorified in us when we are most satisfied in Him."[5] Following Jesus is an active pursuit that is fueled by your love for Him. It requires sacrifice, but He is worth all of you and more.

How thoroughly have you surrendered the parts of yourself to Jesus? How fully are you following Him? Take the following inventory to help you discern opportunities for your growth over the course of this discipleship experience.

Rank the following on a scale of 1 to 4. Write your number next to each statement below.

1	2	3	4
never or disagree	occasionally or somewhat disagree	usually or somewhat agree	always or fully agree

____ **I not only know but also experience the unconditional love of Jesus on a daily basis.**

____ **Spending time in God's Word is like eating food—I need it every day to sustain me.**

____ Communicating with God through prayer comes easily to me and is something I do throughout each day.
____ I experience the power of the Holy Spirit as He lives through me on a daily basis.
____ I regularly bring to God any thoughts and desires I have that are unpleasing to Him, so He can renew my mind with truth.
____ When I experience unpleasant emotions, I share them with God and let Him comfort me and reorient me.
____ What I consume through my mouth and eyes and how I move and rest my body show honor to God.
____ Hallmarks of my closest relationships are love, forgiveness, and healthy communication.
____ I regularly and authentically engage with a small group of Christ-followers for Bible study, encouragement, and accountability.
____ How I spend my time, money, and talents pleases God.
____ God has made me His witness, and I regularly engage in this role He has given me.
____ A deep desire I have is to bring glory to God. I seek to steward my whole life well because I know I am significant in His story.

Now add the totals for each number to get your total score and write it here: ______. The highest possible score is 48.

Lastly, circle or highlight the statements that represent the top three areas of growth for you. These correspond with the twelve topics you will be exploring in this discipleship experience. Now invite God to transform you in these areas.

Quote this week's verse, Mark 12:30. Then, pray it aloud to Him like this:

Father, You are my Lord and my God. Help me to love You with all my heart, with all my soul, with all my mind, and with all my strength. In Jesus's name I pray, amen.

Optional passages for more conversations with God:

Day 6: Luke 7:36-50
Day 7: Psalm 103

Week Two
GOD'S WORD

Then he said to them all, "Whoever wants to be my disciple must deny themselves and take up their cross daily and follow me. For whoever wants to save their life will lose it, but whoever loses their life for me will save it."

LUKE 9:23-24

Jesus said in the verse you will be memorizing this week that if you're going to follow Him as a disciple, you should take up your cross and follow Him every day. Your cross is not the same as Jesus's cross. His death on the cross was a once-for-all substitutionary payment for sins.

Your cross is one you are to bear every day to benefit both your relationship with God and your relationships with people. Just as Christ sacrificed Himself, He calls you to deny yourself, sacrificing your selfishness. Your cross is not a long-term hardship that's unique to you specifically—"this is just my cross to bear, I guess," some people say. There is a linked purpose between Jesus's physical death on the cross and your cross, the symbolic death to yourself. The purpose of both is the glory of God.

Cross bracing is a construction technique in which braces are crossed to support a frame. Cross braces are often made of metal or wood. This type of bracing is used on many different types of items including ships, buildings, and furniture. Braces are not as strong separately as they are when intersected and held together in the form of a cross. This is why the Roman empire used wooden crosses for crucifixions. Only a cross could sufficiently support the weight of a criminal's body as to cause prolonged, painful death.

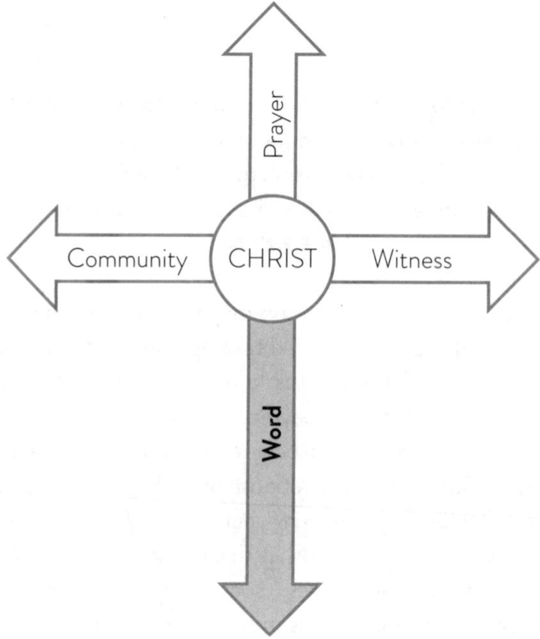

Look at this diagram of the Disciple's Cross. It includes four spiritual disciplines that keep you rooted in the foundation of God's love for you: God's Word, prayer, Christ-centered community, and witnessing. The vertical brace of the cross illustrates the two primary ways you relate to God. The horizontal brace shows your relationship with two groups of people—other believers and those who are far from God. The vertical and horizontal braces are inseparably connected, and point to the daily importance of relating rightly with God and other people.

Remember God's greatest commandment that you memorized last week? Say Mark 12:30 aloud now.

Which brace does it relate to? Underline one:

Vertical Horizontal

Now read the verse that follows it: "The second [greatest commandment] is this: 'Love your neighbor as yourself.' There is no commandment greater than these" (Mark 12:31).

Which brace does this verse relate to? Underline one:

Vertical Horizontal

Rightly relating to God and people are certainly linked; it's why Jesus ranked these as the number one and number two commandments. For the next two weeks, we will focus on the vertical bar of the Disciple's Cross—being in the Word and in prayer—and near the end of our group experience, we will return to the horizontal bar of Christ-centered community and being a witness. This week, our focus is being in the Word, as shown in the diagram.

PRAYER

Heavenly Father, thank You for carrying the cross for me. I want to faithfully carry the cross You've called me to as Your disciple. Jesus's death and resurrection has made a profound difference in my life—carrying a cross for You is the least I can do. I confess that I'm not as consistent as I want to be. Please help me deny myself, take up my cross, and follow You every day this week. Help me be willing to lose control of my life because I believe You can do better with it than I can on my own. Help me to grow in learning and obeying Your Word as a regular discipline in my life. In Jesus's name, amen.

Day One

DAILY INTIMACY WITH CHRIST

Today's passage for your conversation with God: John 15:1-17

I hope you are benefiting from putting in the effort to journal your conversation of what God said to you and what you said to God from each day's passage. If you haven't been writing it out, start today with John 15:1-17. Having a daily conversation with God makes every day count for eternity!

According to Andrew Murray, "True abiding consists of two parts—occupying a position into which Christ can come and abide, and abiding in Him so that the soul lets Him take the place of the self to become our life."[1] *Abide* or *remain* is how most English versions of the Bible have translated Jesus's imperative in John 15:4 which you read in today's passage. Jesus emphasizes its importance by repeating the word four more times in just three verses (vv. 4-7).

Abide isn't a word I use very often, so when I read John 15, I paraphrase Jesus's words as "Be intimate with me every day." When you use the word *intimate*, you might reserve it only for a marital relationship. That's reasonable, but Jesus desires to be closer to you than any other human relationship—even closer than a spouse. This verse is the basis of our family's vision statement, which is, "To daily be intimate with Jesus Christ through loving, obeying, and surrendering to Him." When Jesus tells you to abide in Him, it's not an obligation or admonishment; it's an invitation.

Glance back at the Disciple's Cross on page 30 and notice that "Christ" is the center. This symbolizes the importance of your life revolving around Christ. Being a disciple is not about adopting Christianity as a religion or practicing a set of rules. The Master of the universe wants to have a dynamic, personal relationship with you!

If you could meet anyone on earth and spend the day with him or her, who would you choose?

Maybe you wrote the name of a celebrity, actor, athlete, or president. Imagine what that day would be like. How many people would be in his or her entourage? Do you think that person would appear rushed because his or her time is so precious and his or her schedule so demanding? If you wanted to spend every day for the rest of your life with that person, it seems impossible that he or she would agree to that, right? Yet Jesus gladly offers this arrangement to you. He's given His Holy Spirit to live inside anyone who's repented from his or her sins and experienced His salvation. He goes with you, never leaving or forsaking you (Hebrews 13:5). Many times when I pray during my morning run, I thank God for running next to me. He is real, present, and always available.

How much time do you typically spend aware of the abiding presence of Jesus on an average day?

How much time do you want to spend aware of His presence on an average day? Is there a gap between the two answers? If so, why?

Spending time alone with God is the foundation of your day and is vital to your growth as a disciple. This is why I encourage you to make your highest priority each day to spend time alone with the Master of your life. In order to sufficiently prioritize Him, it's best to meet with Him as soon as you wake up—before you get busy with lesser things. Listening to God through reading His Word and sharing your heart with Him through prayer should be hallmarks of your time with God. Ideally, this is just the first of many times you interact with God throughout your day. If you want to have consistent time alone with God each day, it will help you to do some planning—first, schedule a regular time for it; second, find a regular place to have it; and third, decide on a regular process for it.

What time do you usually get up in the morning?

If you are not already spending time alone with God daily, what adjustments would you need to make to get up fifteen minutes earlier tomorrow morning?

Name the best place for you to spend time with God:

If you're not in the habit of spending time with God every day, who could you ask to keep you accountable to do so over the next month?

I usually spend time with God while drinking my coffee and eating my breakfast. My "process" includes worshiping with music, reading the Bible, memorizing and/or reviewing Scripture verses, and journaling prayers to God based on the verses I've read. One best practice I try to follow is "Scripture before phone" each morning so that the first message I get each day is not a text, social media, video, or news but rather God's words.[2] That means I use a physical Bible in the morning instead of my Bible app.

I encourage you to involve journaling your conversations with God according to the day's passage throughout this discipleship journey. Try to do this in the morning. If you still have time then, you can also work through the day's content (that is, what you are reading right now). But if you don't have enough time in the mornings, try working through each day's content during a break at work, over lunch, or in the evening.

What do you envision your process looking like for your daily time with God during this *MasterLife Together* experience?

Spending time with God daily is the first and most important of four spiritual rhythms[3] our family has adopted—all of which serve to increase our intimacy with Christ. God designed much of His creation to function rhythmically—think about sunrises and sunsets, seasons, ocean tides, sleep cycles, and your heart beat. You too will function at your best by establishing rhythms in your life. Later in this discipleship experience you will learn about the rest of our spiritual rhythms:

1. Daily Divert (spending time with God)
2. Weekly Withdraw
3. Monthly Move-out
4. Annually Abandon

Practice this week's memory verse by saying and/or writing the first part of it a few times:

Then he said to them all, "Whoever wants to be my disciple must deny themselves and take up their cross daily and follow me."

LUKE 9:23

Day Two
GOD'S WORD

Today's passage for your conversation with God: 2 Timothy 3:12-17

Isn't it amazing that God speaks to you? You may think, "God has never spoken to me," but certainly the problem is not that God is silent, but rather that your ears are not attuned to listen. It's easy to take God's Word for granted and allow it to become commonplace, but hearing from God is a privilege. God's Word is completely and perfectly recorded in the Bible. That's not to say that God can't speak in other ways—through people, relationships, circumstances, etc.—but it always aligns with what He's said in the Bible. That's why it's important to spend time listening to what God may say to you uniquely and specifically.

In today's passage we see that all Scripture is inspired, or breathed, by God. That means we don't get to choose parts of the Bible we're not going to believe because they are difficult to understand or accept. A survey found that only 6% of Americans have a "biblical worldview"—half as many as thirty years before then.[4] Barna Group defines a biblical worldview as "believing that absolute moral truth exists; the Bible is totally accurate in all of the principles it teaches; Satan is considered to be a real being or force, not merely symbolic; a person cannot earn their way into Heaven by trying to be good or do good works; Jesus Christ lived a sinless life on earth; and God is the all-knowing, all-powerful creator of the world who still rules the universe today."[5]

Reread the definition of a "biblical worldview" provided above and underline any of it that you don't believe fully. What is keeping you from believing those principles?

Unfortunately, the percentages of people with a biblical worldview are similarly underwhelming among Americans who identify as Christians. Only 21% of those attending evangelical Protestant churches have a biblical worldview. The study finds even smaller proportions in mainline Protestant (8%) or Catholic (1%) churches.[6] To develop a biblical worldview, you need to devote yourself to God daily through time in His Word.

One evangelical statement of faith defines God's Word in the Scriptures this way:

The Holy Bible was written by men divinely inspired and is God's revelation of Himself to man. It is a perfect treasure of divine instruction. It has God for its author,

> salvation for its end, and truth, without any mixture of error, for its matter. Therefore, all Scripture is totally true and trustworthy. It reveals the principles by which God judges us, and therefore is, and will remain to the end of the world, the true center of Christian union, and the supreme standard by which all human conduct, creeds, and religious opinions should be tried. All Scripture is a testimony to Christ, who is Himself the focus of divine revelation.[7]

God's Word is sufficient as the ultimate authority for a believer in all matters of faith and practice—what we believe and what we do.

Today's passage gives four benefits you'll receive from being rooted in the Bible: teaching, rebuking, correcting, and training in righteousness (2 Timothy 3:16-17). To reword those as questions, you can ask of any Scripture:

1. What does this teach me?
2. What should I not do?
3. How do I get right?
4. How will I obey?[8]

How could these questions help you get more out of your time in God's Word?

Many people do not believe in absolute truths and further state that to claim the existence of such is arrogance. Second Timothy 4:3-4 says that people will increasingly gravitate toward whatever is convenient for them rather than embrace truth. The reason you can humbly uphold the Bible is because you received it by revelation (2 Peter 1:20-21). It doesn't matter what you say; it's what God says that counts. Your interpretation of the Bible could certainly be wrong, but the Bible itself is always right.

Spending time in God's Word is an essential part of relating to God as you follow Him. The goal of being in the Bible is not more head-knowledge about a religion. Jesus rebuked those who read the Scriptures for this end: "You study the Scriptures diligently because you think that in them you have eternal life. These are the very Scriptures that testify about me" (John 5:39). Being in God's Word is the means by which you can know Jesus better and follow Him more closely.

Try to memorize the first part of this week's memory verse:

Then he said to them all, "Whoever wants to be my disciple must
deny themselves and take up their cross daily and follow me."

LUKE 9:23

Day Three
GRASPING GOD'S WORD

Today's passage for your conversation with God: Psalm 119:9-16

If I were to hand you a Bible, how many fingers would you use to grasp it? Your pinky finger alone won't suffice to hold such a large book. If you don't grasp it with your whole hand, it will fall to the ground. Likewise, you need to engage a multipronged approach for your heart and mind to wholly grasp God's Word.

Psalm 119 exalts God's Word and reveals how much the psalmist truly loved it. Like the psalmist, you should strive to grasp God's Word well so that it grabs hold of your heart and leads you toward true and full life. The illustration below shows how to fully engage with God's Word.

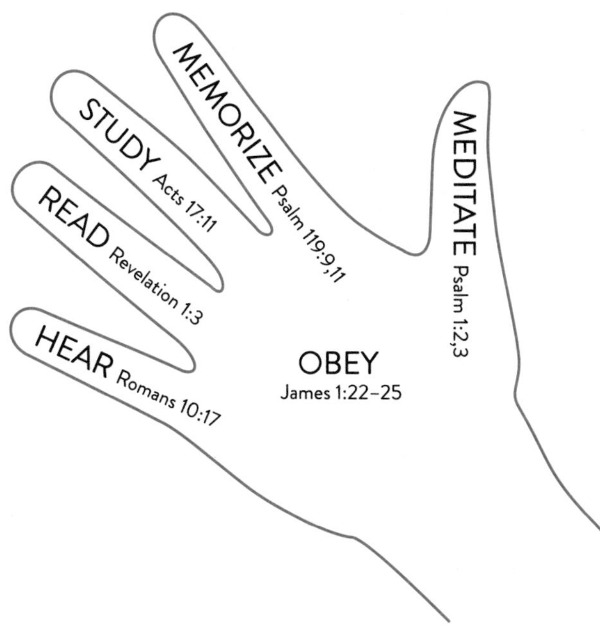

READ: If you've never read the entire Bible, I strongly encourage you to do so. Many plans are available to help you read the whole Bible in one year's time. Reading the whole Bible as a teenager was the first giant leap I took in following Jesus.

HEAR: You might prefer listening to the Bible more than reading it. If so, search online for audio Bibles. There are great resources to help those who do not prefer to read or cannot. I met a blind woman in Asia who had listened to the entire Bible because she had her son read it to her. Where there's a will, there's a way.

STUDY: The goal of studying isn't to learn more facts about the Bible; it's to know God better. When I want to study verses in-depth, I read them in multiple Bible translations. Use whatever Bible translations help you to best connect with God. You may like one that is easier to understand such as the New Living Translation, although it isn't as strict on how precisely it translates each word. Many great biblical commentaries and devotional books also exist. It's best if you read a commentary or devotional after you read the Bible verses—and never in place of reading the Scripture itself.

MEMORIZE: We'll spend more time tomorrow on this topic.

MEDITATE: Some non-Christian meditation practices urge you to empty your mind, but Christian meditation fills your mind with the Bible. In the Old Testament's original language of Hebrew, the words for *meditation* originally used in both Joshua 1:8; Psalm 1:2; and today's passage in Psalm 119:15 involve the Scripture being said out loud.[9] Singing songs that include Scripture helps you repeat the truths of God's Word as they take root deeper into your heart. These verses also speak to the importance of meditating on Scripture every day and night. For example, when I go to sleep, I'm usually meditating on just one different word or phrase of Psalm 23 (made possible in the dark because I have it memorized) and delighting in God's life-changing truths.

OBEY: James 1:22 reminds us, "Do not merely listen to the word, and so deceive yourselves. Do what it says." Some Bible verses involve commands we are to obey that are straightforward with no gray area. Where there are gray areas, God's Word still has useful principles that can be applied to every situation. Consider how every Scripture can be applied to your life, keeping in mind that you should follow each of them in light of what the rest of the Bible says. Resist the temptation to overlook any chapter in the Bible, because it's all inspired by God. The Bible is not merely a collection of truths for you to believe; its truths are meant to be acted upon.

I like how Franklin Graham said it: "Reading God's Word informs the mind; studying God's Word transforms the heart; obeying God's Word reforms the will."[10] This is why you should seek to grasp God's Word increasingly.

Think about it this way: how many times do you usually eat in one day? Most people eat breakfast, lunch, and dinner—and even some snacks. No matter how busy you are, you make time to eat because your physical life depends on it. Even if you're up against a deadline at school or work, your hunger pangs remind you to eat some food. Yet how many times do you use busyness as an excuse to not spend time with God?

How many times do you usually take in God's Word in one day?

Think of a time you ate a huge feast. How long was it before you ate again?

If you're like most people, you don't often skip meals! Yet how many believers try to get by with one weekly sermon as their only intake of God's Word? A well-preached sermon is just a single delicious banquet; it's not enough to feed you for an entire week. You must feed yourself on God's Word and not solely depend on other people to feed it to you. Frequently take in God's Word—your spiritual life depends on it!

Later in Psalm 119:103, the psalmist praised God, saying, "How sweet are your words to my taste, sweeter than honey to my mouth!" Can you say the same?

Ask God to show you one specific action step that would help you better grasp God's Word, and write it below. (For example, you may start going to bed earlier in order to have time alone with God every morning.)

Say the first part of this week's verse by memory, and then add the second part of the verse by saying and/or writing it down a few times:

> Then he said to them all, "Whoever wants to be my disciple must deny themselves and take up their cross daily and follow me. For whoever wants to save their life will lose it, but whoever loses their life for me will save it."
>
> **LUKE 9:23-24**

Day Four
MEMORIZING GOD'S WORD

Today's passage for your conversation with God: Matthew 4:1-11

You learned yesterday that memorizing Scripture is one of the six ways to grasp God's Word, and today I hope you will see why.

How many times in today's passage did Jesus quote God's Word when He was tempted by Satan?

How many times did Satan quote God's Word (although out of context)?

How many Bible verses do you think you have memorized that you can currently recite accurately?

For that last question, in addition to a number I hope you also thought, "not enough"! Jesus is fully God but also fully human, so He probably had to work to memorize Scripture, just like you do. Jesus's first words as a toddler were probably not the entire book of Genesis! So you can't use the excuse, "I could never be like Jesus. He knew everything."

Can you imagine Satan tempting Jesus and Him replying, "Hmmm, that's a good point. I've read somewhere about that before in the Bible. I can't remember exactly what it says, but I think it's in Deuteronomy or Psalms somewhere?" If Jesus and even Satan have verses memorized, you are wise to consider memorizing some yourself.

Read the list below and put a star next to the one that is most compelling to you.

Why should Jesus's disciples memorize Bible verses?

1. To know God more intimately. Jesus said in John 15:7, "If you remain in me and *my words remain in you*, ask whatever you wish, and it will be done for you" (italics mine).
2. To increase obedience and decrease sin by resisting temptation as you read in Psalm 119:9-11 yesterday and in Matthew 4:1-11 today.
3. To share the gospel with people who don't follow Jesus. You have more credibility when you really know God's Word in the moment. At Pentecost, the apostle Peter quoted three different Scriptures, apparently from memory (Acts 2:14-41). Three thousand

people accepted Christ after Peter spoke those words. I once asked an unsaved passenger beside me on a train to help me review my Bible verses. He agreed and heard me recite all the verses I had memorized from the book of Romans.

4. To always have God's Word with you. Some Christians are imprisoned for their faith in hostile places and not allowed access to a Bible. The only Word of God they have is what they have memorized. Jesus said in John 14:26, "the Advocate, the Holy Spirit, whom the Father will send in my name, will teach you all things and will *remind* you of everything I have said to you" (italics mine). How can the Holy Spirit remind you of something Jesus said if you never learned it in the first place?
5. To redeem the time that would otherwise be wasted (Ephesians 5:16). Life is short and evil is pervasive, so you should not waste your precious time. You have idle times when you're waiting for someone, taking a break, or standing in a line of people. Avoid the gravitational pull toward your phone and instead spend time memorizing God's Word.

Which verses should I memorize?

All are worth memorizing, but start by choosing verses that God is is speaking to you as you spend time with Him. Be sure to read the verses before and after the ones you want to memorize to understand its context and original meaning. Think about choosing and memorizing a "life verse," similarly to how I've chosen Mark 8:35. You will likely want to memorize verses that give you victory over a specific sin or address a specific circumstance in your life. I've memorized verses God gave me about the type of person I should marry (Philippians 4:8), when I was to move somewhere (Exodus 33:14-15), and when I was to accept another vocational position (Psalm 107:7,30).

Is there a tool that will help me?

Yes! All you need to make a simple, practical tool is verse cards. I recommend you buy them and a packet online by searching "Topical Memory System and The Navigators." You will get to practice using this proven system during the rest of our discipleship experience.

Write the reference of the verse you want to memorize in the middle of a verse card. On the bottom left corner write today's date, and on the bottom right corner write the date that is exactly two months later. Flip the card up and over, and then write out the verse. Here's an example:

Luke 9:23-24 *month / day / year* *month + 2 / day / year*	Then he said to them all: "Whoever wants to be my disciple must deny themselves and take up their cross daily and follow me. For whoever wants to save their life will lose it, but whoever loses their life for me will save it."

For your convenience, we have included verse cards for all the Scriptures you will memorize during *MasterLife Together* at the back of this workbook. Cut out the Luke 9:23-24 card now. Write today's date in the bottom left corner. Then write the date two months from now in the bottom right corner.

Also cut out the Mark 12:30 card that goes with week 1, and follow the same process with the date you began memorizing it last week. If you prefer larger verse cards, you can create your own using index cards.

You always want to memorize the reference in addition to the verse. You will review the verse every day for the first two months—which is why you write the date you started memorizing the verse on the card as well as the date two months later. After two months, you will remember it well, and you can begin to review that verse weekly (instead of daily).

After your first two months of Scripture memory, you will have two sets of verse cards to review each day: the newer ones that you need to review every day and the older ones that you need to review weekly. If you memorize just one Bible verse per week (like you're doing during this study), you'll have over fifty verses memorized in just one year—more than the average Christian memorizes in his or her lifetime!

A few things that have helped me best use this system: After you can correctly quote the reference, verse, and reference again, find a friend to check your accuracy on the verse. Better yet, ask them to memorize it with you! Pray about the verse, meditate on God through the verse, and obey what God is saying in it. Do not memorize Scripture solely as a mental exercise. There are three secrets to memorizing Scripture long-term: Review! Review! Review! Repetition is the best way to engrave the verses on your heart and mind.

Using your new verse card, practice saying Luke 9:23-24 until you have it memorized.

See page 284 in the appendix for Scripture memory best practices, purchasing options, and/or to help you share this tool with others.

Day Five

OBEYING GOD'S COMMANDS

Today's passage for your conversation with God: John 14:15-24

Three times in today's passage, Jesus linked our love for Him with our obedience of Him: "If you love me, keep my commands" (John 14:15); "Anyone who loves me will obey my teaching" (John 14:23); and "Anyone who does not love me will not obey my teaching" (John 14:24). Too much of what passes for discipleship is primarily knowledge-based. The result is "disciples" with big heads and no muscles. Believers are taught but not held accountable to do anything based on what they've learned.

When we served as missionaries in Asia, our missionary friends focused on obedience-based discipleship because while a person needs some knowledge to obey God, a full understanding can only come after obeying Him. Adding obedience to knowledge is an improvement, but the Bible actually points to something even better: love-based discipleship. If you prioritize growing in your love for Jesus, you will be eager to both know and obey Him more. Where your love goes, your thoughts and actions will follow.

The best indicator of spiritual maturity is how much you love and obey Jesus. Today we will focus on some of the most important steps of obedience that God commands (see chart on the next page). You need to take the first two steps (salvation and subsequent baptism) only one time, while the other eleven steps are to continue over your lifetime. To be clear: you cannot earn salvation by doing these good works, nor can you lose salvation by evil deeds (Ephesians 2:8-9).

The first seven steps were organized by missionary George Patterson, who highlighted these principles to instruct brand-new believers.[11] In addition to these, I've included six steps that I prioritize when discipling a new believer. Each is listed with its corresponding Scripture references. The first reference (for example, Mark 1:15-17) is the command and the second one (for example, Luke 19:1-10) shows people following it:

THIRTEEN STEPS OF OBEDIENCE

	COMMAND	EXAMPLE
1. Repent and believe in Jesus for salvation.	Mark 1:15-17	Luke 19:1-10
2. Be baptized.	Matthew 28:18-20	Acts 8:26-39
3. Pray.	Matthew 6:9	Matthew 6:5-15
4. Go and make disciples.	Matthew 28:18-20	John 4:4-42
5. Love.	Matthew 22:37-39	Luke 10:25-37
6. Take the Lord's Supper.	Luke 22:19-20	Luke 22:7-20
7. Give.	Luke 6:38	Mark 12:41-44
8. Study the Bible and obey it.	John 15:7	Acts 17:10-12
9. Grow in a church.	Hebrews 10:24-25	Acts 2:38-47
10. Grow in character and holiness.	Matthew 5:8	Colossians 3:5-14
11. Be filled with the Holy Spirit.	Acts 1:5-8	Acts 2:1-21
12. Rejoice when persecuted.	Matthew 5:10-12	Acts 7:54–8:4
13. Be ready for Jesus's return.	Matthew 24:42-44	1 Thessalonians 4:16–5:11

Which of these do you find the most difficult to obey and why? Are there any you're ignoring entirely?

In which area would you like to see growth and maturity?

Write the name of someone you will ask to keep you accountable for what you wrote above.

In this discipleship experience, we will spend a whole week on some of these individual commands. I want to spend just a moment now on the important command of baptism. Although Jesus commands all His followers to be baptized, baptism is the hardest step of obedience for some to take. Some people say they believe Jesus privately, but they don't want to risk the possibility of being ostracized, impoverished, or killed because of a public demonstration through baptism. Jesus wasn't ashamed to die publicly for us, so we should not be ashamed for people to learn that we are following Him (Luke 9:26). Some people were sprinkled with water as babies before they could make their own choice to follow Christ. However, every baptism in Scripture was done by immersion and happened after the person accepted Christ's salvation (that is, not as infants). Immersion by water is significant because it is a symbol to show that as Jesus died, was buried, and rose again; likewise, our old flesh has been crucified with Christ, and we now walk in the newness of life in Christ. Baptism doesn't save a person, but every person who is saved should obey Jesus's command to be baptized.

In addition to the thirteen steps of obedience mentioned above, there are many other life-giving commands in God's Word for you to obey. A simple tool you can use to interpret and apply Scripture in your life is called the sword method.[12] Hebrews 4:12 says, "the word of God is alive and active. Sharper than any double-edged sword, it penetrates even to dividing soul and spirit, joints and marrow; it judges the thoughts and attitudes of the heart." Look at the diagram below. This illustration's vertical questions help you learn from a passage and the horizontal questions help you apply it to your life. You can use this method for yourself and those you disciple to discover how to personally follow God's ways—not because someone else said so but because God said so.

Let the Bible regularly penetrate your mind and heart—and then watch God transform your life and worldview. As Jesus said, "Blessed rather are those who hear the word of God and obey it" (Luke 11:28).

I want to challenge you to read at least one of the optional passages below and use it to try out the sword method before your next group session. Simply write down the four questions in the diagram and answer them according to the passage.

Review this week's verse using your verse card until you have it memorized. Be prepared to quote it from memory during your next group session.

Note: A mini composition book or a pocket-sized notebook is recommended for week 3.

Optional passages for more conversations with God:

Day 6: John 8:21-59
Day 7: Hebrews 4

Week Three
PRAYER

"If you remain in me and my words remain in you, ask whatever you wish, and it will be done for you."
JOHN 15:7

What do you think Jesus is doing at this very moment?

The Bible says He is praying for people (Romans 8:34; Hebrews 7:25). Might He even be praying for you at this moment? When you pray, you enter into living fellowship with Jesus—joining Him and appealing to His friendship.

Jesus spent time teaching His disciples how to pray. The first two words of Jesus's model prayer—"Our Father"—are of utmost significance (Matthew 6:9-13). He does not say, "*My* Father." You are never praying alone—you are joining Jesus and all His redeemed who live in unceasing prayer.

Jesus invites you into a relationship with the Father. He wants you to be reminded of God's fatherly, tender, infinite love each time you pray—as if to awaken your childlike trust.[1] When your heart is filled with the fatherly love of God, you will not hesitate to bring your needs, sins, and temptations to Him. You will pray with confidence and joyful expectation.

After saying, "Our Father," Jesus prays that God's name, kingdom, and desires will be glorified and fulfilled on earth as they are in heaven. He teaches that the aim of your prayers should always be the glory of the Father. God will not be honored if the objective of your prayers is anything but His glory. As you pray, God is aligning your identity, treasures, and desires with His. He is conforming you to His image, for the praise of His glory.

It is only after praying all this that Jesus models requesting something of His Father. The three things He instructs you to ask for are needs specific to each part of your being. For your body, you are to ask for the provision of daily bread; for your soul, you are to ask for deliverance from Satan and a pulling toward God; and for your spirit, you are to ask for forgiveness. Jesus was perfect and thus never in need of being forgiven, but He modeled the importance of *you* daily keeping a clear conscience before your Father.

Jesus did not just teach His disciples how to pray. He taught them how to know the Father through prayer. Prayer holds a significant place in your life as a disciple. Take a look at the diagram and notice that prayer is the upward support of the cross. It is the way by which you communicate with your Father and come to know Him.

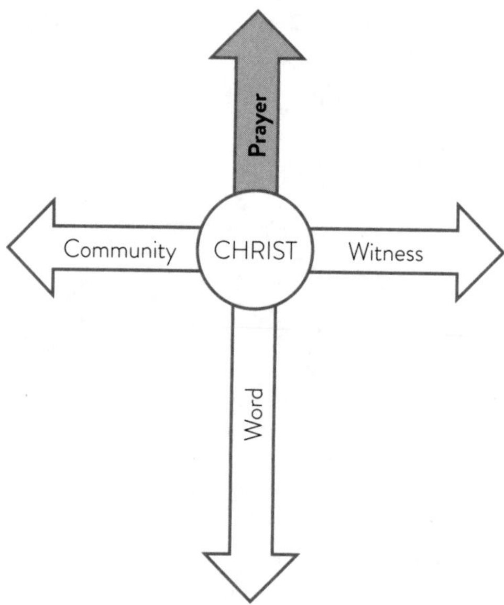

PRAYER

Lord, may your Father-like love awaken my child-like trust. May the spontaneous breath of my heart cry out that Your name, kingdom, and desires become first loves in my life. Move my heart to have more conversations with You, more fellowship with You, and deeper friendship with You. In Jesus's name, amen.

Day One
THE PURPOSE OF PRAYER

Today's passage for your conversation with God: Matthew 6:5-13

The first part of today's passage teaches us this important truth: prayer is meant to be an intimate, faith-filled experience with your Father. One in which you believe He cares about you and you share your heart with Him accordingly—as though face-to-face, despite not being able to see Him. The strength and fervency of your feelings are not what matters in prayer—what does is the love and power of the Father whom you entrust with them.[2]

Jesus says, "Your Father knows what you need before you ask him" (v. 8). Even though God knows what is on your heart, He desires to hear you express it. We see this same desire when we look at the life of Jesus throughout His three years of public ministry. Have you noticed how many questions He asked people? Over three hundred are documented in the four Gospels! He wants to hear from people and hear from their hearts.

Prayer's primary purpose is not the exchange of information but rather intimacy with your Father. When you pray, you bring delight and glory to God and deepen your relationship with Him. Prayer stirs your affections for Christ.

Cut out the John 15:7 verse card at the back of your workbook, and write today's date on it, along with the date two months from now, as described on page 41. Read the verse aloud several times to begin memorizing it.

Notice in John 15:7 the prerequisite to receiving what you ask for in prayer: that you remain in Him and His words in you. Remaining in Christ gives you the right and power to ask for what you desire in prayer. Your power in prayer will correspond with the extent to which you abide.[3]

The idea of abiding or remaining in Christ can be illustrated by thinking about a refrigerator or microwave. If it is not plugged in it will not work, even if you turn it on. It will accomplish nothing without its power source. Abiding means staying plugged into your Source—the One from whom the power comes. It means going through your day aware of the presence and power of the Holy Spirit living in you.

Our kids have enjoyed playing on a zip line we hung between two trees in our yard. After several years of transporting people from one tree to another, the cord of the zip line has actually carved itself inside our tree—I can put my hand flush against the tree trunk where the wire is attached, and I am not able to feel it. This is what abiding in Jesus looks like.

As you press yourself and your burdens against Him each day, you are slowly growing into Him. Jesus will increasingly conform your will and desires to His.

The apostle Paul reminds believers to pray constantly and about everything (Philippians 4:6; 1 Thessalonians. 5:17). Only when you remain in Christ—pressing yourself into Him like our zipline does our tree—will you be able to pray constantly and about everything.

Reread John 15:7 now, along with this verse that follows it: "If you remain in me and my words remain in you, ask whatever you wish, and it will be done for you. *This is to my Father's glory*, that you bear much fruit, showing yourselves to be my disciples" (John 15:7-8, italics mine). Jesus emphasizes that when you abide in Him, your prayers bring the Father glory. Jesus also says praying helps you bear fruit. In your daily conversation with God, you are listening to what God is saying to you in His Word and praying that He will help you do it. Prayer is the means by which you express your reliance on Him to transform you and others through you.

Prayer is not intended to involve God in your plans, but rather to involve you in God's plans. Richard Chenevix Trench wrote that prayer is not about you getting your will done in heaven, but God getting His will done on earth. It is not overcoming God's reluctance but laying hold of God's willingness.[4] Prayer changes many things—perhaps the most important of which is you.[5]

Ask God to reveal to you who or what you have turned to meet your deepest needs, and fill in the following blanks:

I primarily depend upon ______________________ to meet my need for love.

I try to ______________________ in order to feel like I belong.

I depend upon ______________________ to make me feel secure.

I look to ______________________ for approval.

I worship or value______________________ more than God sometimes.[6]

Confess to God how you have looked to other people and things to meet your deepest needs, and then receive His forgiveness. Now ask Him: "What are some things I need most from You in this season of my life?" List at least one need He reveals pertaining to each part of your being as follows:

Something I want or need for my body (for example, health or finances):

Something I want or need for my soul (such as meaningful activity or wisdom for a decision):

Something I want or need for my spirit (for example, purity or joy):

Now make a list below of people or things that are closest to your heart that you want to pray for most consistently. Some examples could include your family members, your closest friends, your church, a people group unreached by the gospel, and so forth. (You will need this list when you create your prayer notebook later this week.)

Day Two
PRAISE AND THANKSGIVING

Today's passage for your conversation with God: Psalm 91:1-7,14-15

Imagine entering into the presence of the most powerful and benevolent person in the world and having the opportunity to speak. What would you say first? If you are a Christian, you get to do this regularly through prayer. The Old Testament teaches that prayer is an act of coming into God's presence. When you pray, what do you usually say first?

In the presence of the most powerful person on earth, you would almost certainly acknowledge his or her excellence before rattling off your needs. In the same way, when you come into the presence of the Lord Almighty in prayer, it is fitting to begin by praising Him for who He is and thanking Him for what He does. Not only is it fitting, it is also instructed: "Enter his gates with thanksgiving and his courts with praise; give thanks to him and praise his name" (Psalm 100:4).

The word *praise* originates from a Latin word meaning "value" or "price." To give praise to God is to proclaim His merit or worth. Praise is a necessary part of prayer because it takes the focus off you and puts it onto the One who is listening.

Praise focuses on God's character and the ways He works in your life. Reading the Bible is a great way to remind yourself of God's character, and the book of Psalms is especially loaded with descriptions. In its original Hebrew language, today's passage uses four different words to describe God—they are all names with distinct meanings. You will ruminate on each of these names of God today as you practice praising Him.

Read Psalm 91:1 again: "Whoever dwells in the shelter of the Most High will rest in the shadow of the Almighty." *El Elyon* is the Hebrew name that is translated as the "Most High." When the psalmist calls God by this name, he is calling Him the strongest of all gods—the strongest of the strong—and the possessor of heaven and earth.

Think of a time when you experienced God as *El Elyon*. Describe the experience below, or write a prayer asking God to help you experience Him as the strongest of the strong.

Read the second half of Psalm 91:1 again. *El Shaddai* is the Hebrew name that is translated "Almighty," and it means the all-sufficient God. *El Shaddai* first appears in the Bible in Genesis 17:1, when God uses this name to describe Himself to Abraham and promises to bless the nations through him.

Think of a time when you experienced God as your *El Shaddai*. Describe the experience below, or write a prayer asking God to help you experience Him as all-sufficient.

Read Psalm 91:2 again: "I will say of the LORD, 'He is my refuge and my fortress, my God in whom I trust.'" *Yahweh*—sometimes written as *Jehovah*—is the Hebrew name that is translated "LORD" (written in all caps), and it is the personal name of God that He revealed to Moses in Exodus 3. It means "I am that I am" and is a way for God to say He is the ultimate Being. Many Bible translators honor God's personal name with such respect that they will not translate it directly as *Yahweh*, but instead write LORD. (The word *Lord* written in lowercase letters is the Hebrew word *Adonai*, meaning "the master," or "the God with authority.") Jesus used the title of *Yahweh* for Himself in John 8:58, saying "before Abraham was born, I am!"[7]

Think of a time when you experienced God as *Yahweh*. Describe the experience below, or write a prayer asking God to help you experience Him as the God who is with you all the time.

Read the second half of Psalm 91:2 again. *Elohim* is the name translated "God, in whom I trust" and means the strong, covenant-keeping, Creator God. *Elohim* is the name for God used in Genesis 1:1.

Think of a time when you experienced God as *Elohim*. Describe the experience below, or write a prayer asking God to help you experience Him as your promise-keeping Creator.

Pause now and enter God's presence. Praise Him for the times you just described when He has been your *El Elyon, El Shaddai, Yahweh,* and *Elohim.*

Meditating on other biblical names of God will further extend your praise. Consider these: *Jehovah Jireh*—the God who sees and provides; *Jehovah Shalom*—the God who brings peace; *Jehovah Sabaoth*—the God over all hosts of angels and armies; and *Jehovah Rapha*—the God who heals.

Thanksgiving goes hand-in-hand with praise, often coming more naturally, as it is more tangible. Still, it is easy to get so busy presenting your requests to God that you neglect thanking Him for what He's already done. How much do you enjoy hearing someone thank you for something you've done for him or her? How much more so must the Giver of all things delight when you take time to thank Him for His limitless gifts?

Not everything you ask for in prayer will be granted with a yes. Sometimes you will have to wait. Other times what you want is not part of His plan and He will say no. But He always hears and answers you—and He grants many of your requests just as you ask.

List two prayer requests for which you have already seen God answer as you asked. Take time to thank Him now.

Take out your verse card for this week, and memorize the first part of it as follows:

If you remain in me and my words remain in you.
JOHN 15:7

Day Three CONFESSING YOUR SIN

Today's passage for your conversation with God: Psalm 51:1-10

King David wrote today's passage after he slept with a woman named Bathsheba, whose husband was away at war. When Bathsheba became pregnant, David also had Bathsheba's husband murdered to cover up his sin. A prophet named Nathan came to rebuke David and told him there would be serious consequences, including the death of the son Bathsheba bore him (2 Samuel 11–12).

This story points back to Adam and Eve's sin. They too chose their own pleasure over pleasing God. They too felt the need to cover up. They too were rebuked and suffered serious consequences. But in both situations, the grace of God was on full and immediate display. The Lord made garments to clothe Adam and Eve, and blessed them with children (Genesis 3:21). Eve declared, "With the help of the LORD I have brought forth a man" (Genesis 4:1). David and Bathsheba, too, were given the gift of another son—Solomon—whom the Lord named *Jedidiah*, which means "the beloved of Yahweh."

Just as He did with Adam and Eve and with David and Bathsheba, the God of mercy and grace draws near when you sin. He shows you mercy by not giving you the ultimate punishment you deserve for your sin: death. God shows grace by giving something you do not deserve—the gift of an eternal relationship with Him. When your sin is exposed, you can be sure that God's mercy brings it out of the darkness and His grace brings it into the light.

When you confess your sins in light of God's mercy and grace, you experience His joy and healing. When you try to atone or subdue your sins by your own efforts, you instead experience perpetual, sickening self-condemnation.

Unconfessed sin blocks full fellowship with God in the same way that sin—even when it is not disclosed—blocks intimacy between a husband and a wife or a parent and a child. The purpose of confession is to restore your fellowship with God. In confessing, you let God examine your heart to show you the barriers that keep you from experiencing Him to the fullest. The Holy Spirit, whom you will come to trust more as we explore Him next week, will convict you of things that offend your Father as you read God's Word and listen to His voice.

Hebrews 4:12-13 says, "For the word of God is living and active . . . it penetrates even to dividing soul and spirit, joints and marrow; it judges the thoughts and attitudes of the heart. Nothing in all creation is hidden from God's sight. Everything is uncovered and laid bare before the eyes of him to whom we must give account." In other words, sin penetrates all of you—your soul, spirit, and body. It is mostly unseen by human eyes but fully seen by God.

But don't miss what comes next: "We do not have a high priest who is unable to sympathize with our weaknesses . . . Let us then approach God's throne of grace with confidence, so that we may receive mercy and find grace to help us in our time of need" (Hebrews 4:15-16). When you are struggling and vulnerable, Jesus's heart is full of compassion for you. You are fully seen, you are fully known, and you are simultaneously fully loved. Tim Keller said, "The gospel says you are more sinful than you could dare imagine and you are more loved and accepted than you could ever dare hope."[8] You must actively reject the voice of Satan that tells you otherwise—and convince yourself of this truth. Then, you will be able to confess your sin to Him without hesitation and will be able to count on His mercy and grace to help you when you need it most. David, whom God called a man after His own heart, modeled approaching God this way in our passage today.

When Jesus taught His disciples how to pray, confession of sin was one of the components (Matthew 6:12). This confession is different from your initial confession of sin when you received Jesus as your Lord and Savior. At that time of your salvation, God forgave all your sins in the past, present, and future! In teaching His disciples to pray, Jesus was teaching them to confess their daily sins for the sake of their fellowship with a holy God and their witness to the world. God justified you in Christ once-for-all; He sanctifies you over a lifetime.

First John 1:9 says, "If we confess our sins, he is faithful and just and will forgive us our sins and purify us from all unrighteousness." The Greek word translated *confess* means "to agree with." When you confess your sins, you are coming into agreement with God that what you did was wrong. And notice that He cleanses you from not only what you knew you did wrong, but from all your unrighteousness.

Pause now to come into the presence of God. Greet Him with praise and thanksgiving. As David did, acknowledge that God desires truth in your inner parts and wisdom in your inmost place. Ask God to show you where you are weak and vulnerable to sin and write what He says below. Read Galatians 5:19-21 if you aren't hearing His voice, and see if any of the sins listed there jump off the page to you.

Write a prayer of confession to Him below. Thank Him for having already forgiven you and for restoring your fellowship with Him.

David wrote in Psalm 139:23-24, "Search me, God, and know my heart; test me and know my anxious thoughts. See if there is any offensive way in me, and lead me in the way everlasting." Each morning during my quiet time, I think about the day before and ask God to show me my sin. I write it down, confessing it to Him. While reflecting on the day before, I also write down things I am thankful for. As I write both my sins and my thanksgivings, I am thanking Him for His forgiveness and His daily gifts.

Now you try it. Think of the last twenty-four hours, and fill in the blanks below:

I confess: ____

Thank You for: ____

____

Using your verse card, practice the first half of John 15:7 that you memorized yesterday, and then memorize the second part of the verse as follows: "Ask whatever you wish, and it will be done for you."

Day Four
PRAYER REQUESTS

Today's passage for your conversation with God: Matthew 7:7-12

As I have learned in years of receiving Christian counseling, an important part of close relationships is identifying and sharing your wants and needs. If you don't, your relationships will lack intimacy and be fraught with unmet expectations. Sharing wants and needs should be reciprocal.

Expressing your wants and needs to God is an important part of your relationship with Him too. God will not be sharing any needs with you, because unlike anyone else, God has no needs. But be certain that He does have wants and loves to share them with you. This is why listening to God should be a key component of your prayer life. Read 1 John 5:14-15 written below, and notice the phrase "according to His will."

> This is the confidence we have in approaching God: that if we ask anything according to his will, he hears us. And if we know that he hears us—whatever we ask—we know that we have what we asked of him.
>
> **1 JOHN 5:14-15**

The Greek word translated *will* means "wants," and is the same word Jesus prays in His model prayer when He says, "Your will be done" (Matthew 6:10). God's Word is full of His wants. To start—like any loving father—He wants good things for His children. You are His child, and He wants good things for you.

Pause and come into the presence of Jesus. What do you want from Him? Write it below. Then ask Him, "What do you want from me?" and consider what Jesus is asking you to do in accordance with His Word.

What I want from God:

What God wants from me:

In His model prayer, Jesus told us we should ask our Father to meet our daily needs. And in today's passage, Jesus says, "Ask and it will be given to you."

Our teenage son Joshua recently asked me to buy him an energy drink. He certainly didn't need an energy drink (like I did). But because he is my son, and he wanted it enough to ask me for it, I bought it for him. I would not have bought that drink if a stranger had asked me for it. And I would not have bought it for him had he not specifically asked. Prayer and its answer—the child asking and the Father giving—belong to each other. So prayer has two parts—a human side (asking) and a divine side (giving).

Your part in prayer is to ask and to believe that He will answer your request, as 1 John 5:14-15 states on the previous page. The famous theologian Andrew Murray said, "We may and must most confidently expect an answer to our prayer."[9] God's part in prayer is giving an answer, and you can be sure that He will.

Believing that He will answer you, and coming to Him as His son or daughter, ask your Father now for the want you wrote above. Either write out your prayer or describe this experience with Him below.

Neglecting to share your wants and needs with God is an active declaration of your independence from God. E. M. Bounds said it well: "Every day spent in prayerlessness is a day spent in functional atheism."[10]

Ask God how He wants to grow your prayer life. What needs to change?

Now, pause to imagine what it would be like if you fully obey what He just told you for the next month. Describe the impact this could have on yourself and those you are praying for.

In addition to praying for ourselves, we have the privilege of intercession, which is when we pray for God to meet the needs of another person.

Make a list below of people or things that you want to pray for weekly or monthly but can't commit to pray for daily. Some examples could include extended family, friends, neighbors, missionaries, organizations, justice issues, countries in peril, and so forth. (You will write these in your prayer notebook during tomorrow's lesson.)

When you pray for yourself and others, God uses you as His vehicle to accomplish His will. You help fulfill His wants—just remember He fulfills them according to His time, not yours. Prayer must often be heaped up until God sees that its measure is full.[11] Prayer can instantly move a mountain, but more often it happens one shovel-full at a time. You must learn to give the Father time.

God collects and treasures every one of your prayers (Revelation 5:8). Just as water constantly dripping onto a rock over a long period of time eventually makes a hole, your consistent prayers over time bring about significant and permanent change on earth and in heaven. A prolonged process does not mean God is holding back from you. He doesn't want to just change your circumstances; He also wants to change *you* through the process of prayer.

When you pray, you are joining Jesus and His army in a raging battle against Satan. As you pray, remember that the battle is temporary and that it belongs to the Lord; you are praying for victory, but also from victory (as seen in 2 Chronicles 20, the optional passage for day 7 this week).

Use your verse card to practice John 15:7 until you have it memorized.

Day Five
A PRAYER TOOL

Today's passage for your conversation with God: Matthew 14:13-23

Note: A mini composition book or a pocket-size notebook is recommended for today's experience. I prefer a paper notebook over a digital prayer notebook because I already spend enough time looking at my phone; however, if you prefer a digital version, search "Prayer Notebook" among available apps.

I want to give you some context for today's passage. The events you just read took place during a very busy season in the middle of Jesus's three-year earthly ministry. Jesus had just found out that His cousin and dear friend, John the Baptist, had been beheaded for following God. As you read, Jesus responded by withdrawing privately to be alone with His Father. But so many followed Him that He found Himself in a large crowd and showed great compassion toward them all day long and into the night. At that point, He felt urgency to get alone with His Father to pray and spent the entire day and much of the night on a mountainside doing so.

Jesus prioritized prayer. Do you? If not, what keeps you from praying more?

Jesus kept a full schedule. He had a big job. His earthly father had passed away when Jesus was between the ages of twelve and thirty, making His mom a widow, and He was the oldest child of at least four younger brothers and two younger sisters. In addition to His family, Jesus had twelve disciples He cared deeply for. "But Jesus often withdrew to lonely places and prayed" (Luke 5:16).

Today you will create a tool called a prayer notebook. A tool is something you hold in your hand that helps you do a certain task. For many years, this tool has helped me to pray. Here are some of the benefits I've found:

- More consistency in prayer, leading to deeper intimacy with God
- Structure to pray for more people
- Increased variety and specificity in what I pray for
- Accountability to pray for new needs as they arise
- Greater ability to see God at work in my life as He responds to my prayers

Pause and ask the Lord to bless and multiply your prayer life through this tool. Say John 15:7 from memory and then declare its personalized version aloud as follows: "If I remain in You and Your words remain in me, I can ask whatever I wish and it will be given to me."

Follow the instructions below to divide your pocket-size notebook into three sections: daily, weekly, and monthly. I recommend writing in pencil so that you can more easily update requests in the future. (If you do not have a small notebook, you can use normal paper, and yours will be a prayer list rather than a portable notebook. Fold several pieces of paper in half twice so they have four even sections. Each section will simulate a prayer notebook page.)

The first section is for your daily requests—those people or things closest to your heart. Each person or thing will have its own page. I recommend putting your own name on the first page. Then turn back to day 1 on page 16 and write each person or thing you listed, at the top of a new page, in the order you would like to pray for them. After you have created a page for each thing you wrote, go back and list one or a few prayer requests on each page. For example, under my daughter Jenna's name, I might write, *Growing love for Jesus, Honesty,* and *Godly friends.*

Now add a few more pages to this section, and write *Etc.* at the top of them. Leave these pages blank for now. When something comes up you want to pray for temporarily such as a decision you need wisdom for or if someone asks you to pray for his or her surgery next Friday, you can add it here for daily prayer. You might want to write a Bible verse you're believing for that situation. When God answers your prayers, you can write in the results and date so you'll have a record of God's faithfulness. After your Etc. pages, you have completed the first section of your notebook.

The second section is for your weekly requests. You will have seven pages in this section—one for each day of the week. Add these pages (Monday, Tuesday, etc.) to your prayer notebook now. Then write in your notebook under each consecutive day the various requests you wrote out until all of them are included in this weekly section. For example, under the "Sunday" heading I might write *My small group*, *Pastor Will*, *Shanks (Missionary family in Asia)*, and *Racial justice*.

The third section is for your monthly requests. I have found it helpful to put a paperclip or tab on the first page of this monthly section of my prayer notebook, so that it is easier to flip to. Start by writing a circled or underlined *1*, *2*, and *3* vertically on the first page, giving space between each number (see below). On the second page, write *4*, *5*, and *6*; then keep going with three numbers—representing dates of the month—per page until you get to thirty-one. If you have the time right now, list people or things you know you would like to pray for but don't have the capacity to pray for daily or weekly under consecutive numbers, starting with 1. If you don't have time right now, you can leave the space for requests (between the numbers) blank for now, but try to fill it out soon. You can always add to this section as your prayer life develops. Here is an example of what this might look like:

1
Uncle Cliff and Aunt Krista
Mike and Elyse (neighbors)

2
Persecuted believers in Asia
Coworker Johnnie (atheist)

3
Ukraine
Jag (mailman—Hindu)

Your prayer notebook is now complete! Here's how to pray through it: Begin on the first page of your first section and flip through each page, praying for one request on each page. Then turn to the page in the second section that corresponds with what day of the week it is and pray for all the requests written on that page. If you have added monthly requests, then turn to the page in the third section that corresponds with what date of the month it is and pray for the requests listed under that date.

This prayer tool is intended for daily use, but resist an all-or-nothing mindset. You can be in any position when praying through it—kneeling, laying, sitting, standing, walking, and so forth. It is helpful to get into a rhythm of praying at the same time each day—such as during your quiet time, during your commute to work, before bed, or even during a morning run like I do. I want to challenge you to commit to pray through your prayer notebook once before your next group session. Bring it to this week's group session as well.

Make time in the next few weeks to ask the people you pray for every day what they would like you to pray for them. Also ask God what He wants you to pray for each of them. Add what you hear to their daily pages in your prayer notebook. An appendix is included on pages 272-73 that describes how to make this prayer notebook, and can be used for your own reference and to help you pass this tool on to others.

Optional passages for more conversations with God:

Day 6: 2 Chronicles 20:1-30

Day 7: Luke 18:1-8

Section Two

YOUR RELATIONSHIP WITH YOUR INNER SELF

Week Four

YOUR SPIRIT AND THE HOLY SPIRIT

Be filled with the Holy Spirit.
EPHESIANS 5:18B (NLT)

Today begins a new section of your discipleship experience. Over the next three weeks, you will be exploring your innermost being—your spirit and your soul. These are the parts of you that are most essential to who you are yet no one sees. When you look in the mirror, you see only your physical body. But what do you think God sees when He looks at you?

Throughout His Word, God points us toward what is unseen: "So we fix our eyes not on what is seen, but on what is unseen, since what is seen is temporary, but what is unseen is eternal" (2 Corinthians 4:18). He beckons us to pay attention to our innermost being. Jesus said, "You clean the outside of the cup and dish, but inside . . . are full of greed and self-indulgence . . . First clean the inside . . . and then the outside also will be clean" (Matthew 23:25-26). In other words, if the cup is clean on the outside but is filthy inside, its external cleanliness is nullified. May these truths remind you of the importance of your spirit and soul as His disciple.

Notice in the diagram that the very center of your being is your spirit. It is your core, and the topic of this week's study. Let's look a bit closer at the verse you will be memorizing this week related to your spirit. In context, the apostle Paul gave this command to the church in Ephesus describing how they should live differently from those who are far from God. He first told them what not to do and why: "Don't be drunk with wine, because that will ruin your life" (Ephesians 5:18a, NLT). Then, just as straightforwardly, he told them, "Instead, be filled with the Holy Spirit." The use of the word *instead* implies that the Spirit can completely fill every part of you. The phrase *be filled* is significant. It is a command, not a suggestion. It is written in a passive voice—meaning you can't fill yourself with the Holy Spirit; God alone can fill you. It is also written in the present continuous tense—meaning you are to keep on being filled on a regular basis. Although you received all of the Holy Spirit (His entire person) when you received Jesus as your Lord and Savior, you must let Him keep on filling all of you (your entire person).

Three weeks ago in this discipleship journey, you experienced receiving from God. This week, you will experience anew the highest and most wonderful gift you began receiving from Him at salvation: His own Spirit of life, the Holy Spirit. His special work is to convey Christ and everything in Him to you.

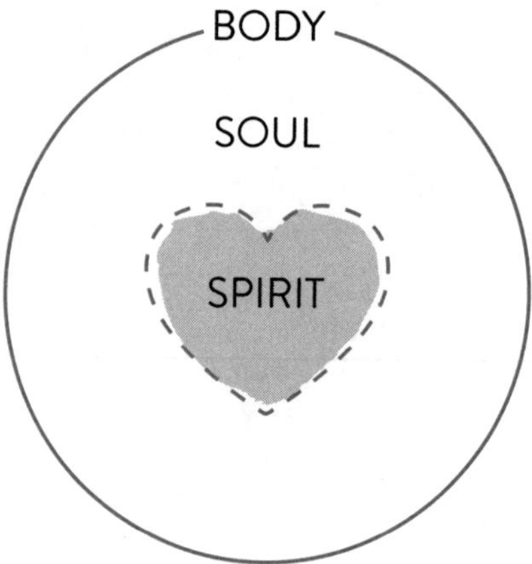

PRAYER

God, only You living in me as the Holy Spirit can satisfy me. It is You, Lord—not just before me and above me, but united with me—that I need. I want Your Holy Spirit to fill more of me, to possess me more completely. I need Your unceasing guidance. I trust You for this, Father. I cannot do this filling myself, so I am asking You to do it and thanking You for this immeasurable gift. In Jesus's name, amen.

Day One

THE DEEPEST PART OF YOU

Today's passage for your conversation with God: John 14:15-21

To open our discussion of something so core to our being, let's go back to Genesis: "Then the LORD God formed a man from the dust of the ground and breathed into his nostrils the breath of life, and the man became a living being" (Genesis 2:7). God distinctly created man's body from dust and man's spirit from His breath. It seems that Adam's body and spirit combined to make him a living being—specifically, a soul, as defined by the Hebrew word *nepes* used for "living being." Adam's body helped him relate to the physical world, his spirit helped him relate to God, and his soul bridged the two. The same is true of you—your body connects you to the world, your spirit connects you to God, and your soul connects your body and your spirit.

If you're like me, differentiating between your spirit and soul is a bit tricky, but we see them distinguished as distinct words throughout both the Old and New Testament. The Greek word in the New Testament translated as soul is *psyche* and it means your mind, will, and emotions. After exploring your spirit this week, you will spend the following two weeks exploring your soul.

The words in the Bible translated as spirit—*ruah* in Hebrew and *pneuma* in Greek—are the same words used elsewhere in Scriptures (sometimes along with the adjective "holy") to mean Holy Spirit. In today's passage, Jesus said to His disciples, "I will ask the Father, and he will give you . . . the Spirit [*pneuma*] of truth" (John 14:16-17).

The context of today's passage is significant. The time had come for Jesus to die. He had just finished sharing a meal with His disciples, washing their feet, and telling them about His impending death. Twice Jesus told them, "Do not let your hearts be troubled" (John 14:1, 27). He chose this tender moment to tell them that although He had to leave them, He would not leave them alone. He promised to give them His very own Spirit—the Holy Spirit—who would make His home inside each of them.

Jesus's eternal Spirit would come into their spirits—the innermost and core part of their beings—and would forever connect them to Jesus. Paul later said of Him, "The Spirit himself testifies with our spirit that we are God's children," brought about our "adoption to sonship," and is the One by whom we cry "Abba, Father" (Romans 8:15-16).

The Holy Spirit is just as alive today and longs to make His home in the spirit of every human being. He longs to connect each one with his or her Creator—his or her Abba Father, but He waits until a person chooses to receive Christ for salvation before entering. He longs to give each person He created a sense of belonging.

At your core you too feel a need to belong. How have you been seeking to meet your need for belonging?

If you have received Jesus as your Lord and Savior, you have already received the precious and eternal gift of His Holy Spirit. Your spirit has been filled with His. He longs to remind you that you are God's son or daughter—and that you belong to Him.

Pause now and ask God to remind you that you belong to Him. Give it a minute to sink in. How does it feel to know you belong to Him?

Only in Christ do you gain an identity worth writing about. In the first two chapters of Ephesians, believers in Jesus are identified in thirty-one glorious ways. It is the Spirit of God in you that contains every one of these excellencies and bestows them to you as an inheritance (Ephesians 1:13-14).

Read about yourself according to Ephesians 1 and 2 below and underline the parts of this identity that you struggle to fully accept as you read these biblical truths.

> I am blessed, loved, holy, forgiven, free, and showered with kindness, wisdom, and understanding. I am saved, created anew in Christ, and given His peace. I am united with Christ, chosen by Him, purchased by His blood, and seated with Him in heaven. I am part of the body of Christ and am carefully joined together with the rest of His Church as God's holy temple. I am without fault in God's eyes. I have been adopted into God's family and am called His masterpiece. I am near to God, pleasing to Him, called by Him, and filled with Him. I have a rich and glorious inheritance given by God and am a citizen of both His kingdom and heaven. I belong!

God desires to give you the new and glorious identity you just read about and to etch it deep into your heart.

Cut out the Ephesians 5:18b verse card at the back of this workbook. Practice saying it a few times: "Be filled with the Holy Spirit."

Day Two
THE HOLY SPIRIT

Today's passage for your conversation with God: John 16:5-15

In today's passage, Jesus continued teaching His disciples about His Spirit, whom He promised to send them. *Counselor* and *Spirit of truth* were the words He repeatedly used to describe His Spirit to them. Jesus knew His disciples would not be able to follow Him without a lot of help—not then, and not now.

List some circumstances in life where you could use wise counsel. Based on those areas identified, where does your heart need to be reminded of what is true?

Ask the Holy Spirit for counsel and truth in the places you need it right now and thank your Father for giving you the incomparable gift of His Spirit.

What would it be like if you received a free counselor who was available twenty-four hours a day, seven days a week and who never led you in the wrong direction?

If you belong to Jesus, this Counselor, whose name is the Holy Spirit, is already yours—whether you are accustomed to depending on Him or not. Either way, you have yet to experience all He can and will do in your life. He has unlimited power, but it is certainly possible to quench or stifle Him by your own apathy or pride (1 Thessalonians 5:19).

The Holy Spirit is a Person of the Trinity—Father, Son, and Spirit—who indwells the bodies of followers of Jesus. Specifically, He is fully God, just like God the Father and God the Son. The Holy Spirit is a He, not an "it" or a "power." Like God the Father, the Holy Spirit is invisible, yet He has chosen to inhabit our bodies as His "temple" (1 Corinthians 6:19). He guides and directs, reveals the will of God, and can be grieved. In other words, He is a Person, not an impersonal force. The Holy Spirit indwells you and should be evident in your personality and actions.

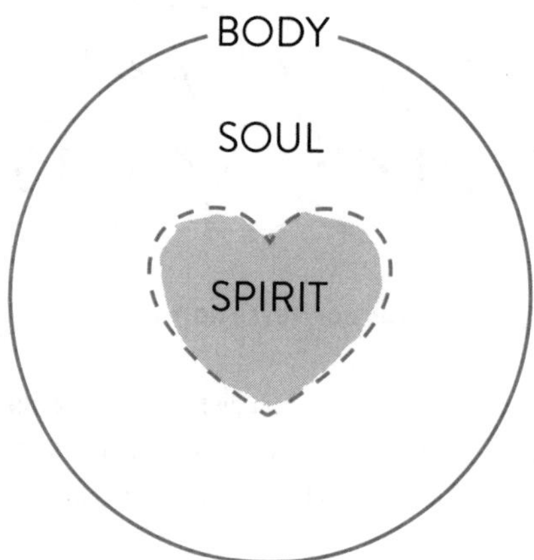

Look at the diagram. You received the Holy Spirit at the same time you received Jesus as your Lord and Savior—and because He is a whole Person, you received all of Him into the deepest part of you. Your spirit has been made new! What's more, His presence will conform you into the image of Christ.

As you read what God's Word says about His Spirit, you will discover that He is an incomparable gift. Last week you read Matthew 7, where Jesus taught about prayer. The Gospel of Luke adds more detail than Matthew: "Which of you fathers, if your son asks for a fish, will give him a snake instead? If you then . . . know how to give good gifts to your children, how much more will your Father in heaven give the *Holy Spirit* to those who ask him! (Luke 11:11-13, italics mine). Later Jesus, speaking of His Spirit, told His disciples to "wait for the *gift* my Father promised," and even later Peter said to those who would repent and believe, "You will receive the *gift* of the Holy Spirit" (Acts 1:4, 2:38, italics mine).

The Holy Spirit is a gift like no other. He is your Helper, your Comforter, and your Teacher. He imparts to you life, hope, and spiritual gifts. He reveals Jesus—and "all the truth"—to you (John 16:13). He also reveals God's thoughts, His love, and things that are to come. He empowers you to live as Jesus's disciple and love those around you. Don't try to follow Jesus by your own strength; ask the Holy Spirit to empower you to follow Him. The Holy Spirit wants to live Jesus's life through you, but you must let Him![1]

You have all of Him—but does He have all of you? Are you regularly inviting Him to fill all of you so that your entire being is flooded with the presence of God as shown in the diagram? Are you surrendering all of yourself to Jesus and His authority?

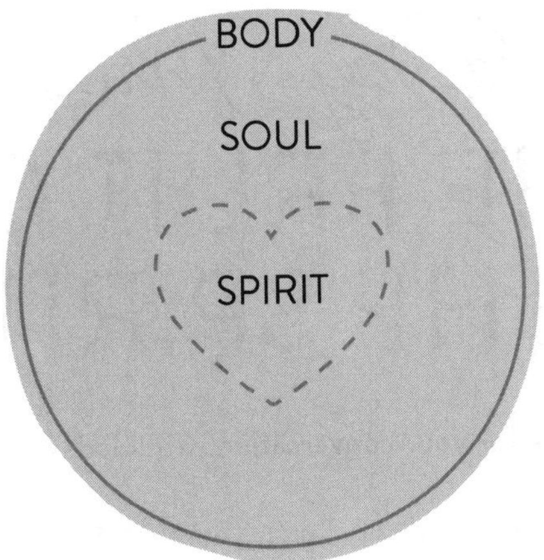

L.L. Letgers said, "Evidence that you are filled with the Spirit is that Jesus becomes everything to you. You see Him. You are occupied with Him. You are fully satisfied with Jesus . . . and you rest in His Lordship."[2]

Practice saying this week's verse a few times out loud, giving special emphasis to the phrase *be filled*. This is a command from God. Consider what a gift it is to be filled with the Spirit and reflect on the thankfulness you have for God's indwelling Spirit. Sit in the reality that the Holy Spirit is filling you with His life and freedom (2 Corinthians 3:17).

Reflect on your experience below.

Why is it beneficial to reflect upon the ongoing work of the Spirit in your life?

Day Three
THE FRUIT OF THE SPIRIT

Today's passage for your conversation with God: Galatians 5:16-25

As more of you is filled with the Holy Spirit, you become more like Jesus. One of the Holy Spirit's primary roles is to produce Christlike character in you, which He calls the fruit of the Spirit as you read in today's passage.

Spiritual growth involves all of God—Father, Son, and Spirit—working together. In John 15, Jesus clarifies other roles for us as well—His own, His Father's, and even yours. God made the garden, so He is the Gardener. Jesus is the Vine. You are one of His branches. If you remain, or abide, in Him, the Holy Spirit produces abundant, lasting fruit on your branch and gives you a joy that cannot be surpassed. If you do not remain in Jesus, you will wither and can do nothing.

When we lived in Asia, our next-door neighbor Raina had a trellis over part of her driveway, on which grape vines grew. When we would go over to visit her, my little kids would always jump up and try to grab the small but plump purple and green grapes hanging above them. I always scolded them, but Raina was always delighted that they liked her grapes and would scold me instead. The fruit brought her joy—and likewise brought joy to my children and to all who tasted it. In the same way, the fruit of the Spirit brings the Gardener glory and delight while also attracting those who see it.

The fruit of the Holy Spirit is not as tangible as grapes. If it was, people like me would try to check off each fruit's box. Instead, His fruit are Christlike qualities produced in our spirit and can be cultivated without limit! The fruit of His Spirit displays the difference God is making in our lives.

Only a living vine can produce fruit—and only the Holy Spirit can produce the fruit of the Spirit. As God imparts life to you through His Son, the Holy Spirit makes you loving, joyful, peaceful, patient, kind, good, faithful, gentle, and self-controlled. These are all qualities that Jesus displays in their fullness.

What are some examples of Jesus embodying the fruit of the Spirit?

Who is a person you know that embodies the fruit of the Spirit?

For me it is my husband Matt, and I am not just saying that because he is my coauthor. The Holy Spirit produces those qualities in Matt as he abides in Jesus. The fruit comes as a package rather than individually and is ever-growing as he abides. The fruit in his life is not only pleasing to God but is also a tremendous blessing to our family. Matt leads us like Jesus leads His church because the Holy Spirit is continually producing the character of Christ in Him. He is not perfect, but the presence of Christ in him is evident.

In your own strength, you may be able to temporarily muster up some conditional love or a few of the qualities you read about. Attempting to produce the fruit of the Spirit on your own is like buying apples and tying them onto a tree. They might look good from a distance but will soon rot. To grow fruit "that will last" (John 15:16), you must intentionally abide—letting His Spirit water your roots. You are powerless to live the Christian life on your own. But Christ is ready to live it through you through His Spirit!

When you are filled with His Spirit, you cease striving and focus instead on receiving from, relating to, and responding to God. The Spirit-filled life is a moment by moment relationship with Jesus, like a ballroom dance—the Holy Spirit leads and you follow.[3] As Paul encouraged in today's passage, your responsibility is to keep in step with Him (Galatians 5:25).

How would the Holy Spirit living inside you say that you treat Him? [Circle one]

as a guest | **as a servant** | **as a tenant** | **as an Owner and Master**

On a normal day, how well are you keeping in step with the Spirit?

not at all | **occasionally** | **often** | **almost always**

How regularly do you fit the description of someone who is filled with the Spirit—loving, peaceful, patient, kind, good, faithful, gentle, and self-controlled?

not at all | **occasionally** | **often** | **almost always**

In which settings is it most difficult for you to be filled with the Spirit and displaying His fruit? [Circle those that apply]

at home | **with family** | **with friends** | **at work**

at church | **running errands** | **other:** ____________

If your answers, like mine, are less than stellar, don't let Satan fill you with an unhealthy shame. Rather, press into God's presence as Hebrews 4:16 says: "Let us then approach God's throne of grace with confidence, so that we may receive mercy and find grace to help us in our time of need." The fruit of the Spirit is gentleness, remember? Let His Spirit empower you to treat even yourself with His fruit. It is always His kindness that leads you to repentance (Romans 2:4).

Ask God to help you experience His Spirit at work in you right now. Ask Him the following questions, and journal responses below.

How can I hand over control of my life to You, Holy Spirit? Where am I denying Your leadership?

How can I stay more in step with You?

How do You want to transform me? And what do I need to change in my beliefs and behavior to be transformed?

Practice saying Ephesians 5:18b, "Be filled with the Holy Spirit," with another person.

Day Four
THE IMPACT OF THE HOLY SPIRIT

Today's passage for your conversation with God: Acts 2:1-11

Nowhere can you see the impact of the Holy Spirit more clearly than in the lives of Jesus's disciples in the book of Acts. Prior to receiving the Holy Spirit, they were not able to fully grasp all that Jesus was teaching them. They often lacked patience and indulged their pride. Rather than receive the wisdom of Jesus's teaching, they bickered amongst themselves. They were unable to perform miracles. And in Jesus's most painful hour, many deserted Him and denied knowing Him.

As you read in today's passage, encountering the Holy Spirit changed everything. As you continue through the book of Acts, you see the disciples were bold and humble. They were willing to identify as followers of Jesus—knowing their very lives were at stake. They got along with one another and generously shared their possessions. They performed miracles and attracted new people daily.

The Holy Spirit always comes with power. Notice what the angel said to Mary about Jesus's conception: "The Holy Spirit will come upon you, and the power of the Most High will overshadow you" (Luke 1:35). Jesus spoke similarly when He described the impact of the Holy Spirit: "You will receive power when the Holy Spirit comes on you; and you will be my witnesses in Jerusalem, and in all Judea and Samaria, and to the ends of the earth" (Acts 1:8). The apostle Paul, who experienced the power of the Holy Spirit in dramatic fashion, spoke further of His power to the Romans: "If the Spirit of him who raised Jesus from the dead is living in you, he who raised Christ from the dead will also give life to your mortal bodies because of his Spirit who lives in you" (Romans 8:11).

Paul knew the Holy Spirit's power firsthand. Speaking of his life before receiving the Spirit, he said, "I too was convinced that I ought to do all that was possible to oppose the name of Jesus . . . and that is just what I did . . . I put many of the Lord's people in prison, and when they were put to death, I cast my vote against them . . . I was so obsessed with persecuting them that I even hunted them down in foreign cities" (Acts 26:9-11). Contrast that with Paul's words after he had received the Holy Spirit: "Compelled by the Spirit, I am going to Jerusalem, not knowing what will happen to me there. I only know that in every city the Holy Spirit warns me that prison and hardships are facing me. However, I consider my life worth nothing to me; my only aim is to finish the race and complete the task the Lord Jesus has given me—the task of testifying to the good news of God's grace" (Acts 20:22-24).

When Paul received the Holy Spirit, everything in his life changed—his identity, thoughts, desires, feelings, relationships, mission, and even his body. Paul was fully committed to Jesus. He testified that his message and preaching "were not with wise and persuasive words, but with a demonstration of the Spirit's power" (1 Corinthians 2:4).

Paul also said referring to the Holy Spirit: "I have been crucified with Christ and I no longer live, but Christ lives in me. The life I live in the body, I live by faith in the Son of God, who loved me and gave himself for me" (Galatians 2:20). Faith is being certain of what you do not see (Hebrews 11:1). Like Paul, you must exercise faith to believe the Holy Spirit lives in you.

How much faith do you have right now that He lives in you?

little **some** **a lot** **full**

Ask Him to increase your faith as needed.

When you received the Holy Spirit, you received God's power—and not just some of His power but all of it. (Remember, the Holy Spirit is a whole Person who cannot be divided up.) You may be tempted to think you need to know more or do more to access the Spirit. This kind of thinking could not be further from the truth. You have all of the Spirit's power right now because you are all His.

Describe the evidence of the Holy Spirit's power in your life from the day of your salvation to the present.

The disciples who formed the early church did not have much. They didn't have many buildings, much money, political influence, or social status. They were "unschooled, ordinary men," and yet when people saw what they accomplished they knew they "had been with Jesus" (Acts 4:13). Equipped with the power of the Holy Spirit, the disciples turned the whole world upside down. You are equipped with this same power to change the world in this generation!

How would your life look different if all of the Holy Spirit's power was used in you?

Read this week's verse a few times and then try saying it from memory.

Day Five
THE SPIRITUAL BATTLE

Today's passage for your conversation with God: Romans 8:5-15

You have the Spirit of life and He has set you free. As long as you live in this world, however, you live behind enemy lines. Satan is the god of this age who rules over those living in darkness in the world (2 Corinthians 4:4, 1 John 5:19). Jesus said of him, "He was a murderer from the beginning," and "when he lies, he speaks his native language, for he is a liar and the father of lies" (John 8:44).

Satan wages his war around you and against you. His ongoing work in the world around you is obvious—just watch the news. His primary tactic against you personally is to lead you to indulge what the Bible calls "your flesh." The "flesh" is shorthand for our sinful nature and its desires. It's your old way of thinking and behaving before you received Christ. Before Christ made you new, you lived by your flesh; its memory dies hard. Living by the flesh is simply living by your own abilities and energy to meet your needs.

As you read in today's passage, "You, however, are not in the realm of the flesh but are in the realm of the Spirit, if indeed the Spirit of God lives in you" (Romans 8:9). To give you some context, Paul is comparing those who are in Christ and have His Spirit (that is, believers) to those who aren't and don't. You have the choice to walk in step with the Spirit or to walk according to your flesh: "The flesh desires what is contrary to the Spirit, and the Spirit what is contrary to the flesh. They are in conflict with each other, so that you are not to do whatever you want" (Galatians 5:17). The Holy Spirit does a far better job being in charge of your life than you do.

The Holy Spirit working through you changes the outcome of the battle. Though you are still at war, you are a victor, so don't yield to a victim mentality. "The one who is in you is greater than the one who is in the world" (1 John 4:4). Satan cannot touch you because Jesus keeps you protected (1 John 5:18). "God is faithful; he will not let you be tempted beyond what you can bear. But when you are tempted, he will also provide a way out so that you can endure it" (1 Corinthians 10:13).

The Holy Spirit is your Protector. The four disciplines in the Disciple's Cross are some of His weapons, and you will find other pieces of the armor of God in Ephesians 6:14-18 such as the belt of truth, the breastplate of righteousness, the shield of faith, and the helmet of salvation. Our weapons have been forged by the Holy Spirit. We're not just defending our faith; we're advancing God's kingdom. "Though we live in the world, we do not wage war as the world does. The weapons we fight with are not the weapons of the world. On the contrary, they have divine power to demolish strongholds" (2 Corinthians 10:3-4). *Demolish* comes from a Greek word meaning "a taking down" or "a pulling down." A stronghold is an idea, a thought process, a habit, or an addiction through which Satan has set up occupancy in your life or in the world—a place where he has a foothold to take more ground (Ephesians 4:27).

Using the definition you just read, what are some strongholds you've allowed into your life?

Strongholds are challenging, but don't let yourself be defeated by them. As any enemy does, Satan attacks those he feels threatened by. If you are linked to Jesus and living by His Spirit, the devil sees you as an enemy. There is not a stronghold in your life that the Holy Spirit doesn't have the power to pull down. You are a coheir with Christ and all of His victory has been granted to you. Rather than focusing on strongholds, focus instead on Jesus and His power that is in you. As a mentor once told me, "Instead of pressing against your sin, press into your Savior."

Look over your answer to the previous prompt and pray that the Spirit would give you power to overcome your strongholds.

Believe by faith that He is at work. Be encouraged by the promise found in today's passage: "The Spirit helps us in our weakness. . . . [He] himself intercedes for us through wordless groans" (Romans 8:26). Trust Him with the process rather than fixating on the outcome.

I can almost hear Paul admonishing you and me now: "Be strong in the Lord and in his mighty power. Put on the full armor of God, so that you can take your stand against the devil's schemes. For our struggle is not against flesh and blood, but against the rulers, against the authorities, against the powers of this dark world and against the spiritual forces of evil in the heavenly realms" (Ephesians 6:10-12).

Be encouraged that you are on the winning team and that you fight from victory. Read below how Paul concludes Romans 8, and underline truths you need to remember.

> And we know that in all things God works for the good of those who love him, who have been called according to his purpose. If God is for us, who can be against us? He who did not spare his own Son, but gave him up for us all—how will he not also, along with him, graciously give us all things? Who will bring any charge against those whom God has chosen? It is God who justifies. Who then is the one who condemns? No one. Christ Jesus who died—more than that, who was

raised to life—is at the right hand of God and is also interceding for us. Who shall separate us from the love of Christ? Shall trouble or hardship or persecution or famine or nakedness or danger or sword? No, in all these things we are more than conquerors through him who loved us. For I am convinced that neither death nor life, neither angels nor demons, neither the present nor the future, nor any powers, neither height nor depth, nor anything else in all creation, will be able to separate us from the love of God that is in Christ Jesus our Lord.

ROMANS 8:28,31-35,37-39

Write out Ephesians 5:18b below from memory.

Optional passages for more conversations with God:

Day 6: Ephesians 6:10-20

Day 7: Acts 4:1-31

Week Five

YOUR SOUL

PART 1: MIND AND WILL

Do not conform to the pattern of this world, but be transformed by the renewing of your mind. Then you will be able to test and approve what God's will is—his good, pleasing and perfect will.

ROMANS 12:2

I hope you feel a closer connection to the Holy Spirit than ever before as you head into this new week. His presence and partnership with you in this discipleship journey not only allows for your transformation but also accomplishes it! I pray that you are increasingly confident in His desire and ability to transform you. This week and next, He will be especially precious to you as you explore the complexity of what makes up the rest of your inner being—your soul. As the diagram shows, your soul houses your mind, will, and emotions—and unfortunately, they don't have their own rooms. Your thoughts, desires, and emotions are intertwined and difficult to untangle. This week, you will explore your mind and will, and next week you will explore your emotions. My prayer is that you will increasingly love God with all of them.

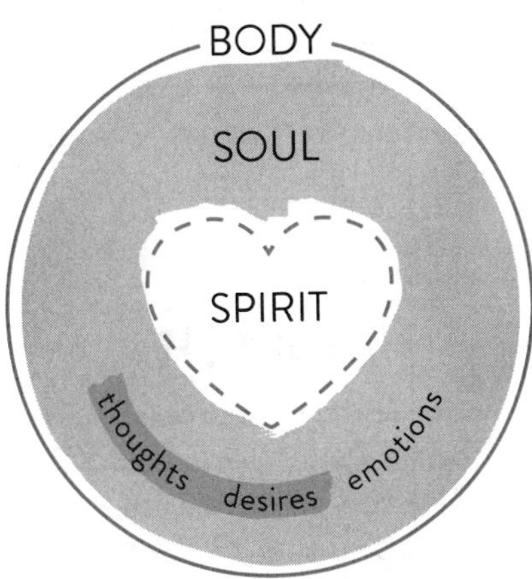

The verse you will memorize this week speaks clearly of both your mind and your will. A few weeks from now, you will be memorizing the verse that comes before it: "Therefore, I urge you, brothers and sisters, in view of God's mercy, to offer your bodies as a living sacrifice, holy and pleasing to God—this is your true and proper worship" (Romans 12:1). Paul first urges the believers in Rome to give their bodies to God as an act of worship. It is in this context Paul pleads with them to also give God their minds so they could be renewed. Renewed minds would transform them, and only then would they be able to know God's will and carry it out.

You need a renewed mind because the enemy lies to you, just like he did to Adam and Eve in the garden. God told them they would die if they ate the fruit from a certain tree, and Satan told them the opposite. They believed Satan's lie rather than that God had their best interests at heart. God has your best interests at heart, too, and what He says to you is always true—no matter what Satan says.

Jesus said, "True worshipers will worship the Father in the Spirit and in truth, for they are the kind of worshipers the Father seeks" (John 4:23). He told this to a deeply broken Samaritan woman. Standing before her was Truth Himself. His Spirit was ready to indwell her with the same transforming Truth. God gave her everything she needed to be a true worshiper.

God has done the same for you. You have His Word, which is "alive and powerful" (Hebrews 4:12 NLT). You have His Son—who is Truth (John 14:6). And you have the indwelling of His Spirit, who sets you up to worship Him and to display His worth throughout your entire being. But you must cooperate. The dotted line—albeit imaginary—that separates your spirit from your soul represents a crossroads. It is your transformation that is at stake. And it begins with the renewing of your mind and will.

PRAYER

Father, thank You for designing me to worship You. Thank You for giving me Your Spirit of Truth. My mind and will are Yours. Only You can move freely through the tangled mess of my fleshly thoughts and desires. But I want You to! Make me more aware of what I am thinking, and show me the lies that I have been believing. Transform me from the inside out, Father, so that my thoughts and desires will reflect Yours. In Jesus's name, amen.

Day One
YOUR SOUL

Today's passage for your conversation with God: Psalm 139:1-16

Today, you read some of my favorite verses in the Bible. I remember latching onto this chapter at an early age, and memorizing them before I even knew Scripture memory was a "thing." As a young girl, I felt unseen and unknown. I was crippled by all sorts of fears. I felt different, less-than, and unfixable. But this ever-so-personal psalm brought me great comfort; its truths covered me like a weighted blanket. The God who made me not only saw me, but He also knew me—and at the same time, He wanted me.

My soul ached for love. It still does. And so does yours. In your inmost being—described by David in today's psalm as your thoughts, your movements, and your ways—you long to be accepted and counted worthy.

You do not just have a soul; you are a soul. Your soul is the essence of you. It is the "being" part of you. The gravitational pull of the world you live in will keep your focus elsewhere—more precisely, on your doing. For that reason, and also because your soul is unseen, it is easy to neglect it. But just as you must attend to the engine underneath the hood of your vehicle, it is critical that you attend to your soul.

To better understand your soul as it relates to the rest of your being, let's compare the three parts of your being to the three parts of a tree—its roots, trunk, and leaves.[1] You learned last week that your spirit is the deepest part of you and is made alive by the Holy Spirit. Your spirit is like the roots of a tree—unseen but vital to your life. Your physical body is like the leaves of a tree—the first thing most people notice but also what continually changes according to the season. The trunk of the tree connects its roots to its leaves and gives the whole tree its unique shape. In the same way, your soul—made up of your thoughts, desires, and feelings—gives you your unique personality.

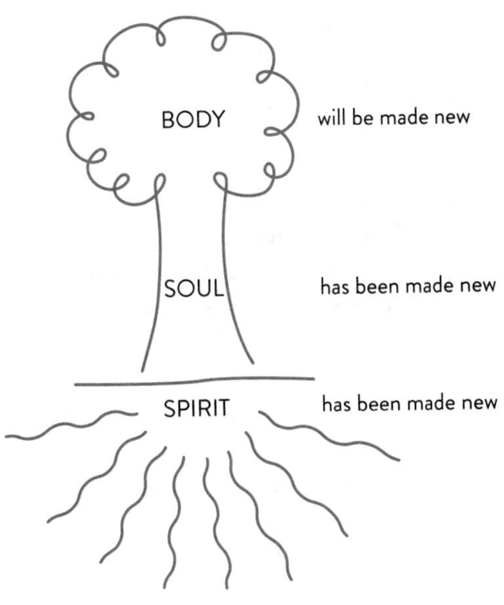

According to today's passage, where did you first exist? (See v. 13.) Why does that matter?

You are formed in your mother's womb, which is why God shows us the sanctity of life from conception. Abortion, infanticide, suicide, and murder are all efforts to snuff out a soul prematurely.

Why should it matter that God created your soul and determined your personality? (See v. 13.)

God was intentional when He made you, and He never makes a mistake. For this reason, you should neither boast in nor take pity in the personality He chose for you. Personality tests can certainly be a helpful lens to understand your tendencies, but keep in mind that there is no one else like you in the history of mankind, nor will there ever be. Your unique personality has a purpose. The Holy Spirit wants to use your strengths and redeem your weaknesses to live out a one-of-a-kind Jesus-life through you. He wants to fully redeem your unrepeatable life.

Your spirit has already been made new. And your body will be made new, although not until heaven. Your soul, though, is unique in that it is being made new now! The degree to which your soul is being made new is the degree to which you are submitting yourself to the Holy Spirit's ongoing work of transformation.

Cut out the Romans 12:2 verse card located at the back of this workbook and date it according to the instructions on page 41. Read the first part of the verse out loud a few times and try to memorize it: "Do not conform any longer to the pattern of this world, but be transformed by the renewing of your mind."

The roots determine the growth. The trunk of a tree cannot simply decide it wants a new shape and transform itself. Only its roots can affect such change. In the same way, your soul cannot be transformed without the life-giving power of the Holy Spirit. He wants to transform you by renewing your mind—but in His love, He will not force your transformation. You must choose to cooperate with Him.

Most of your beliefs were formed before you knew God. At that time, you were enslaved to sin. Your mind was subject to fear and death and was unable to submit to the Spirit of life and peace (Romans 8). Influenced by Satan, the world, and your own sin, your soul was formed in darkness. This is why your mind and mine need to be renewed.

When you repented, believed, and gave yourself to God, His Spirit brought you from death to life: "If anyone is in Christ, the new creation has come: The old has gone, the new is here" (2 Corinthians 5:17). Jesus said: "If you hold to my teaching, you are really my disciples. Then you will know the truth, and the truth will set you free. Everyone who sins is a slave to sin. Now a slave has no permanent place in the family, but a son belongs to it forever. So if the Son sets you free, you will be free indeed" (John 8:31-32,34-36).

In Christ, you are new and you are free. You have the mind of Christ (1 Corinthians 2:16)! You are no longer bound to Satan. Still, 1 Peter 5:8 warns you to be clear-minded and alert because "your enemy the devil prowls around like a roaring lion looking for someone to devour."

As the seat of your identity, your soul is the place where the strongholds we talked about last week often take root—and the soil of your mind is especially fertile. Satan will try to remind you of who you used to be, but John Newton put it well: "I am not what I ought to be, I am not what I wish to be, yet I am not what I once was, and by the grace of God I am what I am."[2]

Of all the parts of me, my mind is Satan's favorite playground. His lies whirl around like a merry-go-round unless I am intentional to stop them. The lies he spoke to me as a little girl still tempt me today: "You are less-than. Not enough. Unlovable." These lies related to my identity are the ones with the deepest and most destructive roots.

Look at the "Who I Am" chart on the next page.[3] Think back to your childhood and/or to your life before you knew Christ. Ask the Holy Spirit to reveal to you one or more lies (whether listed in the chart or not) Satan etched on your soul related to your identity, and write them below:

Tomorrow you will explore ways these lies have affected your life as you continue to look "under the hood" of you. Finish your time today by praying the following:

PRAYER

Father, only You know what all is inside of me—because it was You who purposefully knit me together in my mother's womb. Help me believe in the deepest part of me that You made me both fearfully and wonderfully. Father, only You can erase the lies Satan has etched on my life. I am asking You to do so now and to write Your truth in their place! I entrust You now to renew my mind as I cooperate with Your Spirit. In Jesus's name, amen.

WHO I AM

LIE	TRUTH	SCRIPTURE
I am unworthy.	I am worthy and accepted.	Psalm 139 Romans 15:7
I am alone.	I am never alone.	Romans 8:38-39 Hebrews 13:5
I am a failure.	By God's grace and power I am adequate.	2 Corinthians 3:5-6 Philippians 4:13
I have no confidence.	I have boldness/confidence.	Proverbs 3:26; 14:26; 28:1 Ephesians 3:12 Hebrews 10:9
I am depressed and hopeless.	I have all the hope I need through Jesus Christ.	Psalms 27:13; 31:24 Romans 15:13; 5:5 Hebrews 6:19
I am not good enough.	I am complete in Christ.	Ephesians 1:10 Colossians 2:10 Hebrews 10:14
I am a fearful person.	I am free from fear.	2 Timothy 1:7 1 Peter 5:7 1 John 4:18
I am in bondage.	I am free in Christ.	Psalm 32:7 John 8:36 2 Corinthians 3:17
Sin controls me.	I am dead to sin.	Romans 6:6; 17:18
I am insignificant.	I matter to God.	Psalm 139:17-18 Romans 5:8 1 John 4:16-18

Day Two
YOUR BELIEFS

Today's passage for your conversation with God: Hebrews 11:1-16

You read about faith in today's passage. It is defined as "confidence in what we hope for and assurance about what we do not see" (Hebrews 11:1). You may see the word *faith* as something connected only to the spiritual part of you. But today I want to challenge you to extend its importance beyond that. The root word for faith and belief are the same in the New Testament. Today, you'll see that your beliefs are at the core of your soul and affect every part of you.

Let me illustrate this with a story: A couple built a new house in a neighborhood where garbage service wasn't yet available. Weeks went by as they stayed busy cleaning and furnishing their new home. Their trash began to accumulate, and they decided to store it in their basement where it would be out of sight, out of mind. Little did they know, mice were also accumulating downstairs, feasting on the contents of each bag tossed down. The day came when the couple invited their friends over to see their new home. Although the home was exceptionally clean and filled with brand new furnishings, their guests could not get past the smell. The odor from the basement had permeated every room. The outcome could've been different.

Imagine if rather than using the basement to store trash, the couple used the oven in their basement kitchen to bake a loaf of yeast bread. Its smell would have filled their entire home with a delicious aroma. Even if the first floor wasn't perfectly tidy, the smell coming from the oven would have made their guests want to sit down and stay awhile.[4]

Your beliefs—like the contents of this couple's basement—are unseen, but permeate all of your being and affect not only you but also those around you. It is your beliefs that form the dotted line connecting your spirit to the rest of your being, as shown in the diagram. What you believe colors the rest of your experience. Your beliefs color the way you interpret all of life.

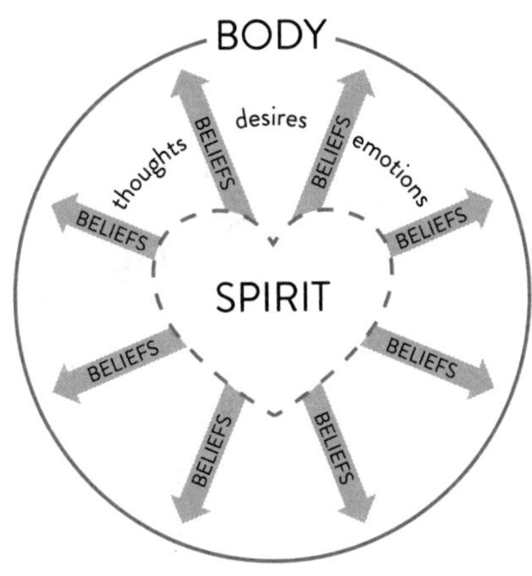

If you grew up believing you were deathly allergic to chocolate, you would probably never taste its splendor. How tragic it would be to find out decades later that it was a lie. A lie you believe as true will affect your life as if it were true—even though it is a lie.[5]

The people commended in today's passage were ordinary men and women who chose to believe what God said was true even when it contradicted their own logic, opinions, and desires. They chose to view their lives through the lens of the faithfulness of God. Their belief made them willing to follow God no matter what might happen or how they felt. And God was pleased.

What these men and women were commended for believing wouldn't be classified as purely "spiritual" things. Abel believed God by offering his best resources to Him. Noah believed God by building an ark. Abraham believed God by moving to an unknown land and fathering a baby as a senior citizen. Rahab believed God by welcoming spies.

Your beliefs affect you and others, for good or for bad. Your beliefs determine your thoughts, which determine your emotions, which determine your behavior. Your behavior in turn reinforces your beliefs, and the cycle continues, as shown in the diagram. Your beliefs about God, yourself, and your circumstances are not meaningless or inconsequential. Beliefs are practical because they determine your values, which influence the decisions that shape your life.

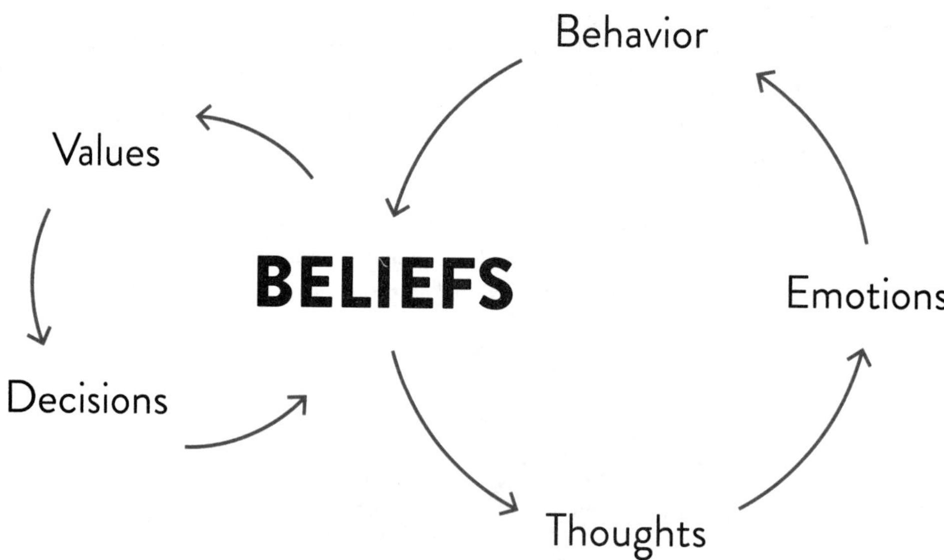

Rewrite the untrue belief from yesterday's exercise that Satan etched on your soul. (For example, I'm not good enough.)

What thoughts have resulted from that belief? (For example, I need to do more.)

What emotions have resulted from those thoughts? (For example, anxiety.)

What behaviors have resulted from those emotions? (For example, over-functioning and under-enjoying.) Do these behaviors reinforce your original belief, creating a vicious cycle?

Now I want you to write what is true about you—the correct belief that is exactly opposite to the one Satan has etched on your heart—listed in the second column of the "Who I Am" chart on page 88. (For example, I am complete in Christ.)

Imagine really believing what you just wrote is true, and answer the following questions accordingly:

What are some thoughts you might have as a result of this belief? (For example, I am allowed to rest.)

What emotions would result from those thoughts? (For example, a weight lifted; peace.)

What are some behaviors that might result from those emotions? (For example, engaging in more fun; being present.) Do these behaviors reinforce your new, biblical belief?

I hope you are able to see from this exercise that what you believe matters a lot. God wants you to know and believe what is true. Your transformation depends on it.

Use your verse card to practice saying the first part of Romans 12:2, and believe that it applies to you! "Do not conform any longer to the pattern of this world, but be transformed by the renewing of your mind."

Day Three
YOUR THOUGHTS

Today's passage for your conversation with God: 2 Corinthians 3:17–4:18

I hope you caught this truth in today's passage: the Spirit of God is transforming you into the likeness of Christ. One of the ways He is doing that is through the renewing of your mind that is taking place in this discipleship experience.

Notice in today's passage that Satan "has blinded the *minds* of unbelievers, so that they cannot see the light of the gospel that displays the glory of Christ" (2 Corinthians 4:4, italics mine). It is not their eyes that are blind but their minds. But God has "made His light shine in our hearts to give us the light of the *knowledge* of God's glory displayed in the face of Christ" (v. 6, italics mine). In verse 4, Paul uses the word "gospel" but exchanges it with the word "knowledge" in verse 6. Your belief is essential to your receiving of the gospel, and it continues to be essential as you live it out (1 Timothy 2:4).

As you learned yesterday, your thoughts stem from your beliefs. However, your thoughts are often easier to identify than your beliefs. Thoughts cycle through your mind all day long. Some, however, have nothing to do with the task at hand and cycle through your mind like a song on repeat. It is helpful to identify repetitive thoughts you have that are not pleasing to God, as they can lead you to beliefs you need to reexamine in light of God's truth. It is not just the minds of unbelievers that Satan seeks to blind. He often builds strongholds of deception that become habitual thought patterns, keeping you blinded from God's truth.

What are some repetitive, destructive thought patterns that plague you? Write them below. If none come to mind, look at the following list of phrases, and see if any of them trigger a thought you often have:

I'm not . . .
I can't . . .
I'm never going to . . .
I always . . .
I should . . .
What if . . .

If you still have none that come to mind, simply ask God to highlight any destructive thought patterns you have this week. For any thoughts you just identified, write what is true instead below.

Jesus knows and cares about your thoughts. The Gospel writers noted that Jesus knew people's thoughts, whether they voiced them or not. One example is when Jesus told a paralytic that his sins were forgiven in Mark 2: "Teachers of the law were sitting there, thinking to themselves, 'Why does this fellow talk like that? He's blaspheming! Who can forgive sins but God alone?' Immediately Jesus knew in his spirit that this was what they were thinking in their hearts, and he said to them, 'Why are you thinking these things?'" (Mark 2:6-8). In another instance, Jesus healed a man's shriveled hand on the Sabbath in a particular way because the Pharisees were "looking for a reason to accuse" Him, and "Jesus knew what they were thinking" (Luke 6:7-8).

In both of the examples above, Jesus took the initiative to expose lies people believed about Him. He deeply desired that they believe the truth about Him, because He knew it would change everything in their lives. Likewise, Jesus wants to renew your mind with truth about Himself. Lies you believe about Him will rob you of the abundant life He came to give you (John 10:10). Look at the chart below that lists some common lies about God.

WHO GOD IS

LIE	TRUTH	SCRIPTURE
God is not good.	God is always good.	Psalm 34:8-10; Luke 18:19; James 1:17
God is condemning.	God is merciful and saving.	2 Corinthians 1:3; Ephesians 2:4; 2 Peter 3:9
God is distant.	God is always with me.	Psalm 46:1; Matthew 28:20; Hebrews 13:5-6
God doesn't want to be intimately involved in my life.	God cares about every detail of my life.	Isaiah 41:13; Romans 8:28-29; 1 Peter 5:7
God doesn't really love me.	God loves me unconditionally.	John 3:16; Romans 8:35-39; 1 John 4:16

What lies has Satan etched on your soul related to who God is, in the chart or otherwise? Write them below:

God ______________________________

(For example, God doesn't want to be intimately involved in my life.)

Now write some thoughts you have had as a result of that belief. (For example, God doesn't listen to my prayers.)

Now I want you to write what is true about God—the belief that is exactly opposite to the one Satan has etched on your heart—listed in the second column of the "Who God Is" chart. (For example, God cares deeply about every detail of my life.)

Imagine really believing what you just wrote is true. Now write some thoughts you might have as a result of this truth. (For example, God feels compassion toward me.)

Let's think back to the passage you read yesterday in Hebrews 11. The belief of Abel, Noah, Abraham, Rahab, and a host of others, was commended. What they believed was powerful enough to affect their thoughts and their emotions, which led them to action. They each had a choice to make. I love how Warren Wiersbe said "faith is living without scheming."[6] When we believe and think God's truths, we stop trying to manipulate people or situations out of fear or pride. Rather, we trust God that He will work all things for the good of those who love Him and are called according to His purpose (Romans 8:28).

As readers of God's Word, we are not privy to many of its characters' thoughts. But I imagine that Noah, after getting instructions from God to build a boat THAT BIG, initially thought, "Really, God?" When Abraham's wife Sarah found out they would have a son, "[she] laughed to herself as she thought, 'After I am worn out and my lord is old, will I now have this pleasure?'" (Genesis 18:12). I find it interesting that the Lord responds to Sarah saying this by speaking to *Abraham*: "Why did Sarah laugh . . . Is anything too hard for the LORD? . . . Sarah will have a son" (vv. 13-14). God clearly wanted Abraham to know that despite all odds, what He said was actually going to happen. I imagine Abraham chuckled at the thought of Sarah pregnant—and God challenged them both. If you have time, read verse 15—it seems like God wants you to have a chuckle too.

Even if your beliefs are biblical, you will still have thoughts that don't line up with the truth at times. You must "take captive every thought to make it obedient to Christ" (2 Corinthians 10:5). When your thoughts aren't aligned with God's Word, identify them as lies, reject them, and choose to replace them with what is true. This is a continual discipline rather than a one-time decision. As you walk in step with the Holy Spirit, He will help you identify any "stinking thinking." This is critical because, as Warren Wiersbe said, when you sow a thought, you also reap an action. Sow an action, reap a habit. Sow a habit, reap a character. Sow a character, reap a destiny![7]

Try to say the first half Romans 12:2 from memory, and then add the second half and begin memorizing it: "Then you will be able to test and approve what God's will is—his good, pleasing and perfect will."

Day Four
YOUR DESIRES

Today's passage for your conversation with God: 1 Peter 1:3-9,13-16

Let's begin today by saying this week's verse, giving special emphasis to its latter half:

> Do not conform to the pattern of this world, but be transformed by the renewing of your mind. Then you will be able to test and approve what God's will is—his good, pleasing and perfect will.
>
> **ROMANS 12:2**

Your will—your desires and motives—are part of your soul. In the verse you just read, notice that Paul mentions God's will—or His desires and motives—rather than your own. He says it is important to renew your mind so that you will be able to do God's will.

It's not that your will doesn't matter or that God doesn't want you to know His will. Before Jesus went to the cross, He prayed, "Father, if you are willing, take this cup from me; yet not my will, but yours be done" (Luke 22:42). Jesus expressed His own will to His Father. He wasn't excited about drinking the cup of suffering any more than you or I are. Jesus relates to your humanity and earthly desires, and He models to you exchanging your own will for something better: your Father's.

What is a desire that you have? How does this align with God's will and desires for you? As you consider the answers to these questions, pray according to Jesus's model, "Not my will, but Yours be done."

In the verse you are memorizing, it seems like Paul knows you will need a reminder that God's will is better than your own; notice the way he gives special emphasis to the fact that God's will is good, pleasing, and perfect. God knew Paul himself would later need this reminder, as he would find himself time and again in dire circumstances and even facing death. What was true for Jesus at the cross and for Paul in prison remains true today—God's will is sweet, satisfying, and superior even when it doesn't feel like it.

When Jesus saved you, you took yourself off the throne of your own heart and let Him take His rightful place. If He is your Lord, His will trumps yours. But the pull of your flesh will tempt you to dethrone Him again and again. You are a "living sacrifice" (Romans 12:1) and must resist the temptation to crawl off the altar. This is why you need to take up your cross daily—and why Jesus taught you to daily pray "*Your* will be done" (Matthew 6:10, see Luke 9:23; italics mine).

You are learning this week that your thoughts, emotions, and behavior all stem from your beliefs—or to say it another way, from your faith.

What did today's passage say about the value of your faith? (See 1 Peter 1:7.)

Your faith is valuable because God finds pleasure in it—especially when you are believing Him for things you cannot see or feel. Both now and in the future, God receives praise, glory, and honor, and you receive an inexpressible and glorious joy (1 Peter 1:8). Notice this example of how your beliefs affect your emotions.

So how does your will fit into the cycle of your beliefs, thoughts, emotions, and behaviors? In some ways, your will pervades your beliefs, thoughts, emotions, and behavior—because ultimately, you have choices. The place your will most often exerts itself is between your emotions and your behavior, as shown in the diagram.

Regarding your will and desires, James says, "What causes fights and quarrels among you? Don't they come from your desires that battle within you?" (James 4:1). It is always important to get to the why behind the what. No matter how strong-willed you are, the Holy Spirit can produce the fruit of self-control in you that will keep you from acting on any desires that are sinful. You are no longer a victim or slave of your old desires. "Those who belong to Christ Jesus have nailed the passions and desires of their sinful nature to His cross and crucified them there" (Galatians 5:24 NLT). In today's passage, Peter says this: "Do not conform to the evil desires you had when you lived in ignorance . . . be holy in all you do" (1 Peter 3:14-15).

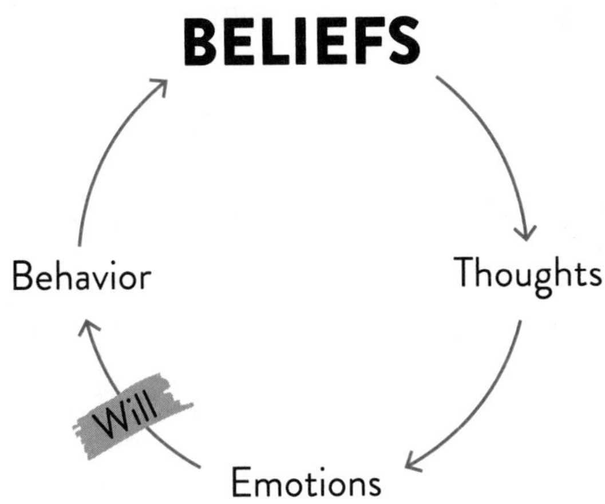

Three of the most foundational human desires are control, comfort, and approval. Which of these fleshly desires do you battle with most? Write it here as a confession to your Father who already knows it, and ask Him to help you desire Him above all else.

During your life on this earth, you do not have control over many things. You cannot control most of your circumstances, much of your health, or other people. You certainly can't control God. That's why self-control is such a wonderful fruit of the Holy Spirit in you! One thing God has allowed you control over is your mind and will. That does not mean it will be easy. You will have thoughts you don't desire, and you will have desires you wish weren't there, but you get to choose what you do with them. These thoughts and desires cannot simply be removed—they must be replaced by greater thoughts and affections. This is the process of renewing your mind. And in doing so, over time, you will find that you increasingly both desire and live out His good, pleasing, and perfect will. This is letting God work out the full effects of His salvation in you "for God is working in you, giving you the desire and the power to do what pleases him" (Philippians 2:12-13 NLT).

Finish today's time with prayer, surrendering your will again to God as the Lord and Master of your life. Consider asking the Lord these questions:

1. **Is my life functionally influenced more by my will or by Your will?**

2. **Will You please help me to want Your will more than mine?**

3. **What can I be, know, or do differently to increasingly yield all of my will to Yours?**

Day Five
TOOLS TO RENEW YOUR MIND

Today's passage for your conversation with God: 2 Corinthians 10:1-5

In today's passage, Paul points out that you should not live by the standards of the world, but rather by God's standards—His truths. Paul reminds you that you're in a battle but you have powerful weapons. The weapons he is talking about are the very ones you have been using these last few weeks—God's Word, prayer, and His Spirit. You will need these weapons to "take captive every thought to make it obedient to Christ" (2 Corinthians 10:5). Your biggest battleground is not your behavior or your circumstances but your mind. External pressures, however, do have a way of revealing the internal reality of your mind.

As I mentioned earlier this week, I have had to battle with Satan over the territory of my mind for many years. In every season of my life, God has guided me to resources and support that have been essential in the battle. One of the things I have learned is that God actually designed the human brain with neuroplasticity, which allows it to be rewired, as science calls it, or renewed as God calls it. Your brain has the scientific capacity to be retrained, and God's Spirit of truth lives in you to empower it. All that is needed is your commitment to cooperate with Him and to proactively use the weapons He has given you.

It is important to Matt and me that we create space here to address the important topic of mental health struggles, as we have experienced them firsthand. Believers are not shielded against having unhealthy brains any more than they are guaranteed immunity from cancer. Your brain is an organ just like your heart or your kidneys, and it can become sick. Sometimes people choose to do things that are detrimental to their mental or physical health—such as illicit drug use or smoking—while at other times we suffer simply because we live in a broken world. While it is true that sin negatively affects our health, most sickness is not a sign of a lack of faith. Even mature believers can have clinical anxiety, depression, or any other mental illness. Satan loves the stigma of mental illness in the church that brings shame and keeps believers from seeking necessary medical treatment. Believers with and without mental illness alike need to renew their minds with truth, because the "father of lies" is our enemy (John 8:44).

I testify to the truth of this week's memory verse—when I cooperate with the Holy Spirit to renew my mind, I am being transformed. Today I want to share some tools that have been helpful for me, and I hope are helpful for you as well.

Scripture Memory. God's Word is a powerful weapon. Memorize Scriptures that remind you of specific truths you need to hear, and review them daily. Post them where you will see them often. Say them out loud when possible—this actually etches them deeper into your heart and mind. Don't be afraid to personalize Scriptures. For example, one I often quote to myself is Galatians 5:1, and I say it like this: "It is for freedom that Christ has set me free. I will stand firm, then, and not let myself be burdened again by a yoke of slavery."

Turn back to the "Who I Am" chart on page 88. For the lie that Satan etched on your heart, write out at least one Scripture verse from the chart that combats it, personalizing it as the Spirit leads. Write it on a verse card and begin memorizing it. (If you have time, you can follow the same process with a truth about God from the "Who God Is" chart on page 94.)

Declarations. These are statements of truth that you want to remember. Just as you do with Scriptures you are memorizing, say these out loud and post them throughout your house. One that is currently on a post-it note in my kitchen, reminding me that I am enough, is, "I am loved, valued, and accepted by God no matter what." One that is currently posted by my desk says, "God cares more about my process than my product. He is perfect, so my writing doesn't have to be." I say this and a few other declarations out loud each day before writing a word. I also incorporate declarations into my morning quiet times. One of the things I currently declare each morning to God is, "I choose to take one day at a time as You have commanded." As you craft these declarations and incorporate them into your life, be sure to root them in specific statements about God's character, His truth, and His feelings about you.

Examine your inputs. What you put into your mind is what will come out of it. How much time do you spend inputting truth compared to the time you spend inputting the "standards of the world" as today's passage mentioned? What type of inputs do you foster when you are on your phone, social media, and other screens? You get to choose what you allow in. Choose inputs that stir up your affections for Christ. Getting off social media and limiting the movies I watch to what our middle-school children are allowed to watch have helped keep my inputs in check.

Christian music. Listen to, or better yet, sing music that directs your thoughts toward God throughout the day. This is a great input of truth, as music helps truth stick in your mind.

Share your struggle with other believers. Because so many emotional wounds are related to lies we have believed, it is important to not only declare what God thinks and says about us but to also hear these truths affirmed and reaffirmed by other people. To receive needed prayer, accountability, and support, you must first be vulnerable with your struggles. Commit to engaging in your church and being part of a small group, as these are excellent inputs of truth that you can build into your weekly rhythm.

Biblical counseling. Every believer could benefit from biblical counseling, but it is especially helpful when you are navigating challenges in your life. The stigma of counseling is a product of the enemy. Matt and I have both benefited greatly from counseling over the years. Some insurance companies will even pay for it! Ask your pastor or people you trust whom they recommend locally, or check out Christian counseling resources online such as the American Association of Christian Counselors at aacc.net.

Monthly Move-outs. A monthly move-out is simply a period of time you carve out once a month to spend uninterrupted time with God. This is one of our family's four spiritual rhythms[8] and is an especially helpful rhythm to keep your mind renewed. It allows space for you to process your inner dialogue with the Lord and re-center yourself in His truth. I recommend a minimum of four hours, but I prefer a full eight. During this special time with God, go back and read all the things God has said to you in the last month—which is easy to do if you are following the two-column conversation with God approach. Other helpful activities for your monthly move-out are found in an excellent book called *Solo* by Steven Smith.

Look at the tools listed above, and put a star next to one or more that might be helpful for you. What is one action step you could implement to make use of these tools?

Try to quote Romans 12:2 by memory. If you can't, use your verse card to practice it until you have it memorized.

Optional passages for more conversations with God:

Day 6: Ephesians 1

Day 7: Ephesians 2

Week Six

YOUR SOUL

PART 2: EMOTIONS

Come near to God and he will come near to you.
JAMES 4:8

You are likely familiar with the term *body language* and can interpret its nonverbal meaning as clearly as spoken words. Your heart too has a language that is vital to your experience of life. Your heart speaks to you through your emotions in the same way your brain speaks to you through your thoughts.

Experiencing emotion is a fundamental part of being human—so it is no surprise that God sees fit to mention emotions throughout the Bible. It is also no surprise that the Bible's most emotionally-laden book—the Psalms—is a favorite of many believers. The raw feelings expressed by the psalmists draws many to regularly consult this book for spiritual and emotional guidance.

You were born with the capacity to feel because you were made in the image of a God who feels. Your emotions, along with your thoughts and desires, which we explored last week, are part of your soul, as shown in the diagram.

Of all the commandments God has given, the one He says is most important is to love Him "with all your heart and with all your soul and with all your mind and with all your strength" (Mark 12:30). It's hard to imagine

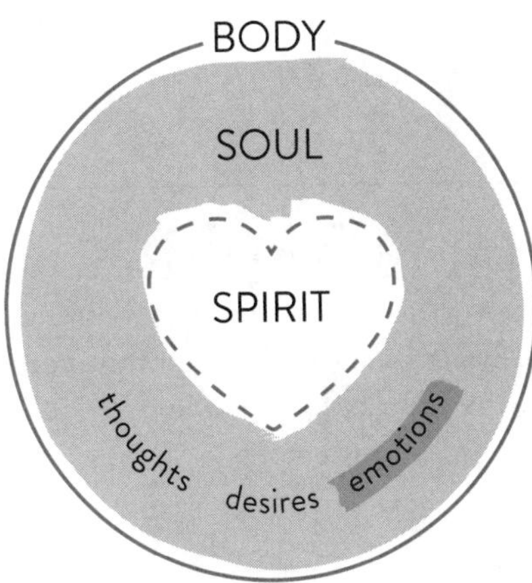

doing that without engaging with Him emotionally. Relationships devoid of emotion are shallow and robotic. According to Peter Scazzero, for this reason and more "emotional health and spiritual maturity are inseparable. It is not possible to be spiritually mature while remaining emotionally immature."[1]

While we've used diagrams to help you conceptualize your inner life, in reality there are no compartments inside you. Your emotions relentlessly reach into every other aspect of your life. As you learned last week, your beliefs lead to your thoughts, which lead to these emotions, which then instigate a myriad of affects throughout the rest of your being. Emotions routinely affect your physical body—think a tingly euphoria, upset stomach, a racing heartbeat, or blushing. They draw out your desires and affect your behavior and choices. They reach into all your relationships—including your relationship with God.

Satan seizes the opportunity to take captive your feelings—which God hopes will be used to draw you near to Him—and uses them as a blockade between the two of you. This isolates you from an intimacy with Christ that Satan knows is so powerful and transforming.

Some people say, "The devil made me do it," but you do not have to be a victim. You can match the fervor Satan shows when it comes to capturing your feelings, and you can do something productive with them. You can bring them boldly into God's presence. You can sit on His lap or lay your head on His shoulder, allowing Him to both bottle up your joy and collect your tears (Psalm 56:8). And if you take time to listen, you will hear Him whisper back precious truths that your soul needs.

The opportunities afforded you to draw near to God through your emotions are plentiful. But what's even more—His capacity to love you and be loved by you is beyond measure.

PRAYER

Father, I desire to follow You with my emotions. Give me wisdom to know how. Give me understanding of the inmost feelings of my heart and the humility to bring them to You. Give me the vulnerability to explore my emotions with my group. In Jesus's name, amen.

Day One
THE PURPOSE OF EMOTIONS

Today's passage for your conversation with God: Psalm 42

Did you notice the way the psalmist in Psalm 42 expressed his raw emotions to the Lord?

Your emotions are a gift from God that enable you to relate to Him, draw nearer to Him, and enjoy Him. Your unpleasant emotions can even help you love Jesus more deeply as you relate to the sorrows He experienced during His life on earth. As an example, I often struggle with feeling like I pursue those I am closest to more than they pursue me. I feel undesired. As I was sharing this painful emotion with God, He spoke to me of the depth of that same feeling He Himself experiences. He who continually pursues every person He creates after already sacrificing His most precious Son for their redemption. How few return His pursuit! And how often am I, too, passive?

Your emotions create a path between your soul and the Holy Spirit that can allow for glorious intimacy. But tapping into this intimacy requires you to pay attention to your emotions and open the door of your soul, making way for you to carry their totality into His presence. Your emotions—both pleasant and unpleasant ones—are poor masters but marvelous servants of connection. In your pain, God is shouting, "Come to Me!"

During His earthly life, Jesus felt the gamut of emotions as you do, yet He did not let His emotions become His master or lead Him to sin. When He was teaching in the synagogue and saw a man with a deformed hand, Jesus felt anger and deep distress at the stubborn hearts of those He was teaching while feeling compassion for this man, whom He then healed (Mark 3:1-5). While hanging on the cross after being abused to the point of death, Jesus felt sympathy toward His abusers and asked His Father to forgive them (Luke 23:33-34).

Similar to how a car has a "check engine" light, your emotions are a signal pointing you to your heart's current reality. It's dangerous to ignore that light or your emotions. They are messengers, reminding you of your need to engage with God. But often, you may be identifying them as messages rather as messengers—and messages of truth at that. Who might be behind this twist of truth?

Satan has not changed since the garden. The father of lies captures your feelings and distorts them into lies that sound good, leading you to doubt what you believe and do what you later regret. And so you pull away from God, and the cycle continues, growing more destructive as it repeats.

Feeling hurt after a friend declines an invitation becomes "he doesn't like me" and later, "I'm not likeable." Your feelings become your master, and you bow to what brings you comfort that day. Feeling rejected after not getting the promotion becomes "I don't measure up" and later, "I am never enough." Your feelings become your master, and you become a workaholic—a slave to perfectionism.

But Jesus's response to His own emotions during His earthly ministry was different. He brought His emotions to His Father, and they became servants of connection, deepening His intimacy with the Father. The rejection Jesus must have felt when His own family came out to publicly "take charge of him" because they thought He was mentally unstable—along with similar rejection from the religious leaders around Him who thought He was demon-possessed and the eventual rejection by all twelve of His closest friends—is the stuff that must have made His heart yearn to stay in His Father's embrace (Mark 3:20-22).

In learning to steward your emotions, it is prudent to first recognize who has been its master. To whose authority have your emotions been submitted? In other words, who do you first go to with your emotions?

No one—I ignore/supress them **Myself—I dwell on them alone**

God **Someone else:** ____________________

How have your emotions served you or led you astray?

Write a prayer of confession and repentance if you have become emotionally numb, self-sufficient, or dependent on someone other than God. Ask God to help you bring your emotions to Him first so that they will serve to connect you more deeply with Him.

Read Zephaniah 3:17 in your Bible. Close your eyes and listen to God's heart for you. Imagine His emotions toward you in this moment. Ask the Holy Spirit to help you engage emotionally with Him for the next few minutes. Ask Him to awaken and activate your emotional space. What do you feel in His presence right now?

Cut out the James 4:8a verse card at the back of this workbook. Practice saying it a few times: "Come near to God and he will come near to you."

Day Two
GOD'S EMOTIONS

Today's passage for your conversation with God: Zephaniah 3:14-20

In today's passage you read of God's joy and delight and how He cared for those experiencing fear, sorrow, and shame. God is compassionate; He cares about your emotions. It is easy to overlook this aspect of His being, especially if you pay little attention to your own emotional interior. God's first recorded publicly spoken words to Jesus were, "This is my dearly loved Son, who brings me great joy" (Matthew 3:17, NLT). It's noteworthy that God proclaimed this joy before Jesus had done any "ministry"—as if to remind His Son and the rest of us that His love springs from our being and not from our doing.

On the very first day of life recorded in history, we read that God spoke light into existence and "saw that the light was good" (Genesis 1:4). In Ecclesiastes, the Hebrew word for *saw* is translated *enjoy*: "There is nothing better for a person than to enjoy their work" and "Enjoy life with your wife" (3:22; 9:9). In the first chapter of Genesis, we read that God enjoys every thing He creates. And to make sure, He adds repeated verbal proclamations of how "good" they each are (Genesis 1:4,10,12,18,21,25).

The Hebrew word used for *good* also means "pleasant." His creation brings Him pleasure! And that pleasure crescendoed when He created man, whom He declared to be "very good"—exceedingly and abundantly good (Genesis 1:31). When's the last time you came into the presence of God recognizing that He takes exceeding pleasure in you?

If you view God as even-keeled, stoic, or even begrudging, reread His Word while engaging your emotions. Throughout Scripture, you can see God experiencing it all: anger, grief, heartbreak, anguish, and weeping, as well as delight, compassion, rejoicing, longing, and tender love. He is the Creator of emotions and knows what they feel like. Jesus, God the Son, experienced the gamut of emotions during His earthly life. He modeled bringing his emotions to the Father.

Read Luke 22:39-46. What emotions do you think Jesus experienced? How did He respond to them?

You were created to delight yourself in the Lord and find pleasure in the good gifts He has given you. The joy that awaits you for all eternity is glorious beyond what you can comprehend. God gives you glimpses of this eternal joy in the temporary pleasures of this life. Have you ever noticed how God designed many of the things needed to sustain life with an unnecessary element of pure pleasure? Think of a restful sleep, a satisfying meal after a long day of work, a big gulp of lemonade after mowing the yard, or the feeling after you finish working out or going on a run. Think of the sunrise and sunset, the fall and spring. Think of the physical experience of fulfilling God's first command—"be fruitful and increase in number" (Genesis 1:28). Wow! God created you with your pleasure in mind and richly provides everything for your enjoyment (1 Timothy 6:17).

Imagine yourself in a beautiful place in nature where you are drawn to worship God. How do these places help you feel and embrace God's presence with you and pleasure in you?

Bring to mind the last time you experienced something wonderful. In response to how you felt, did you also worship God by expressing your feelings to Him? If so, how?

How often is this type of worship a response to your pleasant emotions? Put a star where you land on the following spectrum:

Never/Rarely **Always/Continually**

How does God feel about and/or respond to your emotions, based on the following verses?

Matthew 11:28

John 20:24-28

Hebrews 4:15-16

1 Peter 5:7

What pattern do you notice in the above verses?

Use your verse card to practice saying James 4:8a: "Come near to God and he will come near to you."

Day Three

DISCERNING YOUR EMOTIONS

Today's passage for your conversation with God: Job 10:8-12,18-22

Your legs aren't useful without your leg muscles. Before you began to walk, your muscles were undeveloped and weak. As you practiced standing on them and using them, they became stronger and activated your legs to a more useful state.

In the same way, your feelings aren't as useful without your feeling muscles. Feelings are an inherent part of your being, but they were never meant to exist in a vacuum. Rather, your feeling muscles were created to take you somewhere—more specifically, to Someone. Just as your legs go nowhere without activated leg muscles, your feelings need the engagement of your feeling muscles to discern what you are feeling, to make space for you to really feel it, and to help you process it all with God.

How much time do you make to regularly check in with your feelings? Particularly if you're having a rough day?

Unpleasant feelings left to themselves will weigh you down. But when you activate your feeling muscles to discern and process them, these same unpleasant feelings take you running to the One who designed them in the first place. Paying attention to what you are feeling and taking those feelings to God is a prerequisite for your emotional health. I hope you noticed in today's passage the way Job discerned and shared his emotions with God; this kept him emotionally strong despite his inner turmoil and physical agony.

Giving yourself space to *feel* what you are feeling is an important step to being able to deal with it and then heal. Information and experience are quite different—and the latter is far richer. Here are some ways to create space to feel and strengthen your feeling muscles:

- Ask a new question at the dinner table each evening: "What is on your heart?" instead of "How was your day?"
- Eat one meal per day more slowly, and pay attention to what you feel and experience.

- Journal what was life-giving and life-draining the day before as part of your time with God.
- Reflect on the movements of your heart each evening before bed.
- Do an emotional self check-in at a set time each day.
- Seek out a Christian counselor for built-in opportunities to exercise your feeling muscles.

There are a wide range of emotions you have probably felt at one time or another. Sometimes, there are no words to describe what you feel.

Let's take time to exercise your feeling muscles for a few minutes. As you look at the following chart of emotions, circle one you have felt most strongly in the last few days.

PLEASANT FEELINGS

AFFECTIONATE	Friendly	Loving	Tender
CONFIDENT	Proud	Secure	Empowered
EXCITED	Amazed	Eager	Surprised
EXHILARATED	Thrilled	Radiant	Blissful
GRATEFUL	Moved	Thankful	Touched
HOPEFUL	Encouraged	Optimistic	Expectant
JOYFUL	Pleased	Delighted	Tickled
INSPIRED	Amazed	Awed	Wonder
PEACEFUL	Calm	Quiet	Relaxed
REFRESHED	Rested	Enlivened	Renewed

UNPLEASANT FEELINGS

AFRAID	Dread	Scared	Panicked
ANGRY	Frustrated	Enraged	Resentful
CONFUSED	Puzzled	Torn	Unsure
DISCONNECTED	Bored	Detached	Distant
DISQUIET	Restless	Unsettled	Annoyed
EMBARRASSED	Ashamed	Flustered	Mortified
PAIN	Grief	Agony	Hurt
SAD	Depressed	Hopeless	Discouraged
ANXIOUS	Tense	Overwhelmed	Stressed
FRAGILE	Guarded	Insecure	Sensitive

What impact has this emotion had on the rest of your being? Use the list below.

Physical body:

My choices and behaviors:

My relationships with other people:

My relationship with Christ:

My desires:

My thoughts:

My beliefs:

What pleasant emotions have you experienced this week? Write them below, and thank the Lord for giving them to you.

What unpleasant emotions have you experienced over the last week? Write them below, and ask the Holy Spirit to help you trace them back to your thoughts and beliefs.

Evaluate the state of your feeling muscles by evaluating your awareness of your feelings, the space you give yourself to feel them, and the way you process them. Put a star where you land on the following spectrum:

---

1 (weak) **5 (strong)**

Pray and ask the Holy Spirit to show you a first step in strengthening your feeling muscles. What step is He leading you to take?

Use your verse card to review James 4:8a.

Day Four
PROCESSING YOUR EMOTIONS

Today's passage for your conversation with God: Psalm 55

From yesterday's exercise, you saw how your emotions affect your entire being. Emotions need to be processed and released, and Satan has taught you more than a few unhealthy ways of temporary release. Think road rage, binge-watching a series with a party-size bag of potato chips, or eating a pint of ice cream. William James, a famous psychologist considered an expert on emotions, said it well: "Emotions aren't always immediately subject to reason, but they are always immediately subject to action."[2] You can see this illustrated in the diagram you may remember from last week. Your emotions stem from your thoughts and lead to your behaviors.

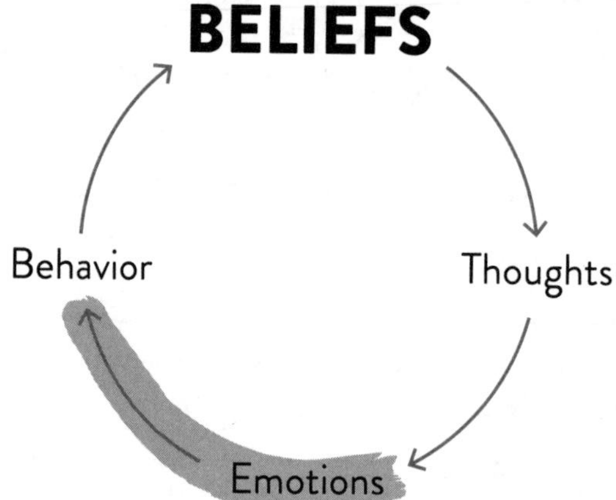

When you were young, you expressed emotions without a filter—as a baby, if you felt tired or uncomfortable, you cried. And when you felt happy, you smiled and cooed. As you grew up, you began to respond differently when your emotions surfaced. Now, when you are overwhelmed with good news and feel like bursting out in song or dance, you probably settle for an inner whisper, "Yay!"

When you feel unpleasant emotions, you probably tend toward one of two initial responses—you combine them subconsciously with your thoughts and spew them out on whoever is near, or you stuff them into deeper crevices of your heart. But to move past your unpleasant emotions, you must first take time to process them.

Your ability to love others well hinges on your ability to embrace, own, and manage your emotions. Without emotions, your relationships will be robotic. But if you let your emotions control you, your relationships will be unhealthy. When you give the Holy Spirit access to your emotions and intentionally process them with Him, your relationships are set up to thrive. You read an excellent example of processing emotions in the presence of the Lord in today's passage written by David, whom God called a man after His own heart. Reread it now and notice how he owns his emotions and bares them to the Lord.

As you learn to bare your whole heart to God, it is helpful to explore any previous pattern of managing your emotions apart from Christ and to learn new ways to use your emotions to connect with Him. One tool you may find helpful is an acronym called NEAR.[3] It is no accident that it aligns with our verse for this week, "Come near to God, and he will come near to you."

The NEAR tool invites you to process your emotions with the Holy Spirit, so He can both comfort and counsel you into truth and then empower you to respond in step with Him.

STEPS IN USING NEAR

N **Name** what you feel. Labeling your emotions brings clarity to them and can help contain what feels overwhelming. Naming them also creates distance between you and what you are feeling, which helps you differentiate your emotions from your identity.

E **Experience and Express** it to God. Take a minute to feel your feelings with compassion toward yourself and without judgment. (Remember—feel, deal, heal.) After you let yourself feel it, vent it all out to God. Don't hold anything back. He already sees and knows, and He desires your honesty and fellowship. David reminds you that his "sacrifice, O God, is a broken spirit; a broken and contrite heart you, God, will not despise" (Psalm 51:17).

A **Ask** God to reveal His truth about *Himself*, about *you*, about *other people* involved, and about the *situation*. Write down each truth He gives you. It might be helpful to ask specifically about each of the italicized categories in light of the emotions you are feeling. For example: "God, what is true about You? What is true about me? What is true about him/her? What is true about this situation?" Consult what Scripture says.

R **Respond** to the Holy Spirit. Ask what He wants you to do with your emotions in light of the truths He has just given you. Record what He says. Maybe it is simply choosing to believe what God says is true despite what you feel is true—to believe greater than you feel. Or maybe it is having a conversation with someone. Or apologizing to someone. Or praying for someone or about something for the next few days.

NEAR can be practiced verbally if you aren't fond of journaling, but writing is a more tangible way of airing your emotions before God and processing them in a godly way with Him.

Which of the two tendencies previously mentioned—spewing or stuffing—comes most naturally to you? Give an example.

In what ways is this emotional response serving you, and in what ways could it be failing you?

The Holy Spirit lives in you and was chosen by God to minister to you (John 14:16-18). What do you learn about the Holy Spirit in the following verses?

John 14:26 ____________________

John 16:13-14 ____________________

Romans 8:26-27 ____________________

What is something that is concerning you right now or evoking unpleasant emotions that would be helpful to process with the Lord? Tomorrow you will have an opportunity to do so using the NEAR process.

Practice James 4:8a by writing it below.

Day Five
PROCESSING EMOTIONS

Today's passage for your conversation with God: Psalm 73

Did you notice in Psalm 73 how the psalmist Asaph brought his anger to God but also reminded himself of God's truth in the moment of his struggle?

God does not grow tired of hearing about your struggles—rather He actually desires to hear your heart. In the book of Job, we see God listening to thirty-five chapters' worth of venting before asking Job a series of questions. God's comparatively brief response moved Job from profound anger and despair to repentance and quiet trust. Remember Jesus asked many questions during His earthly ministry. He is always ready to hear your heart even when it is filled with unpleasantness. He beckons you to come to Him for help sooner rather than later.

Like an invasive vine kudzu in a forest, your unpleasant emotions—stemming just as often from unmet expectations as from wrongs done to you—multiply rapidly and can quickly take over your entire being. If you do not manage them, they will manage you. But you have a chief gardener who longs for you to come to Him for help, and He stands ready to dig up the invasive emotions alongside you. He knows they will return, but with every uprooting, your connection with Him will grow deeper and more closely intertwined.

Something that will hinder this joint uprooting is failing to see that your emotions themselves are morally neutral. As Satan would have it, many people pass their emotions through a moral lens they have constructed, deeming them right or wrong—acceptable or not. In God's Word, you will discover that your emotions are neutral, but how you respond to them can be sinful. The apostle Paul's teaching, "In your anger do not sin" (Ephesians 4:26), is a clear example of this delineation between feeling an emotion and responding sinfully to it. You can also look at the life of Christ, who experienced the full myriad of emotions yet remained sinless. It is hard to imagine Jesus devoid of anger while overturning tables in the temple (Matthew 21:12-13).

While it is your response to your emotions rather than the emotions themselves that can be sinful, you don't have the luxury of ignoring them. Note the second half of the verse in Ephesians previously mentioned: "'In your anger do not sin': Do not let the sun go down while you are still angry." Your feelings matter—they are important—and you are responsible for what you do with them. You will be wise to deal with them before each day ends.

By ignoring your unpleasant emotions, you allow them to take root in your soul. By ignoring your pleasant emotions, you forfeit an opportunity for worship and connection with God. He beckons you to experience pleasure in Him and with Him and to bring Him both the cheerful melodies—like the birds do every morning—as well as the nagging tensions of your heart.

Remember that your feelings are just feelings—don't give them more power than they were meant to have. They do not define you; they are not your identity. I have lived with panic disorder since my college days, and when I am in the middle of a panic attack, it helps me to say something like, "I feel panicked, but I am still OK." Although you may feel truly hopeless, you are in fact not a hopeless person. Although you may truly feel lonely, you are in fact never alone. Your feelings are temporary and changeable.

The NEAR tool you learned yesterday will help you process your unpleasant emotions with the Lord. It is not intended to be used every day, although on difficult days you might need it more than once. When you feel overwhelmed by difficult emotions, it's time to whip out this tool—in the moment if possible or the next day during your time with God.

Fear and shame are two of the most potent emotions. God cares deeply about both and wants you to come to Him first. God says "do not fear" at least 365 times in His Word and often says it preemptively in response to someone's thoughts (Luke 5:10). When you feel shame, let God remind you that His righteousness covers you. Stay with Him long enough to feel its comforting weight and warmth.

When I'm out of whack, I have to make myself stop and journal through NEAR. The Holy Spirit works powerfully in me as I do. Many times I have begrudgingly sat down to journal with my fists tightly clinched in my anger at someone, and then minutes later stood up with tears in my eyes, desiring to embrace them and apologize. At times, the one I am really angry with is God. And His outpouring of truth wrapped in love in these intentional moments lifts a heavy weight off my heart.

Use NEAR to process what the Lord brought to mind in yesterday's homework. Remember, the goal of this exercise is to draw you nearer to God.

N **Name all the emotions you feel when you think about this concern.**

E **Now take a minute to let yourself experience those feelings with compassion toward yourself and without judgement. Now express them honestly to God.**

A **Ask God, "What is true about You? What is true about me? What is true about him/her/others? What is true about this situation?" and record these truths.**

R **How is the Holy Spirit telling you to respond? Record all that comes to mind.**

Use your verse card to review James 4:8a. If you don't have it memorized, review it until you do.

See the NEAR appendix on page 271 to use this tool for your own reference or to help pass it on to others.

Optional passages for more conversations with God:

Day 6: Psalm 69

Day 7: Psalm 16

Section Three

YOUR RELATIONSHIP WITH OTHERS

Week Seven
YOUR BODY

Therefore, I urge you, brothers and sisters, in view of God's mercy, to offer your bodies as a living sacrifice, holy and pleasing to God—this is your true and proper worship.

ROMANS 12:1

This week begins a new section of our discipleship experience. I hope that you have a deeper understanding of your inner self after our last section. This week you will explore your outer self—your physical body. How does your body fit into this section entitled "Your Relationship with Others"? Your physical body is the means by which people identify you and the vehicle through which you interact with them. In addition, you often perceive your body through the lens of how other people will perceive it. My prayer is that this week you will discover what it looks like to "love the Lord your God with all your strength"—or your bodily frame—adding it to the way you are learning to love Him "with all your heart and with all your soul and with all your mind" (Mark 12:30).

The verse you will memorize this week probably sounds familiar, because you read it a few weeks ago—it preceded Romans 12:2. Paul is not just asking but urging the believers in Rome to offer their bodies as living sacrifices to God in the same way they previously had to offer live animals as sacrifices to atone for their sin before Jesus's perfect sacrifice. Can you imagine what the Romans must have pictured and felt when they heard Paul say this? To put your body on an altar was not something you could do without serious commitment. Maybe that's why Paul prefaced this instruction with "in view of God's mercy." Their perspective and yours is critical. You deserve death, but God withheld it from you—transferring it to His Son, whose body was marred beyond description. Jesus literally gave all of His body so that when you offer yours, death is replaced by His eternal embrace.

Your body is the physical boundary to your entire being and houses your soul and spirit—which are the essence of you—as shown in the diagram.

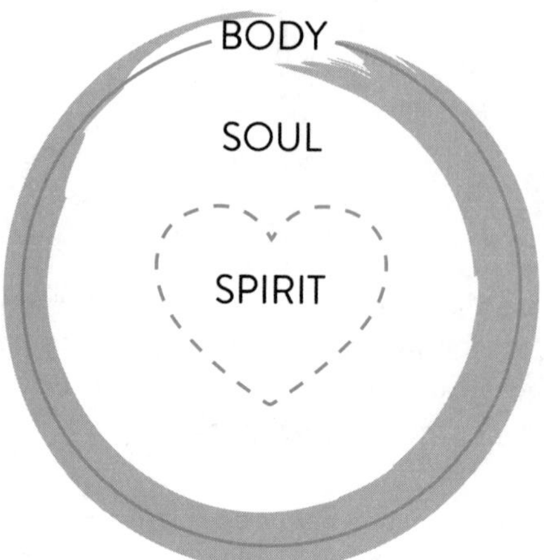

Your body is not the essence of you as Satan would have you believe. Of the three parts of your being, your body is the most temporal. When your physical life on this earth ends, your earthly body will end with it. Yet you will not cease to exist. Your earthly body is temporary and does not define you, but it is a vehicle of your worship.

This week's topics are personal and important, yet discussed far too rarely in our churches—especially from a biblical perspective. As you go through this week's daily content, you will likely be challenged at the level of your beliefs. You can expect your thoughts and emotions to be stirred accordingly. I want to encourage you to lean into Jesus's heart for you as you explore these foundational matters. You will have a natural tendency to want to shift the focus of the content to someone else as you explore newer, uncomfortable territory—but Satan is the one driving that tendency. Jesus wants to have intimate conversations with you about these things.

PRAYER

Father, thank You for my group, and thank You for this journey You have us on together. Prepare my heart for the work You want to do in my life this week, Father. I believe You designed my body with purpose and created it with needs and appetites for a reason. Show me what it looks like to honor You with my body. Give me the desire and the courage to offer every part of my body to You as a living sacrifice. In Jesus's name, amen.

Day One
JESUS'S BODY & YOURS

Today's passage for your conversation with God: Matthew 27:27-31

Jesus gave up His earthly body out of loving obedience to His Father. On days when you feel unworthy, insignificant, or rejected, remember that He laid down His own body as a sacrifice for you. You matter to God—eternally.

Jesus came in flesh like yours. His body grew year by year like yours (Luke 2:52). As a carpenter, He probably did physical labor for much of His life (Mark 6:3). He needed food, water, and sleep just like you do: the Bible records Him being hungry (Luke 4:2), thirsty (John 19:28), weary (John 4:6), and tired—Jesus even slept in a boat during an intense storm (Mark 4:38)! Jesus was faced with sexual temptation and every other temptation, just like you are—yet was without sin (Hebrews 4:15).

And it is in the image of Christ's body that yours was made (Genesis 1:27). Your design, growth, needs, and appetites are not the least bit haphazard.

As you read in today's passage, Jesus suffered greatly for you. He allowed thorns to be pressed into His scalp, and He allowed His mockers to spit on Him. Jesus willingly gave up His dignity by allowing His naked body to be nailed to the cross (John 19:23). His bare, bloody body was lifted high for all to see.

Pause and reflect on the way Jesus gave up His body for you. What does it mean to you to know Jesus sacrificed His body for your sake?

What exactly does Jesus teach concerning your body? One thing He teaches is that your spirit and soul are more valuable than your earthly body: "If your right eye causes you to stumble, gouge it out and throw it away. It is better for you to lose one part of your body than for your whole body to be thown into hell" (Matthew 5:29).

Jesus knows your tendency and mine to care more about the physical than the spiritual. Remember when Jesus healed the paralytic man? He asked those watching, "'Which is easier: to say, "Your sins are forgiven," or to say, "Get up and walk"? But I want you to know that the

Son of Man has authority on earth to forgive sins.' So he said to the paralyzed man, 'I tell you, get up, take your mat and go home'" (Luke 5:23-24). The greater miracle was the healing of the paralyzed man's spirit—which granted him a forever relationship with God. His physical healing was secondary, as it was intended to give evidence to his spiritual healing.

God desires that you too view physical things as evidence of spiritual realities, rather than viewing them as an end in and of themselves. Your earthly body gives evidence that one day you will be given a heavenly body and is designed to point you to your eternity in heaven (1 Corinthians 15:40-44). The apostle Paul highlights how short-term your body is by calling it a "tent": "For while we are in this tent, we groan and are burdened, because we do not wish to be unclothed but clothed instead with our heavenly dwelling, so that what is mortal may be swallowed up by life" (2 Corinthians 5:2-4). Paul knew fleshly suffering firsthand, saying he was given "a thorn in the flesh" (2 Corinthians 12:7). But Paul did not feel entitled to perfect flesh; rather, he said, "I live in this earthly body by trusting in the Son of God, who loved me and gave himself for me" (Galatians 2:20b NLT). God desires that you, like Paul, view your body through the lens of His Word.

Gnosticism, one of the earliest heresies the early church combated, claimed that the material world, including your body, is evil or unimportant. Therefore, they argued that Jesus didn't actually come in the flesh. The truth is that your body is good, important, and also temporary, whereas your soul and spirit are eternal. The fact that Jesus healed so many people during His earthly ministry gives evidence that He cares about people's bodies and physical health. Jesus cares about your body and health too, even though He does not promise you a body without dysfunction or disease. He does not promise you physical health. In fact, right before He allowed His own body to be abused, He said, "In this world you will have trouble. But take heart! I have overcome the world" (John 16:33).

As I type this, my brother Andrew is preaching at the funeral of one of his close friends, Chris, who died suddenly in the prime of his life. Why did Jesus not heal him? Why has Jesus not yet healed the chronic illness in my brain and in my gut? And why does Jesus not always heal you and those you love?

I wish I had a clear answer to these questions. I ask them to Jesus just like I posed them to you. But I can tell you that His embrace is even better than His answers, just as His promises are better than short-term relief. He promises to heal you—just not always on this earth. If Jesus, who died in His flesh at the age of thirty-three, was not entitled to a long life on earth, neither are you or I. Jesus Himself suffered to the point of death. By looking at Him you can know your suffering is not in vain.

Where do you currently need His healing in your physical body? Write it below and ask Him for it, trusting Him to answer you according to His timing. If you don't currently have a need for physical healing, thank God below for the gift of your health.

God does not make mistakes. Your body might be less than ideal "so that the works of God might be displayed" in your life, as Jesus said was true for a man born blind (John 9:3). If so, focus on both His cross and empty tomb—and may you know without a shadow of a doubt that your suffering has purpose and is "not worth comparing with the glory that will be revealed" in you (Romans 8:18). Your suffering will be met with hope that will not disappoint (Romans 5:3-5).

Have you idolized your body—esteeming it too highly, as if your best attempts could make it immortal?

Yes **No**

Have you devalued your body by giving it insufficient attention?

Yes **No**

Jesus honored His Father with His body by going to the cross. Ask your Father to show you what honoring Him with your body would look like and write what He says below.

Cut out the Romans 12:1 verse card in the back of this workbook. Start memorizing the first part: "Therefore, I urge you, brothers and sisters, in view of God's mercy, to offer your bodies as a living sacrifice, holy and pleasing to God."

Day Two
YOUR GENDER

Today's passage for your conversation with God: Genesis 1:26-31

Today and tomorrow's lessons were written by Allison's brother Andrew Franklin. Andrew's life is a testimony to Jesus's ability to bring truth and healing to sexual brokenness. He is a pastor, author, and a leading voice in the church on these topics.

God chose to stamp your body with His very image. In today's passage, you see that gender is a primary way that His image is shown in humanity.

In God's original design, your body, soul, and spirit were intended to work in perfect harmony—your body perfectly expressing your soul and spirit in complete alignment with God. As one theologian expressed: "The body—and only the body—can make visible what is invisible: the spiritual and the divine. It was created to transfer into the visible reality of the world, the invisible mystery hidden in God from time immemorial, and thus to be a sign of it."[1]

If our bodies are meant to express important truths about God, and our gender is a primary way His image is expressed in us, then our genders—and our confidence in them as men and women—really matter!

In the Genesis 1–3 account of creation, it's clear that men and women were created in different ways and with unique purposes. Man is created from dust, infused with the breath of God, and given a commission to name and rule over the rest of creation (Genesis 2:7,19-20). Man begins looking up above at his Sovereign God, then is commissioned to exercise authority over the lesser creatures below. From this we learn that men have a unique calling to name and impart dignity through authoritative words and a unique perspective that tends toward leadership and order.

Men's bodies, likewise, communicate God's story. They are shaped for strength—typically their bodies are more angular and muscular than a woman's. This reflects their purpose and calling before the fall to cultivate and keep the garden of Eden.

Women, likewise, have a powerful formation story and calling. Women are created not from dust but from the side of man himself. Just as God put Adam into a deep sleep and wounded his side to form his bride, so millennia later Jesus would enter the sleep of death, and out of the blood and water that flowed from His wounded side, His bride the church would supernaturally spring forth. If Adam is formed hierarchically, Eve is formed not from above or below, but from the very side of Adam, signifying her greater gift to discern the connectedness and equal dignity of all. This also speaks of women's greater capacity for relationship: while Adam is created from the earth that he is commissioned to work, Eve is created from Adam and called his "helper" (Genesis 2:18): equal in dignity yet supplying what he lacks through the gift of relationship she brings to him.

What does your gender help you see about God? What about the opposite gender?

Although God created our gendered bodies with dignity and a calling, most of us are woefully detached from this dignity. My very name, Andrew, means "strong and masculine," and yet I hated my name for years as I felt it was an expression of everything I wasn't. Why is it so hard for many of us to stand confidently as a man or a woman? The answer to that is complicated in many ways, but it is rooted in the fall into sin described in Genesis 3 and Romans 3.

For men, the gift for work becomes a cursed tendency toward workaholism, stress, anxiety, and meaninglessness regarding vocation (Genesis 3:17-19). For women, the gift for pure relational help and completion becomes a cursed tendency toward disappointment in relationship, a desire for control, and increased pain and heartache in her caretaking calling (Genesis 3:16).

It is important to recognize and take responsibility for how we fail to exhibit the glory God stamped on our gender for "all have sinned and fallen short of the glory of God" (Romans 3:23). Only through purifying our own vision of both genders can we see clearly to help those who are struggling with the brokenness so pervasive in our world today. We need not wallow in shame regarding this but simply ask for forgiveness and cry out for our Redeemer to restore our dignity!

In what ways do you exemplify the curse given to your gender in Genesis 3? Pause and cry out to God, asking Him to give you a godly vision for your gender that glorifies Him.

The arrival of Jesus is truly good news for our insecurities and sins as men and women! In John 4 and John 8, Jesus reveals the ways His love can remove shame from women and restore them to be powerful expressions of His mercy. God also makes women strong relational advocates of Him (see John 4:28-30). Both Jesus's mother Mary and Mary Magdalene profoundly modeled women who received His presence in deep and transformational ways, and thus "birthed" the church as we know it, through Mary's first encounter with baby Jesus (Luke 2:7,19) and Mary Magdalene's encounter with Jesus resurrected (Mark 16:9-11).

The Gospels also reveal Jesus's ability to stabilize and bring meaning to impulsive and empty men. Luke 5:1-11 describes Jesus's encounter with His disciple Peter who had toiled in anxious, sleepless labor, only to find that through simple obedience to Jesus, his work could be overwhelmingly fruitful. Each of the apostles were transformed from passive men—abandoning Jesus at His hour of greatest need—into fiery witnesses, willing to risk their very lives for the sake of Jesus and for the dignity of His bride, the church. We too can become men who sacrifice, serve, and awaken dignity in one another and in the women around us.

Use your verse card to review the first part of Romans 12:1: "Therefore, I urge you, brothers and sisters, in view of God's mercy, to offer your bodies as a living sacrifice, holy and pleasing to God."

See page 277 for more resources on this topic.

Day Three
YOUR SEXUALITY

Today's passage for your conversation with God: 1 Corinthians 6:12-20

If your gendered body displays the character and nature of God, it naturally follows that the way you use your body to express the love of God is of utmost importance. The body severed from the life and inspiration of the Holy Spirit is unable to fulfill the purpose God created us with. While our bodies are incomplete without a spiritual life, the inverse is also true: God wants our spirits to have bodies. His design is intention. God already created beings that have spirits without bodies—they're called angels. And God already created physical beings without a spirit—they're called animals.

God has given you relational desires that only He is able to fully satisfy. Following Him leads you into holy avenues for your needs to be met. As you surrender your temptations, fears, and disappointments to Him, you will begin to learn the way of love that is patient, kind, and not insistent on its own way (1 Corinthians 13:4-5).

The desire for intimacy is a gift from God and one of the many ways you bear His image. However, when it comes to the desire for sexual intimacy, many buy into the lie that sexual desire is inherently bad, and holiness requires killing those desires for intimacy. In God's sovereign wisdom, your desires need not be killed, but rather directed in the right ways.

Your desires are a good gift from God, but they also do not define you. Jesus said only some people can joyfully accept being single and celibate their entire lives in order to be more devoted to the kingdom of heaven, but those who can are participating in something quite valuable (Matthew 19:11-12). Paul said singleness has some advantages if one can remain sexually pure because he or she can focus on pleasing the Lord without divided interests (1 Corinthians 7:32-34). Those who forego marriage to enter into union with God for the sake of building up the church—like Paul chose—are to be commended. Those who choose to enter into a marriage covenant glorify God as well (1 Corinthians 7:38).

God-honoring sexuality and marriage teach us about His love, His pursuit, His faithfulness, and His passion toward His people. From the beginning of Scripture, you will see that a man and woman, brought together under the blessing of God, are meant to exhibit a shame-free joy in their union as they bind themselves together in the physical act of marriage (Genesis 2:24-25). This theme is developed most notably in the poetry of Song of Solomon.

In Genesis 2; Matthew 19; Ephesians 5; and Revelation 21, you will see that the marriage union serves as a powerful, holy metaphor of God's great love for His people. It is no surprise, then, that Satan would seek to defile this witness through sexual immorality and shame.

Let's take a moment to reflect on how Satan may have done this in your own life. Paul says in 2 Corinthians 7:1, "Let us purify ourselves from everything that contaminates body and spirit, perfecting holiness out of reverence for God." What do you allow in your life that contaminates your body and spirit from the holiness God desires?

If you are married, how does the way you love, honor, and show affection to your spouse exhibit the radical, dignifying, sacrificial, honoring love of Jesus?

If you are single, what does it look like to joyfully surrender to Jesus your desire for companionship, giving your undivided all for His kingdom over your comfort? Are you obeying His command to "not be yoked together with unbelievers" (2 Corinthians 6:14)?

Today's passage reveals why we should honor God within the context of sexuality. One reason is that your sexual beliefs and behaviors are a reflection of what you truly believe about God. Do you believe you're the master of your own life or that God is? You do not have the right to do whatever you want with your body (1 Corinthians 6:19-20). Your sexual choices are also spiritual choices.

Sexual wholeness or holiness is not the absence of certain sexual sins; it is fully embracing and living according to the holy metaphor of God's covenant love within your sexuality. You are not alone in your sexual brokenness. Every one of us experiences it in one way or another. No one loves perfectly, but the good news is that Jesus is committed and able to redeem your sexuality and transform the way you love from the inside out! As He did for the woman at the well in John 4 and the woman caught in adultery in John 8, He is able to expose your sin, remove your shame, and set you on a path of wholeness through the knowledge of His all-powerful love and desire for you.

My own story can provide an illustration here. As a young adult with a deep-seated insecurity in my ability to measure up as a man, I (Andrew) longed for other men to love me in such a way as to make me feel secure and desired. The sin I pursued in homosexual relationships only left me feeling more frustrated and empty. I surrendered to Jesus in the hope that He could make me someone who loved others rather than using them, but I had no idea what that would mean for my orientation or relational future. I needed a lot of help.

I committed, in weakness, to repent from my sin and pursue the truth of God's Word. While early childhood relationships had wounded me and made me feel insecure, God used relationships in the church to heal these wounds and walk me into greater levels of security and confidence. Eventually, I was able to shed secondary labels and simply stand my ground as a man. I learned to relate to other men as a brother in Christ willing to encourage and be encouraged; willing to speak the truth and hear the truth; willing to stand in the sufficiency of Jesus's love and to offer His love to those around me.

When I met my future wife Jordyn, we committed to dignify and honor the other as best as we could. When frustrations came up in our relationship, we received counsel from more seasoned couples to help us choose to honor and dignify the other rather than to judge, criticize, or expect the other to meet all our needs all the time. Jordyn's past was as checkered as mine, albeit with different struggles; however, as we submitted to Jesus and walked closely in community with other believers, we were able to stand together on our wedding day, "without fault and with great joy" (Jude 1:24). We were able to look one another in the eye with the joy of Jesus rather than the lust or judgment of the flesh.

Nearly a decade and four kids later, we are still learning the way of holy love and still experiencing the joy of His Spirit binding us together. Although your story is doubtless different from mine, your needs are the same.

Ask the Father if you are abiding in His presence as the true Source of love that you need and long for. What are secondary sources of love, pleasure, or security that you tend to lean on rather than Jesus?

What does accountability look like in your life? Are you walking in the light of consistent confession and repentance with other trusted Christians, or are you wearing a mask of perfection at church and refusing to acknowledge specific sin struggles with others?

Are you submitting to the wisdom of others to help you love in holiness? Or, if you have reached maturity through years of reliance on Jesus, are you offering yourself as a source of wisdom and encouragement to those weaker in their faith?

Try to say the first part of Romans 12:1 by memory, and then add in the second part: "This is your true and proper worship."

Day Four
YOUR CONSUMPTION

Today's passage for your conversation with God: Luke 12:22-34

I have a special passion for today and tomorrow's topics because I am a registered dietitian. Now, drop all your preconceived ideas about the coming content and you'll be off to the right start. As one who knows the science involved, I promise you that following biblical principles—rather than cultural standards—is the best thing for your body, just as it is for your spirit and soul. Today and tomorrow's lessons are a compilation of these principles. Because the messages Satan has pervaded our culture with are the opposite of what God says, I beg you to believe and apply what God's Word has to say more than anything else you read or hear on this topic.

Do not worry about food or your body. Jesus saw fit to share extensively about this topic to a large group of people at the beginning of His public ministry, and you just read what He said in today's passage: "Do not worry about your life, what you will eat; or about your body, what you will wear. For life is more than food, and the body more than clothes" (Luke 12:22-23). Jesus could not have said it more clearly.

If you examine Jesus's life on earth, you will not find Him worrying about His appearance or His next meal. It is interesting, though, that the way Satan first tempted Jesus was to set His heart on food rather than obedience during His forty-day fast in the desert. Jesus resisted him by quoting Scripture: "Man shall not live on bread alone, but on every word that comes from the mouth of God" (Matthew 4:4; see also Deuteronomy 8:3). Jesus modeled giving up food for the sake of dedicated prayer and also instructed His disciples to have pure motives when—not if—they fast (Matthew 6:16-18).

If your thoughts too often revolve around food or your body, the apostle Paul has this encouragement for you: "Since then, you have been raised with Christ, set your heart on things above, where Christ is, seated at the right hand of God. Set your minds on things above, not on earthly things" (Colossians 3:1-2).

How has the enemy tempted you to worry too much about your food and/or your body?

What would change if your heart and mind were consistently set on things above rather than on food and your body?

Honor your body by paying attention to it and nourishing it. Though Jesus does not want you to worry about your body, He does want you to care for its needs. "Do you not know that your bodies are temples of the Holy Spirit, who is in you, whom you have received from God? You are not your own; you were bought at a price. Therefore honor God with your bodies" (1 Corinthians 6:19-20). In context, this passage pertains to sexual immorality, but its principle can be applied more broadly as it is consistent with the rest of Scripture. Jesus cared when the crowds around Him became hungry—He took time to feed them bread and fish, and plenty of it, as indicated by the leftovers (Mark 8:19-20)!

God designed your body to signal you when it needs attention—your stomach growls when you are hungry, you crave water when you are thirsty, you yawn when you are tired. Honor God's design by paying attention to your body and be intentional in responding to its needs. You will feel your best when you eat as you start to feel hungry and stop eating when you start to feel satisfied. Extenuating health conditions and other circumstances can make being more intuitive with your eating challenging or even impossible. But when you can, embrace the gift of these God-given cues to guide your timing for eating in a way that naturally provides energy and vitality. God designed your body to rhythmically need food. Find your own rhythm of eating at regular times each day, and follow Jesus's example of thanking Him for it (John 6:11; Mark 14:22).

How do you think you're doing at meeting your body's needs? Explain.

Enjoy food rather than restricting or idolizing it. God made food for both your nourishment and enjoyment (1 Timothy 6:17b). Have you ever thought about the different colors, textures, flavors, and aromas of various foods? Try to eat your food slowly enough to delight in the creativity and goodness of the God who made it. "So whether you eat or drink or whatever you do, do it all for the glory of God" (1 Corinthians 10:31).

Jesus's first miracle was turning water into wine, and He called Himself the bread of life. He seemed to enjoy eating and drinking, especially with His closest disciples; eating a meal with them was the last thing Jesus wanted to do before His death and one of the first things He wanted to do after His resurrection (John 13; 21).

Satan will tempt you to obsess over what you eat, as you read in today's passage (Luke 12:30). He will tempt you to assign moral value to food so you can boast when you eat "good" or "clean" broccoli and feel shame when you enjoy a "bad" chocolate chip cookie. Jesus told His disciples, "Eat what is offered to you" (Luke 10:8). God made all kinds of foods, and none of them have moral value (Acts 10:15). In various religions, people consider pork or beef as forbidden meats, but "Jesus declared all foods clean" (Mark 7:19). God does, however, want you to be sensitive to other people's convictions, as Paul instructed in Romans 14:21: "It is better not to eat meat or drink wine or to do anything else that will cause your brother or sister to fall."

Paul had this to say to the believers in Colossae: "Since you died with Christ to the elemental spiritual forces of this world, why, as though you still belonged to the world, do you submit to its rules: 'Do not handle! Do not taste!' Such regulations indeed have an appearance of wisdom, with . . . their harsh treatment of the body, but they lack any value" (Colossians 2:20-21,23).

In what ways do you struggle with food bondage or idolatry?

Be mindful of what else you are putting into your body. Food and drink are not all that goes into your body. The average person consumes around seven hours of screen content per day. The more time you spend on screens, the more you will be bombarded by messages that your body isn't enough and the less time you will have to be present in your reality. Examine your intake of everything you view on a screen including social media, TV, and movies. Vices more easily creep into your soul while you are being entertained. "For the world offers only a craving for physical pleasure, a craving for everything we see, and pride in our achievements and possessions. These are not from the Father, but are from this world" (1 John 2:16, NLT).

Be honest with God about what and how much you are consuming on screens, and ask for His response. Summarize your conversation below.

Use your verse card to review Romans 12:1. Try to say it all by memory.

See page 278 for more resources on overcoming bondage related to food and/or screen addiction.

Day Five
YOUR DESIGN

Today's passage for your conversation with God: 1 Timothy 4:1-10

Today you will explore God's principles related to the size of your body and how He designed it to function, along with practical applications.

Accept the body God gave you. God made human bodies to be different shapes and sizes just like He made everything else He created to be different shapes and sizes. God made whales to be large and ladybugs to be small; He made redwood trees to be tall and moss to be short; God made bears to be muscular and jellyfish to be floppy. God created your body just as it is, and it is good, as you read in today's passage (1 Timothy 4:4).

Jesus says this about the details of your body: "Even the very hairs of your head are numbered. So don't be afraid; you are worth more than many sparrows" (Matthew 10:30-31). Manipulating your body to try to make it what you want it to be is putting yourself in God's shoes: "What sorrow awaits those who argue with their Creator. Does a clay pot argue with its maker? Does the clay dispute with the one who shapes it, saying, 'Stop, you're doing it wrong!'" (Isaiah 45:9, NLT). Jesus also said, "Do not judge, or you too will be judged" (Matthew 7:1). Judging your own body, or anyone else's, is sin. You can be in a smaller body and be unhealthy, just as you can be in a larger body and be healthy. It is also important to remember that much of your health is genetic and thus beyond your control. God's Word also speaks strongly to comparison: "For where you have envy and selfish ambition, there you will find disorder and every evil practice" (James 3:16).

What Jesus sees when He looks at you is so different from what you see in the mirror. "The LORD doesn't see things the way you see them. People judge by outward appearance, but the LORD looks at the heart" (1 Samuel 16:7). When Jesus sees you, He lavishes His love on you (1 John 3:1). He sees you dressed in His righteousness (Romans 3:22). Your value does not come from what you see in the mirror but from Him who sees you.

Ask God to help you accept the body He gave you. To do this, consider the love and acceptance God gives you as a fully loved child. How do God's feelings about you shape your feelings about yourself?

Steward God's design by moving your body. God designed your body for movement. Prior to modern history, active labor was required for survival. Times have changed, but your Creator's design hasn't. "For in him [God] we live *and move* and have our being" (Acts 17:28, italics mine). Steward His design by staying active as you are physically able. Jesus led an active life. If the work He has given you is sedentary, find something that is both active and life-giving to you—I like to call it joyful movement instead of exercise—and engage in it on a regular basis. God even designed your body to release feel-good endorphins when you are physically active, which will add to your joy and also improve your quality of sleep. Satan will likely tempt you toward the same two extremes regarding your physical activity as he does regarding work—laziness or over-working. Today's passage offers great perspective: "For physical training is of some value, but godliness has value for all things, holding promise for both the present life and the life to come" (1 Timothy 4:8).

What kind of movement is life-giving for you? When could you make time to engage in this activity?

In heaven your body will be renewed, just as Jesus's physical body was renewed at His resurrection (Romans 8:23). How do you envision worshiping Him with your new body? How could you apply this vision toward the way you worship Him with your current body?

Honor God's rhythm of work and rest. God designed your body to both work and rest. He Himself modeled this rhythm when He created the world in six days and rested on the seventh. The very way He designed the sun to rise and set is a daily reminder of His design.

Jesus too modeled the rhythm of work and rest throughout His earthly life. For most of His life, Jesus worked as a carpenter during the day and surely rested at night. During the last three years of His life, His physical labor shifted to the relational labor of ministry, but He continued a rhythm of activity and rest. His pattern was engaging with people and then withdrawing to be with His Father (Luke 5:16).

Rather than being a curse, work is actually one of God's first blessings to people and is part of how He designed your body to thrive (Genesis 2:15). To recover from your work, God designed you to need sleep. You don't have to earn your rest; God gives it to you as a starting point so you can work from it rather than to it. "In vain you rise early and stay up late, toiling for food to eat—for he grants sleep to those he loves" (Psalm 127:2). Let your need for sleep remind you that you are not God, and honor Him by listening to your body and getting the amount you need.

Ask God if He is honored by your current rhythm of work and rest, circle what He reveals.

Yes **No**

What needs to change for you to better honor Him in biblical rhythms of work and rest?

Say Romans 12:1 by memory. Then, pray it reflectively, as follows:

Father, I now offer my body as a living sacrifice to You, knowing it is holy and pleasing to You. Receive each part of my body as my spiritual act of worship. I both thank you for and give you my (check them off as you offer them to Him):

- ☐ **Eyes**
- ☐ **Ears**
- ☐ **Mouth**
- ☐ **Stomach**
- ☐ **Sexual parts**
- ☐ **Arms & hands**
- ☐ **Legs & feet**

I offer these, along with every cell in my body, to You. In Jesus's name, amen."

See page 278 for more resources related to your body image.

Optional passages for more conversations with God:

Day 6: Men: Luke 5:1-11; Women: John 4:1-30,39-42

Day 7: John 9

Week Eight
YOUR RELATIONSHIPS

"The second is this: 'Love your neighbor as yourself.'
There is no commandment greater than these."
MARK 12:31

"Greater love has no one than this: to lay down one's life for one's friends" (John 15:13). Last week you experienced the way Jesus laid down His earthly body for you out of love for His Father. Love cannot exist between living beings devoid of a relationship. Relationship is the vehicle through which love is expressed and experienced.

God's very being is evidence that relationships are fundamental to our existence. He simultaneously exists as God the Father, God the Son, and God the Spirit. These three are in a dynamic relationship that has always existed and will never end. You were made in His image and are likewise designed to be in a dynamic relationship with the Father, Son, and Holy Spirit.

God designed you to have a love relationship with Him that would be the foundation for every other relationship in your life. He gave you the capacity to have relationships so you can both receive and give love. Your most important relationship is always your relationship with God. He created your spirit, soul, and body first to relate to Him and then to relate to other people. Relationships are actually a need in your life. Your relationships result from your being, as you can see in the diagram.

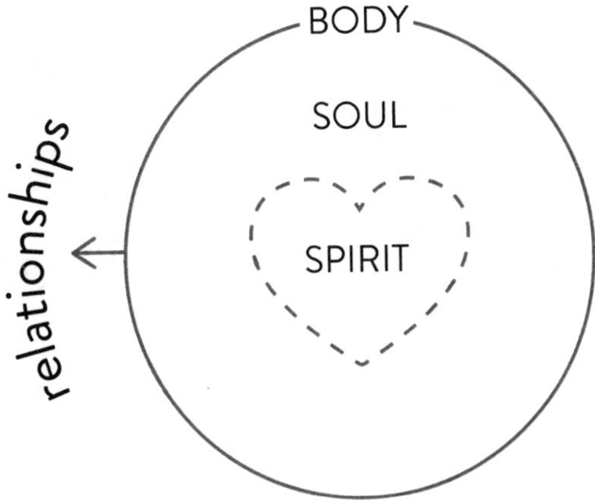

The verse you will memorize this week is a command that, if obeyed, will lay the foundation for healthy relationships in your life. It actually comes after the first verse you memorized in this discipleship experience. To remind you of the context, someone asked Jesus in Mark 12:28, "Of all the commandments, which is the most important?" Try to quote Jesus's reply from memory: "Love the Lord your God with all your heart and with all your soul and with all your mind and with all your strength" (Mark 12:30).

No one asked Jesus about the second most important command—but He deliberately shared it in tandem with the first. To love your neighbor as yourself is the second most important command. When Jesus said this, He was quoting a command first given by God through Moses in Leviticus 19:18: "Do not seek revenge or bear a grudge against anyone among your people, but love your neighbor as yourself. I am the LORD."

You will learn more this week about what it means to love your neighbor as yourself. For now, know that the only way you can obey this second most important command is by obeying the most important command—to love God with all of you. It is through maintaining your vertical love relationship with God that you are able to maintain your horizontal relationships with other people. Your relationships with other people are like a spiritual barometer—if they are consistently unhealthy, your relationship with God needs a check-up. Your relational love is the true evidence that you belong to Christ. Discipleship happens in relationships.

Relationships are messy because people are messy. This week you will explore biblical principles that promote healthy relationships. My prayer is that you will have the courage to examine your closest relationships in light of the gospel—and that in doing so, they might increasingly glorify God.

PRAYER

Father, thank You for creating me to have a love relationship with You. I praise You for the great love You poured out on me at the cross that made our relationship possible. Thank You for the relationships You have given me through this group. You created every person in my life and chose to put me in a relationship with them. I want each of these relationships to bring You glory, Father. Teach me how to love my neighbor as I love myself, and empower me to do so. In Jesus's name, amen.

Day One
LOVE

Today's passage for your conversation with God: Luke 6:27-36

Jesus's teaching in today's passage aligns with His desire for you to love your neighbor as yourself, which is the verse you will memorize this week. After Jesus shared the two most important commandments, a man asked him, "And who is my neighbor?" (Luke 10:29). Jesus took this abstract question and answered it with the story of a specific man: A Jewish man on a journey was abused at the hands of robbers, who left him naked and half-dead on the side of the road. A priest passed by but did not stop to help him. Later a religious Levite passed by but similarly did not stop to help. A Samaritan man passed by next. Samaritans were a racial minority who were typically enemies of the Jews. This Samaritan, however, did not just pass by. He took pity on the man, bandaged his wounds, took him to an inn, and paid for his care.

Jesus asked which of these men was a neighbor to the man who was abused, and the man agreed that it was only the Samaritan who had shown mercy. He then told the man who had asked the question, "Go and do likewise." It is no coincidence that the neighbor was a Samaritan—someone who would have been expected to do nothing to help his enemy. Jesus calls you to love those around you no matter what—like the Samaritan neighbor, and like He did on the cross when He said of His persecutors, "Father, forgive them for they do not know what they are doing" (Luke 23:34). Jesus's definition of a neighbor is anyone in need—regardless of additional affinity.

Jesus loved you when you were His enemy, and He calls you to love your enemies as well, as you read in today's passage. Read what the apostle John says about love: "We love because He first loved us. Whoever claims to love God yet hates a brother or sister is a liar. For whoever does not love their brother and sister, whom they have seen, cannot love God, whom they have not seen. And He has given us this command: Anyone who loves God must also love their brother and sister" (1 John 4:19-21).

Ask the Holy Spirit to bring to mind anyone who is your "enemy" and write their names below.

Without Jesus, it is impossible for you to love these people. But love is the heart of the gospel, and Jesus has given you His Spirit to produce the fruit of love in you that is sufficient even for your enemies. Later this week, you will explore what forgiveness really is and will have the opportunity to experience the healing and freedom it brings to relationships.

Ask God to soften your heart that you might love every person He brings into your life, blessing those who curse you, and being compassionate, "just as your Father is compassionate" (Luke 6:36 NLT).

Love is an act of the will accompanied by emotion which leads to action for someone else's benefit. John teaches that love is to be tangible: "This is how we know what love is: Jesus Christ laid down his life for us. And we ought to lay down our lives for our brothers and sisters. If anyone has material possessions and sees a brother or sister in need but has no pity on them, how can the love of God be in that person? Dear children, let us not love with words or speech but with actions and in truth" (1 John 3:16-18).

Love sourced from God is the best gift you can give to others and is the foundation for healthy relationships. Relationships require two people, however, and both must do their parts to maintain a healthy relationship. You cannot control the people you are in relationships with. What you can control are your beliefs, thoughts, emotions, and behaviors toward them. Do not underestimate the impact of one person taking the initiative to love the other person well in a relationship. Jesus modeled this for us: "While we were still sinners, Christ died for us" (Romans 5:8).

Maturity in discipleship can be thought of as the degree to which you experience harmony or wholeness in relating to both God and other people, especially your enemies. You cannot give to others what you do not have—which is why you must regularly receive love from God to love others well. When your cup is filled to overflowing with His love (Psalm 23:5), you will have love to give out of your saucer. If you make a habit of giving out of your cup rather than your saucer, you will find yourself in a mirage self-sufficiency that leads to bitterness, decaying relationships, and burnout.

Cut out the Mark 12:31 verse card, then say it aloud: "The second is this: 'Love your neighbor as yourself.' There is no commandment greater than these."

On your verse card, underline the words "as yourself." The extent to which you value and love God and subsequently value and love yourself as His image-bearer is the extent to which you are capable of loving God and others well. Far from self-obsession, healthy self-love is believing your worth and stewarding your God-given redemption. God doesn't command us to love ourselves because He expects it—that's our default. "Husbands ought to love their wives as their own bodies. He who loves his wife loves himself. After all, no one ever hated their own body, but they feed and care for their body" (Ephesians 5:28-29). In other words, we eat, shower, and take care of our hygiene because we naturally want what's best for ourselves.

Think about your inner dialogue and the way you treat yourself—your thoughts, emotions, and behaviors. Ask the Holy Spirit to help you discern if you love yourself the way He desires you to, and write what He reveals below. If the answer is no, ask Him to help you learn to love yourself the way He does, creating a foundation for you to learn to love others as He desires. Bask in His love and use it to love yourself. Write a response below.

Day Two

HUMILITY

Today's passage for your conversation with God: Philippians 2:3-11

"He must become greater; I must become less" (John 3:30). This is what John the Baptist said referring to Christ, and in it you will find the path to humility. Humility is the enthronement of God that necessitates the displacement of self.[1] Humbling yourself is recognizing your position of total dependence on God and living that position out in your relationships. Humility paves the way for breakthrough in every area of your life.

It is impossible to be humbled to a greater degree than Jesus allowed Himself to be. As you read in today's passage, Jesus had always been equal to God. In His very nature, He is God. Yet He made Himself nothing. He willingly endured physical and emotional abuse. He gave up all His rights. The gap between His glory and His humiliation is beyond measure. He humbled Himself to such a degree that your humbling will always pale in comparison.

When you grow in humility, you realize how much more you still need to change. Throughout His Word, God warns against the sin of pride and teaches humility. Peter says this: "All of you, clothe yourselves with humility toward one another, because, 'God opposes the proud but shows favor to the humble.' Humble yourselves therefore, under God's mighty hand, that he may lift you up in due time" (1 Peter 5:5-6). Humbling yourself is hard and can only be done with the Holy Spirit's power. Maybe this is why God frequently pairs humility with its reward, as in James 4:10: "Humble yourselves before the Lord, and He will lift you up."

Pride invites opposition; humility invites grace. Ask God to search your heart and reveal any relationships in your life in which you harbor pride (Psalm 139:23-24).

How you view yourself in relationship to the people around you matters. It will always be easier for you to see others' faults than it will be to see your own. You cannot really love someone if you have exalted yourself above him or her, as you read in today's passage: "Do nothing out of selfish ambition or vain conceit. Rather, in humility value others above yourselves" (Philippians 2:3). If you are looking down on someone, you aren't truly loving that person. Humility isn't thinking less of yourself, but thinking of yourself less—meaning you don't have to think poorly of yourself, just don't think about yourself so often.

Humility is a necessary ingredient for biblical love. True love is coming to be *with* someone without your own agenda. It involves giving without expecting anything in return. Jesus modeled this when He came to earth as Immanuel—"God with us" (Matthew 1:23), loving even His enemies to the point of death.

My youngest son Ethan gave me a glimpse of this type of humility. He bought a hamster with the hope that he could hold and play with it often. But "Maple" was too timid and would not come into his hands. Every night Ethan would get teary, wishing he could play with Maple. Growing weary of his nightly sadness, I asked Ethan if he had ever thought about getting a new hamster. Without the slightest pause, Ethan said, "Mom, I could never get rid of Maple. I love him. I'm just sad for Maple because he's afraid of me. I just want him to know that he is safe."

The moment he spoke it, I was struck with the love of the Father. Ethan accepted Maple just as he was. He honored Maple's interests above his own. His love had no agenda. How much more so does God want you and I to know the purity and safety of His love? "See what great love the Father has lavished on us, that we should be called children of God!" (1 John 3:1).

What does the humble, pursuing love of your heavenly Father mean to you?

Approaching your relationships with an attitude of humility creates an atmosphere in which they can thrive. Paul says this: "Live in harmony with one another. Do not be proud, but be willing to associate with people of low position. Do not be conceited" (Romans 12:16). In his letter to the Ephesians, he says, "Be completely humble and gentle; be patient, bearing with one another in love" (Ephesians 4:2).

Write the names of the three to five people you are in the closest relationships with. Reread Ephesians 4:2 (above), and circle the names where Paul's description fits your relationships.

For each relationship you did not circle, ask God to humble you in it. Then ask Him to show you one step you can take to reflect the humble love of God to that person. Write what He tells you below, and make a plan to obey Him.

Use your verse card to begin memorizing this week's verse—but first, quote the verse that precedes it, which you memorized in lesson 1: "Love the Lord your God with all your heart and with all your soul and with all your mind and with all your strength." Then say Mark 12:31: "The second is this: 'Love your neighbor as yourself.' There is no commandment greater than these."

Day Three

COMMUNICATION & CONFLICT

Today's passage for your conversation with God: Matthew 5:21-26; 18:15-17

Conflict within relationships is not a sign of weakness. Quite the opposite, conflict within relationships is necessary for deeper intimacy. Conflict itself is morally neutral. The way conflic t is handled, however, can be either pure or sinful. God's Word has a lot to say about how you should treat other people, evidenced by over fifty "one another" commands in the New Testament alone. As a follower of Christ, you should handle conflict very differently from the way the world handles it; the way you do so is an indication of your maturity as a disciple. God's Word provides timeless instructions for handling conflict. Here are some takeaways from today's passages:

1. **Take responsibility for your emotions** (Matthew 5:21-22). Process them with God before they lead you to sin. The NEAR tool found on page 113 is one way to do so.

2. **Take the initiative to resolve conflict quickly** (Matthew 5:23-24; 18:15). If someone has something against you, take the responsibility to seek out reconciliation. Conflict within relationships is a spiritual matter and will impede your fellowship with God. Regardless of the conflict, it's doubtful you are 100% innocent. Ask God to show you anything you need to seek forgiveness for. Then own your part of the conflict—whether it's your actions or reactions—and seek forgiveness.

3. **Follow the biblical order for resolving conflict** (Matthew 18:15-17). First, try to resolve it one-on-one. If you cannot, add one to two more people to the conversation. Your next step is determined by whether or not the person you are in conflict with is a believer. If your conflict is with an unbeliever, you have now done all that is within your power to resolve the conflict, and you must treat him or her with the love of Christ. This includes forgiving that person, which you will learn more about tomorrow. If your conflict is with a believer and is still not resolved, add a church leader to the conversation. You will learn more about handling conflicts with believers next week.

Ask the Father to show you any relationships in your life where conflict is present and write them below.

From the steps on the previous page, which do you need to take to resolve the conflict? Write the step beside the name above.

I invite you to partner with the Holy Spirit to pursue peace in each of these relationships without delay. This is the path of relational freedom and joy.

Conflict within relationships is most often the result of unmet expectations rather than actual sin. You come into all of your relationships with expectations. Many times these expectations are unconscious, unrealistic, unspoken, and unagreed upon. Expectations in relationships are only helpful if they are clearly communicated and mutually agreed upon. Until then, they are simply hopes. The gap between your expectations and the reality you experience is the story you make up.

When have you struggled in a relationship because of unmet expectations?

Some of your expectations come from important needs in your life such as feeling loved, accepted, and secure. Ultimately, God wants you to come to Him to get these needs met and to yield your expectations to Him. If you look to another person to meet your ultimate need for love, acceptance, and security, you are setting the relationship up for failure by expecting another person to do something only God can do.

The mutual sharing and agreement upon desired, realistic expectations and contributions within a relationship sets it up to thrive. Examples of healthy expectations that could be agreed upon in a relationship include:

- Communicating openly and honestly
- Respecting each other's beliefs, thoughts, desires, and emotions
- Asking for permission
- Giving each other the freedom to say yes and no

Think about the relationship in your life that is most challenging right now. Write that person's name here: ______________. Consider answering the following questions:

1. **Have I spent time with God discerning my expectations and contributions in this relationship?**

   Yes **No**

2. **Are my expectations for this relationship realistic and pleasing to God?**

   Yes **No**

3. **Have I communicated these expectations clearly to the other person with love and respect?**

   Yes **No**

4. **Have we both agreed on mutual expectations for our relationship?**

   Yes **No**

If the answer to any of these questions is no, I invite you to first attend to that step and then continue through all four questions until you can answer yes to them all. At that point, you may find that your relationship is less challenging. If it is not, consider establishing boundaries for yourself within that relationship, which you will explore on day 5 of this week.

What is at least one contribution and/or expectation that would strengthen the relationship you just considered? Write it below and plan a time to share it with him/her.

Use your verse card to review Mark 12:31.

Day Four
FORGIVENESS

Today's passage for your conversation with God: Matthew 18:21-35

Four hundred ninety times. This is how many times Jesus says we are to forgive other people (Matthew 18:21-35). Who would still be keeping count? That's exactly the point—"[love] keeps no record of wrongs" (1 Corinthians 13:5). In today's passage, after the seventy-times-seven reply, Jesus tells a parable that cuts right to my heart. Anytime I refuse to forgive, my sinful pride is immediately exposed. I have been forgiven much, and from everyone who has been given much, much will be demanded (Luke 12:48).

Imagine yourself as the servant owing ten thousand talents (millions of dollars!) in today's passage. Picture the king canceling your debt in full. How does it feel?

What does it mean to you to know Jesus has forgiven you of much more than this? Experience your own forgiveness anew, and record your thoughts and/or feelings.

The whole of the gospel is built around forgiveness. You have been completely forgiven by God through Christ. And God in His perfect love has chosen to forgive not only you but also anyone who would come to Him (1 John 2:2). Forgiveness is a command, not a suggestion. Love and humility—topics you studied earlier this week—prepare your heart to forgive. Because forgiveness is so central to the gospel, it is important that you understand what it really is and how to do it. Satan is behind a host of misconceptions about forgiveness.

FORGIVENESS IS NOT

- Ignoring or forgetting about the wrong done
- Tolerating, excusing, or trying to be polite with the person
- Saying "I forgive you" without meaning it
- Letting time pass
- Keeping silent
- Allowing abuse or continuing in an unsafe relationship

FORGIVENESS IS

- Making a conscious choice to cancel a debt owed to you
- Entrusting the person to God
- Yielding your rights to God, including your right to punish
- Choosing to extend mercy and grace rather than judging, seeking revenge, or keeping score
- Trusting God to redeem the situation

IF YOU WANT TO FORGIVE, TAKING THESE STEPS CAN HELP

- Acknowledge the offense to God and tell Him about the hurt you experienced.
- Express to God your decision to cancel the debt owed and give the person to God.
- Accept the person as he or she is, based on who you know God to be. This includes yielding your expectations to God, trusting Him to meet your needs, and praying God's best for the person.

Although I have given these three steps as a tool, I acknowledge that forgiveness is messy and is some of the hardest work you can do. Forgiving someone requires you to trust in God's character—that He is faithful to work everything out for your good and to bless or punish the other person how He sees fit. Joseph modeled this when he said to his brothers who had tried to kill him, "You intended to harm me, but God intended it for good" (Genesis 50:20a).

Choosing to not forgive is choosing to stay in pain; it is like drinking poison and expecting the other person to die. If you can get to the place where you call your hurt for what it is—unforgiveness—then you can begin to heal. Otherwise, your anger will turn into bitterness that will eventually corrode all the relationships in your life. God's Word warns against bitterness: "See to it that . . . no bitter root grows up to cause trouble and defile many" (Hebrews 12:15). If you harbor bitterness, I invite you to acknowledge it and seek healing. Biblical counseling has helped me deal with bitterness and may help you as well.

Turn back to day 1, where you listed people whom you consider enemies. I invite you to ask God to help you be willing to forgive them now. When you are ready, write the name of each person you want to choose to forgive below. Then go through each of the three steps listed above. Journaling these is helpful, as it is more tangible, but you can also go through each step verbally.

Putting off forgiveness has a corrosive effect on our lives. Jesus taught His disciples to ask for and extend forgiveness daily (Matthew 6:12). This means seeking and offering forgiveness should be a lifestyle rhythm for you as His disciple. The following ten words (said from a repentant heart) can help you get into this rhythm: "I'm sorry I [insert specific sin committed]. I was wrong. Will you forgive me?" You will hear these words often in our home. Keeping short accounts is God's way: "'In your anger do not sin': Do not let the sun go down while you are still angry, and do not give the devil a foothold" (Ephesians 4:26-27).

In some cases, you may forgive someone yet still feel anger toward him or her. Know that your forgiveness is not based on your feelings and your emotions do not define you. Entrust your emotions to your Father. As you continue to renew your mind with the truth and reaffirm your decision to forgive, it is likely that your emotions will eventually reflect His heart of mercy and compassion.

God's forgiveness is one-and-done, but yours probably won't be. The more grievous the sin against you, the deeper your wound will be—and the longer it will take to heal. Forgiveness can be a long process. You can choose to forgive the same person over and over again for as long as you need. Four hundred ninety times, and then some. Jesus is pleased every time. Aim for progress, not perfection.

In closing, it's worth asking, what if the person you are angry with is God? Don't worry; He can take it. Be honest with Him, like David was when he said, "Will you forget me forever? How long will you hide your face from me?" (Psalm 13:1). Listen for God to reveal His heart for you and to correct wrong beliefs you have about Him. The brokenness in the world is not God's doing. Remind yourself of His past faithfulness and His future promises. Then decide to trust in His goodness even when you can't see it and don't feel it. This is faith.

Continue to review Mark 12:31.

See page 278 for more resources on forgiveness.

Day Five
BOUNDARIES

Today's passage for your conversation with God: John 17:1-12

Boundaries were created by God and are a gift from Him. He is a God of order, not chaos (1 Corinthians 14:33). Physical boundaries give order to His creation—for example, God told Job that He "fixed limits" for the sea, saying, "This far you may come and no farther; here is where your proud waves halt" (Job 38:10-11). God also set up spiritual boundaries to establish His authority and give order to society. In the Old Testament, the Law was given to reveal the boundaries within which one could be holy.

The first human boundary-breakers were Adam and Eve. When they ate from the tree God told them not to, they crossed the boundary He had set up for them. People have been breaking boundaries and crossing lines with God and each other ever since. Sin cripples our responsibility and erodes boundaries that protect our well-being.

Boundaries distinguish your separateness from other people, helping you to know what you are and aren't responsible for. They help you take control of yourself and remind you that you can't control anyone else. Another word for boundaries is limits. Discerning and honoring your own personal limits helps you to love people freely and bring your best into relationships. Needs around you will always far surpass your ability to meet them, and without boundaries you will find yourself lost, living someone else's God-given life. Boundaries aren't intended to push others away but to hold you together.

Jesus lived a boundaried life. He regularly withdrew from the crowds, taking time to be away with His Father. He did not heal everyone in the world. In today's passage, you read some of Jesus's last earthly words to His Father, and in them you can see how He lived within His God-given boundaries. He was content with His limited time on earth, His limited influence ("to those whom you gave me"), and His limited responsibilities. At the end of His life, Jesus was able to say to His Father, "I have brought you glory on earth by finishing the work you gave *me* to do" (John 17:4, italics mine).

The Messiah Himself certainly didn't have a faulty "messiah mentality"; He didn't try to do everything for everyone. Jesus must have said no a lot to be able to say an intentional yes to the work His Father had for Him to do. He instructs you, "All you need to say is simply 'Yes' or 'No'" (Matthew 5:37). Jesus said it—"No" is a complete sentence! This is the essence of boundaries—stewarding what is yours, honoring your limits, and allowing others to do the same.

Is your default answer yes, no, or maybe? How would your life and relationships be impacted if your default answer was always no unless you chose to give a Spirit-led yes?

To determine healthy boundaries, it is important to take your physical and emotional capacity into consideration. A container can do nothing to expand its capacity: no matter how hard it may try, a two-liter bottle can hold two liters and no more. In the same way, God created you with a certain capacity, and you will be wise to embrace it. Other factors to consider when determining healthy boundaries are your personality, health, season of life, relational responsibilities, and past woundings.

Boundaries within relationships are biblical. God models relational boundaries in the Trinity—the Father, the Son, and the Holy Spirit are each equally God, yet each have distinct personhood and responsibilities. Every one of the Ten Commandments is a relational boundary—the first four have to do with your relationship with God, and the other six have to do with your relationships with other people.

The fourth commandment contains a clear, important boundary that is often overlooked. It is unfortunate that many believers try to hold to nine commandments and one suggestion: "Remember the Sabbath day by keeping it holy" (Exodus 20:8-11). Obeying the Sabbath commandment means taking one day out of your week to stop working and remember that you are not God but are instead one of His children. Keeping the Sabbath—or "Withdrawing Weekly"[2]—is one of the most important of our family's four spiritual rhythms.[3] It is God's will that you take a day of rest. If you do not have the margin in your schedule to do God's will, something else you are doing must be outside of His will.

What would it look like for you to more fully obey God's command to keep the Sabbath?

In relationships, you are responsible *to* others and *for* yourself.[4] Galatians 6 gives helpful instruction, saying "carry each other's burdens," and "each one should carry their own load" (vv. 2,5). These do not contradict each other as it might seem. The Greek word for *burden* means a heavy weight, while the Greek word for *load* means tasks or obligations. God's Word instructs you to help people when they are in crisis but to entrust them to their own daily responsibilities. You should not be doing for others what they are able to do for themselves. Overfunctioning perpetuates their immaturity, breeds your resentment, and leads to codependency.

Think about your closest relationship and write that person's name below. Then write if you tend to overfunction, underfunction, or function well within that relationship.

If a certain relationship is consistently challenging for you, it might be helpful to determine boundaries you need to have to keep yourself healthy within that relationship. Ask God to help you discern the boundaries He wants you to have. Once you have clarity, mention these boundaries to a few godly people who you trust, and ask for accountability if you need it. When someone crosses the relational boundaries you have set, tell that person he or she did so. If that person repeatedly crosses your boundaries, seek godly counsel to discern how you should respond with appropriate consequences.

Examples of boundaries related to relationships include the following: I can say no, I will respectfully end the phone call if gossip is taking place, I will not listen to yelling or cursing, I will not step in to prevent someone from experiencing the consequences of his or her own choices, and I will take responsibility for my own emotions but no one else's.

With whom do you need to have better boundaries?

What boundaries might help you stay healthy in this relationship?

Try to say Mark 12:30-31 by memory. If you can't, keep practicing until you have it.

Optional passages for more conversations with God:

Day 6: Luke 23:26-49

Day 7: Genesis 50:15-26

Week Nine

CHRIST-CENTERED COMMUNITY

"A new command I give you: Love one another. As I have loved you, so you must love one another. By this everyone will know that you are my disciples, if you love one another."

JOHN 13:34-35

Last week you learned how God created you to live in a dynamic relationship with Him and others and how your relationships flow out of your being—your spirit, soul, and body. This week you will explore the most eternal and essential of all the human relationships in your life: your relationship with other believers. Engaging in Christ-centered community is one of the four spiritual disciplines that will keep you rooted in His love and living as His disciple. This is why "community" is one of the cross bars—along with God's Word and prayer—in the diagram to the right. You will learn the final spiritual discipline in the cross frame in two weeks.

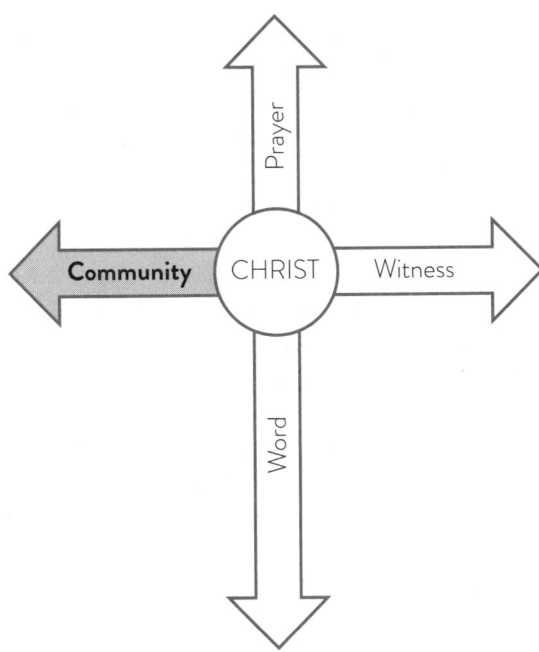

In the creation account, the only thing God called "not good" was for the man to be alone. God wasted no time before He said, "I will make a helper suitable for him" (Genesis 2:18). God knew Adam would need other human relationships, but it seems He wanted Adam to come to this realization for himself. Rather than immediately creating Eve, God asked Adam to name the creatures He made. Despite being surrounded by living creatures, Adam was lonely. He longed for companionship, but "no suitable helper was found" (Genesis 2:20). God caused Adam to fall into a deep sleep, took one of his ribs, and formed Eve from it. When God then presented Eve to Adam, how much greater his delight must have been after knowing loneliness!

Just like Adam, it is not good for you to be alone. God has made provision for your need for human relationship. Eve was merely a solitary, earthly bride, but you are one of a multitude of Christ-followers who forever comprises the bride of Christ.

Not only do you belong to this bride, but you also need it. Together you are sustained until the wedding day in heaven comes. On that day, your relational needs will find their ultimate fulfillment and satisfaction in the embrace of your groom—Christ. I love John's description in Revelation 19:6-7: "Then I heard what sounded like a great multitude, like the roar of rushing waters and like loud peals of thunder, shouting: 'Hallelujah! For our Lord God Almighty reigns. Let us rejoice and be glad and give Him glory! For the wedding of the Lamb has come, and his bride has made herself ready.'"

Christ loves the global church—everyone in the world who follows Jesus as Lord and Savior—and your local church. And you are called to love His bride—the church—according to the verses you will memorize this week. Jesus spoke them to His disciples during the last meal He shared with them before going to the cross. To fully appreciate His message, it is helpful to look at the verse that precedes them, where Jesus says, "Where I am going, you cannot come" (John 13:33). This is the context of Jesus's "new" command to love one another. The one thing that connected all of the disciples was Jesus—and He was about to be gone.

Jesus's disciples knew they needed Him. Now He wanted them to know that they also needed each other, and that the world needed to witness it. Because of that, the evil one's strategy has been to divide Christians against one another so that the world would think we act no differently than them. In the absence of Jesus's physical presence, the evidence of His love bringing His followers together and sustaining their unity is the way that "everyone will know" we are His (John 13:35).

PRAYER

Father, thank You for letting me be a part of Your bride. What a delight to belong. Thank You for providing relationships for me with other people who follow You. Thank You for the small group I am going through this discipleship experience with. I ask You to transform us as we continue to journey together and allow us to experience the fullness of joy You intended for Your bride to share. In Jesus's name, amen.

Day One

THE BODY OF CHRIST

Today's passage for your conversation with God: 1 Corinthians 12:12-27

In today's passage, you read that you are part of the body of Christ—Paul's favorite descriptor of the church, one he used twenty-four times in his letters. When you made Jesus your Lord and Savior, you received His Spirit and became part of His body. He is "the head of the body, the church" (Colossians 1:18). As a part of the body of Christ, you belong both to Him and to every other part of His body.

Your physical body is made up of many parts that cooperate with each other to sustain your life. Each part makes a valuable contribution within your body, but when separated from it, loses its functionality and worth. An eyeless body can cope, but a bodiless eye is unimaginable. Eyes need a body that will bring them blood and receive their nerve impulses. The most beautiful eyes in the world, when detached from a body, are lifeless and worthless.[1]

So it is with the body of Christ, of which you are a part. If at any point you disconnect yourself from it, not only will you be unable to operate as you were designed, but the rest of the body will also suffer. You do not function alone but with a vast multitude of disciples representing different ethnicities, cultures, social statuses, and denominations. Your joint head is Christ: "From him the whole body, joined and held together by every supporting ligament, grows and builds itself up in love, as each part does its work" (Ephesians 4:16). Like the brain within your physical head, Christ controls and directs His entire body. Like the blood in your physical body, the Holy Spirit flows throughout the body of Christ and supplies what is needed to maintain life.

The human body is a fascinating creation that is outmatched in beauty and complexity only by the body of Christ. While every human body has its limits and is deteriorating, Christ's body is unstoppable in its mission and ever-increasing in its glory.

Pause and envision the global body of Christ. Imagine its diversity and scope with every member being knit together with Jesus as the head. Feel yourself belonging to the multitude. Play one of your favorite worship songs and consider how the truths of this song are true for this global body despite our differences. Consider searching online for a global edition of "Revelation Song." Describe your experience below.

Our family was able to experience the body of Christ in a way few are privileged to on this earth when we moved to an Asian country with a two-month-old and a toddler. We arrived with no existing relationships (with the exception of one couple we had spoken to a handful of times), no language skills, no tolerance for extreme heat without consistent electricity, and just a few suitcases. The degrees and aptitudes we came with were completely nullified the moment we stepped foot in this country that was so opposite of the place we called home. Jesus was the only reason we were there and was obviously going to be the only reason we would stay. But we could never have stayed had it not been for the body of Christ.

Far from home, we needed the body of Christ to be our family. Stripped of all our comforts and painfully shaved of our perceived "rights," we needed the compassion of the body and the wisdom of those who had already been humbled. We needed the meals they shared with us and the truth they spoke into our lives. We needed their help raising our kids and the tears they cried alongside us. The body of Christ was a lifeline for us overseas and was one of our hardest goodbyes when God called us to move back to the United States.

Once we had tasted the richness of Christ-centered community, we were desperate to continue the feast through the new local church God called us to. We made it a priority to plug into a small group that allowed for weekly interaction, and we formed intentional relationships within it. We created margin in our schedules to invite people into our home. We didn't shy away from asking people for help when we needed it, as we are still many hours away from family. It took time, admittedly, but God blessed our desire to connect with His people and provided a new community for us—one that has once again become a lifeline.

God designed you to not only need the community of His body but also to thrive in it and help others to do the same. Engaging in Christ-centered community means belonging to and participating with the body of Christ in shared attitudes, interests, and goals made possible by the unity of the Spirit. Christ-centered community is more than just being active in a church, although that is where it begins. The word the Bible uses to describe this kind of community is *koinōnia*, which is most often transliterated as fellowship. In tomorrow's passage, you will read the first mention of this word in the New Testament.

What impact has Christ-centered community had on your life since you began this small group discipleship experience?

Cut out the John 13:34-35 verse card at the back of this workbook. Practice the first part by saying it a few times: "A new command I give you: Love one another. As I have loved you, so you must love one another."

Day Two
CHURCH

Today's passage for your conversation with God: Acts 2:42-47

To give you some context for today's passage, Jesus had recently resurrected and ascended into heaven. His disciples were staying in Jerusalem waiting to receive the Holy Spirit, who then came and filled the place they were sitting, resting on each of them and allowing them to speak in other languages. Jews from every nation were in town for a Jewish feast, and when they heard the disciples speaking their own languages they came together in bewilderment. Peter stood up and boldly invited them to repent, be baptized, receive the Holy Spirit, and join them as disciples. About three thousand of them did on that day, and the church was born.

They did not know each other. They were from different places. They spoke different languages. And yet, "All the believers met together in one place and shared everything they had" (Acts 2:44, NLT). The Holy Spirit came in such power among them that their differences were insignificant in light of their new identity as followers of Christ. They began to function not just as a group but as a family. In doing so, they were aligning with what Jesus had taught them before His death, when as He pointed to His disciples, He said, "Here are my mother and my brothers. For whoever does the will of my Father in heaven is my brother and sister and mother" (Matthew 12:49-50).

You read in today's passage that the first church "devoted themselves to the apostles' teaching and to fellowship, to the breaking of bread and to prayer" (Acts 2:42). This is the first mention of the word *fellowship* in the New Testament, and it means "joint participation in a community." The early church didn't "go" to church, they *were* the church and devoted themselves to following Christ together. In doing so, they shared meals and material goods with glad and sincere hearts, reaping the favor of the community at large. "And the Lord added to their number daily those who were being saved" (Acts 2:47).

The fellowship of the early church attracted onlookers. True biblical community today does the same. Those who are far from God cannot see Him, but they can see other believers (at least in places reached with the gospel), and the way they live reflects their belief in God. Believers, then, have a great responsibility. The local church—a people, not a place—is how God chooses to put His glory on display to those who are far from Him.

I want to press pause for a minute, because there could be no better example of what your memory verse this week is all about. Try to say the first part by memory, and then add the second part (italicized here):

A new command I give you: Love one another. As I have loved you, so you must love one another. *By this everyone will know that you are my disciples, if you love one another.*
JOHN 13:34-35

Draw a picture of a church here.

What you drew demonstrates how you define and describe church. Did you draw a building? Did it have a steeple or a cross on it? Did you include people in your drawing? If your illustration didn't include people, you missed the most visible indication of a church. The church always needs a place to gather, whether it be its own building, a home, school, or outside under a tree, but the church is a people, not a place.

If you are not a member of a local church, make it a priority to find and join one that is biblical in doctrine and proactive in mission. I have heard too many people say, "I love Jesus, but I don't want to have anything to do with the church." We should sensitively listen to people's hurts from their experiences with church—but saying that is like someone saying to my husband, "I love you Matt, but I don't want to have anything to do with your wife." God wants you to commit to meeting regularly with His body as a part of a local church.

Before the church was established in the book of Acts, Jesus promised, "I will build my church, and the gates of Hades will not overcome it" (Matthew 16:18). Church was Jesus's idea, not man's creation, and He is the primary builder of the church. Admittedly, some churches have failed because people have formed them into something much different than what He intended. There is no perfect church on earth, and even if there was, it would no longer be perfect once you joined it! Every believer is imperfect, but God is most glorified as we grow in Christlikeness together. Jesus's main concern in building His church wasn't how many people attended a worship service on Sunday mornings, but rather overcoming the gates of Hades. *Hades* is synonymous with the grave and is sometimes translated as *hell* in the New Testament. Jesus's resurrection fashioned not just an institution on earth but also a forever family in heaven.

What was the early church good at—in being or doing—that isn't happening enough in your current church?

What, if anything, do you believe God wants to change in your church?

What do you sense God may want you to do about that?

Day Three
SMALL GROUP

Today's passage for your conversation with God: Hebrews 10:19-25

Jesus came from a tight-knit community. Growing up in the Middle East, He lived in a culture that valued collectivism—one that is quite the opposite of the individualistic culture of the West. Here's proof: Once, when His family was on a multiday journey, it took Jesus's parents more than a day to realize He wasn't with them (Luke 2:42-46). They just assumed He was with relatives or friends, until they looked and He wasn't. And He was only twelve years old!

Living in community involves caring for those within it as you would your biological family. It requires a regular investment of your time. You read in today's passage what the author of Hebrews said: "And let us consider how we may spur one another on toward love and good deeds, not giving up meeting together, as some are in the habit of doing, but encouraging one another—and all the more as you see the Day approaching" (Hebrews 10:24-25). You were not intended to live the Christian life alone. Jesus certainly didn't. You need community because you need to encourage others and be encouraged so that you will "hold unswervingly to the hope" you profess (Hebrews 10:23).

Jesus modeled living in this kind of community throughout His public ministry. He chose twelve disciples and spent much of His time with them. He invited them to join Him for meals and celebrations as well as ministry. These disciples, along with a few women who traveled around with Jesus, were a sort of "inner circle" for Him. Jesus chose to disciple people in a small group rather than one-on-one. Benefits of small group discipleship include increased accountability, support, diversity, collective wisdom, and a decreased risk of codependency. Small group discipleship also allows you to simultaneously mentor those younger in the faith and be mentored by those whose spiritual maturity exceeds yours.

Authenticity and vulnerability are hallmarks of small groups that thrive. Jesus modeled these in His relationship with His twelve disciples. A prime example is when He took His disciples along with Him to the garden of Gethsemane in one of His darkest hours, admitting to them, "My soul is overwhelmed with sorrow to the point of death," and asking them to pray (Mark 14:34). Jesus did not try to hide His weakness or grief from them. And He did so knowing these men He was fully opening Himself to would soon deny even knowing Him. Jesus's vulnerability was unsurpassed.

Today's passage speaks to the confidence available to you before God and beside others because of the finished work of Christ. Your small group should be a place where you can confess your sins to your brothers and sisters and be reminded of the grace Jesus offers you. "Nothing in all creation is hidden from God's sight. Everything is uncovered and laid bare before the eyes of him to whom we must give account" (Hebrews 4:13). Your heavenly Father already sees you, knows you, and loves you. If you have the courage to also open yourself up to being seen and known by other believers you can trust, you will get to experience a love that is transformative and restorative.

Satan wants nothing more than for your sin to lead to shame that keeps you walled off from community—the very place where your healing can begin. Shame is defining yourself by your shortcomings, and Satan produces it in your life to try to keep you from forgiving yourself. So you hide behind a mask like an actor. The ancient Greek word for *actor* is where we get the word *hypocrite*, which meant "an interpreter from underneath." Are you wearing a figurative mask, pretending to be someone you're not? Isolation is Satan's workshop, but the antidote is found in James 5:16: "Therefore confess your sins to each other and pray for each other so that you may be healed."

Small groups who embrace vulnerability are able to more fully experience the sufficiency of Christ. I love how Dietrich Bonhoeffer describes the healing available through vulnerability: "Who can give us the certainty that, in the confession and the forgiveness of our sins, we are not dealing with ourselves but with the living God? God gives us this certainty through our brother. Our brother breaks the circle of self-deception. A man who confesses his sins in the presence of a brother knows that he is no longer alone with himself; he experiences the presence of God in the reality of the other person."[3] Small groups are where we break down the lies of the enemy and grasp the love of God in tangible form.

Have you ever confessed sin in your life to another believer or small group?

Yes **No**

If you have, describe the benefits of that experience below. If you haven't, what has kept you from doing so, and would you be willing to in the future?

How authentic and vulnerable are you with your small group? Rank yourself on the following spectrum, and then consider asking God to help open you up to more vulnerability:

1 2 3 4 5 6 7 8 9 10

I mask my true feelings **I am 100% honest and real**

Belonging to a small group with Christ at its center will fast-forward your growth as a disciple and allow you to contribute to the health of the body and the discipleship of others. Ideally, groups have twelve people or less, which helps facilitate more intimate dialogue. More important than whether you meet at a church building or in a home is finding a place where members of the group feel comfortable openly sharing their hearts. As a foundation, small groups should spend time studying God's Word together and praying for each other. Serving and having fun together are also important functions. A consistent and simple format for group times can be helpful, such as the following three-thirds process we have used in the leader guide of this discipleship experience:[4]

1. Looking Back: worship, mutual care, accountability, and casting vision (one-third of group time)
2. Looking Up: learning or doing something new (one-third of group time)
3. Looking Ahead: application, goal setting, and prayer (one-third of group time)

We hope you've been going through this resource as a part of a small group. If so, how have you benefited from the group aspect of this discipleship experience?

Using your verse card for John 13:34-35, try to say the first part of this week's verse by memory, and then add in this second part: "By this everyone will know that you are my disciples, if you love one another."

Day Four
UNITY IN THE BODY

Today's passage for your conversation with God: Ephesians 4:1-16

Jesus deeply desires unity within His church. His last prayer before going to the cross was for just that. Jesus prayed, "That all of them may be one, Father, just as you are in me and I am in you . . . so that they may be brought to complete unity. Then the world will know that you sent me and have loved them even as you have loved me" (John 17:21, 23).

Today, you read Paul's exhortation to the church in Ephesus that echoes Jesus's heart for unity. Paul painted a tangible picture of this unity when he said that from Christ, the "whole body, joined and held together by every supporting ligament, grows and builds itself up in love, as each part does its work" (Ephesians 4:16). The basis for our unity as believers, expressed by Jesus in John 17 and Paul here, is the person and work of Christ. When believers are divided, it is because their center is no longer Christ.

Satan relentlessly attacks unity among the church. No doubt, he wants to "steal and kill and destroy" this vehicle God has chosen to accomplish His mission (John 10:10). Unfortunately in some churches, members argue with each other and fail to resolve conflict biblically. They feel entitled to their opinions and preferences, undermining the authority of their pastors. Some local churches and denominations fixate on their differences and isolate themselves from others. All the while the world watches and Satan grins.

But now the good news: the church has all it needs to unite what Satan has divided. The Holy Spirit circulates through the body of Christ, producing His fruits of love, joy, and peace in sufficient supply to unify and fortify it. Christ is leading His church in triumphal procession and through us is spreading everywhere the fragrance of the knowledge of Him (2 Corinthians 2:14).

Conflict within the body of Christ is to be expected, and when handled biblically, it provides a healthy opportunity for the church to grow in intimacy and maturity. Last week on day 3 you read Matthew 18:15-17, which gives you the following biblical process for resolving conflict with a believer who sins against you:

1. First, try to restore him or her one-on-one.
2. If you cannot, add one to two more people to the conversation.
3. If you still cannot, add a church leader to the conversation.
4. If you still cannot, treat him or her as an unbeliever. At this point, church discipline is appropriate. The church will be holier and have a better testimony when you "expel the wicked person from among you" (1 Corinthians 5:12-13).

Some biblical translations of Matthew 18:15, rather than saying, "If your brother sins against you," simply say, "If your brother sins, go and show him his fault." Therefore, this same four-step process can be applied if you are in a relationship with a believer who you know is caught in sin and the Spirit leads you to confront him or her out of love. As you read in today's passage, "speaking the truth in love" is a mark of maturity (Ephesians 4:15). Be sure to bathe the confrontation in prayer and the conversation in humility.

Pause now to reflect on your relationships with believers. Ask God to show you any relationships where conflict is present or where He may want you to speak the truth in love, and write their names below.

Consider which of the three steps above you might need to do for each relationship, writing the number(s) beside each name. Ask God to equip you to follow through.

If all your conflicts are currently resolved, what is an action the Lord is leading you to take to help a relationship with another believer be even better?

Much of the conflict we experience in the body of Christ is due to the way individual members use their tongues. When you are in the middle of a conflict, ask the Holy Spirit to produce His fruit of self-control in you so you will not sin when you speak, and you will know when you should not speak at all.Read these passages that highlight the importance of taming your tongue:

- "The tongue also is a fire, a world of evil among the parts of the body. It corrupts the whole body . . . with the tongue we praise our Lord and Father, and with it we curse human beings, who have been made in God's likeness . . . My brothers and sisters, this should not be" (James 3:6,9-10).
- "Don't use foul or abusive language. Let everything you say be good and helpful, so that your words will be an encouragement to those who hear them . . . Get rid of all bitterness, rage, anger, harsh words, and slander, as well as all types of evil behavior. Instead, be kind to each other, tenderhearted, forgiving one another, just as God through Christ has forgiven you" (Ephesians 4:29,31-32, NLT).
- "The tongue can bring death or life; those who love to talk will reap the consequences" (Proverbs 18:21, NLT).

When have your words caused unnecessary disunity between you and another person?

Learning to speak less will greatly benefit your relationships, especially during conflict. Not only does it keep your tongue in check, but it also allows you to listen. You will reap much wisdom if you learn how to listen well, as God's Word instructs: "Everyone should be quick to listen, slow to speak and slow to become angry" (James 1:19), and "To answer before listening—that is folly and shame" (Proverbs 18:13). Jesus asked many questions during His earthly ministry and modeled attentive listening.

If you are struggling to communicate with someone on an important topic, tell that person how much you value the relationship and then ask if he or she would be willing to participate in a reflective listening conversation with you to help the relationship move forward. Reflective listening is a useful tool for difficult conversations, and is also a powerful gift of love. Here's how to do it: One person listens to the other person share what's on his or her heart for a minute and then reflects back what he or she heard. The person sharing then affirms, denies, or adds to that reflection. Continue this pattern until the person has shared for five to ten minutes. Then switch so that the other person is able to express what's on his or her heart for the same time frame. It's sometimes helpful to involve a third person to assist in difficult conversations. Preserving unity is an active pursuit that requires humility and hard work, but its purpose is significant as this week's memory verses highlight.

What is one concrete action you can take to preserve unity in the body of Christ?

Use your verse card to review John 13:34-35.

Day Five
PRIORITIZING COMMUNITY

Today's passage for your conversation with God: 1 Thessalonians 2:1-12

Today's passage highlights the depth of Paul's commitment to his fellow believers in Thessalonica, as well as their reciprocity. Paul, along with Silas and Timothy, prioritized spending time with them despite "working night and day" as tentmakers to earn a living (Acts 18:3; 1 Thessalonians 2:9). They shared life together and identified as family. Paul used the terms *mother* and *father* to describe the way he cared for them, leaving no doubt that he invested himself fully in them. Paul viewed the gospel and his fellow believers as treasures entrusted to him. He labored that they might live lives worthy of the God who called them.

As Paul demonstrated, Christ-centered community requires commitment and intentionality. A key ingredient you will need to consistently engage in Christ-centered community is time. If Satan can't make you disobey the commands of Christ, he will try to make you too busy to obey them. Last week, you learned how boundaries can be helpful within relationships. Today, you will see how boundaries can also help you to manage your time.

Today's church has much to learn from the early church, and its unparalleled devotion is a worthy start. Despite everything else going on in their individual lives, "Every day they continued to meet together" (Acts 2:46). In addition to meeting together they also daily searched the Scriptures (17:11), cared for others' physical needs (6:1), and increased in number (2:47; 16:5). Many in today's church are not even committed to meeting together once a week.

Reflect on your level of commitment to engaging in Christ-centered community. Is it a true priority to you, or is it something you participate in when it's convenient? Put a star where you would rank yourself on the following spectrum:

1—not committed **5—highly committed**

You cannot add hours to your day, but you do get to choose how you spend the hours you have. Parkinson's Law is true: "Work expands so as to fill the time available for its completion."[5] Boundaries help you contain the time you spend on activities that are necessary and urgent so that you can prioritize spending time on things that are the most important.

If you don't have the margin to engage in spiritual disciplines including Christ-centered community, or if your life is chaotic and your relationships could use a tune-up, explore your boundaries. Any area where you are experiencing problems in your life could indicate a need for clearer boundaries.

SIGNS YOU ARE LIVING OUTSIDE OF HEALTHY LIMITS

- Not having time to spend with God daily
- Being unable to be fully present with people
- Feeling indispensable
- Always being in a hurry
- Being regularly irritable about simple tasks in life such as waiting in line
- Feeling consumed by someone or something

EXAMPLES OF BOUNDARIES THAT HELP PRIORITIZE KINGDOM VALUES

- Work—I will limit my work hours and take a weekly Sabbath so I can spend time with those I love.
- Sleep—I will get to bed by 10 p.m. on on the night before my church gathers so that I can worship with them every week.
- Relationships—I will show up to my small group every week even if it's not convenient.
- Finances—I will honor my budget each month and tithe at least ten percent.
- Physical—I will partake in joyful movement for thirty minutes three times a week to keep my body active.
- Technology—I will put my phone to bed at 8 p.m. and not use it until after my morning time with God.

Where are you embracing wise boundaries to prioritize community with other believers?

Where could you stand to establish clearer boundaries?

Pray over your previous two responses. What is a first step that you need to take?

God will at times take you beyond your limitations in supernatural ways. Your boundaries should never be your god. Remember, you establish boundaries to make room for the things God has called you to. It is helpful to periodically ask the Lord these questions:[6]

1. Which of my limits should I receive as God-given reminders to continue trusting Him?
2. Which of my limits might God be asking me to break through by faith so that I might become the person He intends or so that others might know and trust Him?

BENEFITS OF HEALTHY BOUNDARIES THAT FOSTER MORE INVOLVEMENT IN CHRIST-CENTERED COMMUNITY

- Being able to rejoice with those who rejoice and weep with those who weep (Romans 12:15)
- Being able to pray for others more regularly
- Being able to bless and serve others during their times of need or as the Holy Spirit prompts you
- Being able to have the ministry of presence—being present even without words—during difficult times in others' lives
- Being able to have fun with others

Paul encourages you to "look carefully then how you walk, not as unwise but as wise, making the best use of the time, because the days are evil" (Ephesians 5:15-16 ESV). God will bless your commitment to spending time in community with believers. You will be strengthened and encouraged, because "as iron sharpens iron, so one person sharpens another" (Proverbs 27:17). As you prioritize your time and live within your God-given limits, may you be able to say like David, "Lord, you alone are my portion and my cup; you make my lot secure. The boundary lines have fallen for me in pleasant places; surely I have a delightful inheritance" (Psalm 16:5-6).

Use your verse card to review John 13:34-35 until you have it memorized.

Optional passages for more conversations with God:

Day 6: 1 John 4:7-21

Day 7: 1 Thessalonians 3:7-13

Section Four

YOUR RELATIONSHIP WITH THE WORLD

Week Ten
GOD'S MISSION

"Therefore go and make disciples of all nations, baptizing them
in the name of the Father and of the Son and of the Holy Spirit,
and teaching them to obey everything I have commanded you.
And surely I am with you always, to the very end of the age."
MATTHEW 28:19-20

As a disciple, you should always be growing in knowing, being, and doing what the Master wants. So far in this experience, we've focused on being His disciples, but it's time now we turn our eyes toward doing what God has called us to do. The remainder of this experience focuses on what God wants to do through you to further His mission. You can see the next step in this discipleship process illustrated in this diagram below.

Everyone is on a mission: some are trying to climb the corporate ladder; others are trying to win someone's love, amass a fortune, earn an award, or achieve the next milestone. Many people give their lives to a mission with no eternal value.

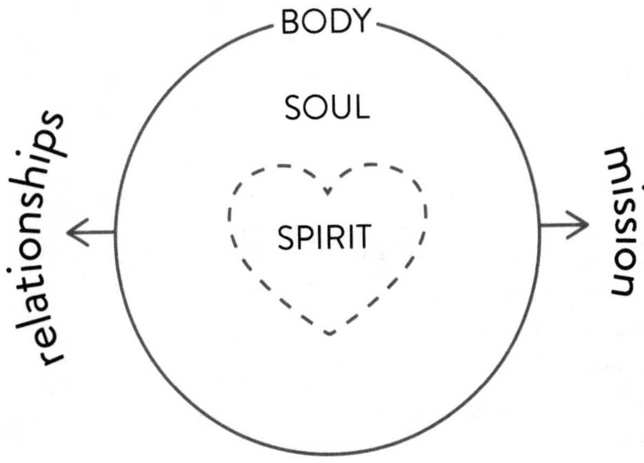

As a disciple, your mission is to glorify God and edify people. This is not "mission impossible." Rather, it's the Great Commission that Jesus gave to all believers in Matthew 28:19-20, which you'll memorize this week. This mission culminates in the second coming of Christ. What a thrill that this could be accomplished in your lifetime!

Someone once said to Jesus, "If you can do anything, help us." His shocked reply was, "If you can? . . . Everything is possible for one who believes" (Mark 9:22-23). You get to go after this mission along with the other members of the most diverse group of people in history—a global movement with momentum building over thousands of years—the church. This week, you'll explore how you can fulfill your portion of His mission as an individual and together with other disciples. As you do so, you will find yourself most fully alive, because this mission is what you were made for.

God gave His mission as a nonnegotiable directive to all of His disciples. To quote Pastor J. D. Greear, "The question is no longer if you are called; only where and how."[1]

Jesus said in Luke 14:25-33 that He wants you to go all-in as His disciple, not halfway. Decide now if you're really committed to being on His mission. It could look like succeeding in the corporate world so you can generously give more money to ministries, teaching the next generation, adopting an orphan, or establishing a shelter for homeless people.

To be fully on mission with God, it is important to regularly pray these dangerous yet thrilling words: whatever, wherever, whenever, whoever, however. Too often, we draw a circle in our prayers around what we're willing to do and resist God doing anything through us outside that circle.

You may be either paralyzed or energized by such a monumental responsibility that ripples into eternity. What you can't be is neutral. Even your passivity—a decision to do nothing for God's mission—is a choice that deprives other people of the blessings He intended to give them through you.

PRAYER

Heavenly Father, thank You for giving me a life of purpose, value, and meaning. Help me to not waste my life. Change in me whatever You need to. Whoever You want me to serve, I will. Wherever You lead, I'll go. Whatever it looks like for me to align with Your perfect will that's what I want to do. Whenever You want me to make a major adjustment in my life, please make it clear and grant me a willing heart to sustain me. Yes, Lord. In Jesus's name, amen.

Day One
GOD'S MISSION

Today's passage for your conversation with God: Matthew 28:16-20

The overarching mission of God in the past, present, and future is to redeem people to Himself for His glory. When Adam and Eve sinned, God sought them, spoke with them, clothed them with the skin of an animal, and promised a Son who would crush Satan's head. Two thousand years ago, God walked among us in the person of Jesus who sought us, spoke with us, clothed us with His righteousness through the sacrifice of His own body, and conquered Satan by resurrecting from the dead. Before He ascended back to heaven, Jesus gave a mandate to every one of His followers—including you—to go and make disciples of all nations, as you read in today's passage. The Great Commission is a mandate to all disciples for all time.

To live under a mandate is to be entrusted with a task of lasting significance. When a man or woman is elected to office by an overwhelming majory, it is said he or she has a mandate to govern. Yet the impact and significance of an elected official is confined by term limits, legislation, and other factors outside of his or her control. Jesus is not limited by anyone and neither is His mandate, which extends to "all nations" and "to the end of the age." The mission mandate Jesus has given you is of far greater eternal significance than any mandate people entrust to a president.

In the Great Commission, Jesus is giving you authority and entrusting you with responsibility to fulfill God's purpose for all of history. The collective force of all the promises, covenants, and works of God constitute a powerful mandate that empowers the entire people of God to co-labor with Christ for the fulfillment of His purpose.[2]

Cut out the Matthew 28:19-20 verse card in the back of your workbook and say it out loud a few times to begin memorizing it.

Notice that Jesus did not command you to teach future disciples everything, rather He said, "[Teach] them to obey." Jesus wants His disciples to learn obedience. Some believers assume they are saved to only sit and soak; but according to Jesus, disciples are called to go and make. Believers are Jesus's "Plan A" to accomplish His mission on earth. Christ is grieved when His disciples settle for anything less than what He created them to join Him in accomplishing. His Great Commission is truly a co-mission.

How have you already personally been obeying Jesus's Great Commission—in going, discipling, baptizing people, and teaching them to obey? [Circle one.]

not at all **a little** **want to do more** **a lot** **always**

Whether or not you are on mission, God is always on mission. My granddad Avery Willis and Henry Blackaby outlined His mission and how we should respond in *On Mission with God.*[3]

GOD'S WAYS	OUR BEST RESPONSE
God is always at work around you to accomplish His mission.	Expect God to encounter you to reveal what He is doing near you or among distant peoples to reconcile a lost world to Himself.
God pursues a continuing love relationship with you that is real and personal. He loves you more than He wants to utilize you for a task.	Accept God's invitation for a covenant relationship.
God invites you to get involved in His work when He reveals Himself and His work to you.	Agree to be on mission with God when He calls you to Himself.
God speaks to you by the Holy Spirit through the Bible, prayer, circumstances, and the church, to reveal Himself, His purposes, and His ways.	Let God prepare you for His mission as you learn His ways with others.
God's invitation for you to work with Him always leads you to a crisis of belief that requires faith and action.	Obey as God sends you where He can best work through you to accomplish His mission.
You must make major adjustments in your life to join God in what He is doing.	Receive God's empowerment as you make the life changes that open you to co-labor with Him.
You come to know God by experience as you obey Him and He accomplishes His work through you.	Follow God as He guides you on His mission to reveal Himself and to reconcile a lost world to Himself.

Reflect on which of God's ways you have or have not yet experienced, and put a star by the statement that is most relevant to you now. Write below how He would want you to respond.

God has never once paused His mission or abandoned His people. He keeps moving, wooing, saving, working miracles, fulfilling His promises, keeping His covenants, defeating evil, and transforming those who have eyes to see and ears to hear Him. He will never grow weary, run out, or give up. All around the world, God is on the move. And He is inviting you to join Him.

Day Two

YOUR VOCATION

Today's passage for your conversation with God: Nehemiah 6:1-9

Work is not a consequence of the fall but is part of how God designed humans to thrive. God gave Adam and Eve work to do before they sinned. Adam was to name all the animals and take care of the garden (Genesis 2:15,20). Adam and Eve were also told to multiply and rule responsibly over the earth (Genesis 1:28).

You are also called to do great work by God. Greatness is not always equated with visibility—many people accomplish great things in relative obscurity. You influence people more than you probably realize. Though your position or your work on the earth may not have changed when God saved you, your purpose for life definitely got an upgrade. As a believer in Christ, you have been made for a great mission. You are "created in Christ Jesus to do good works, which God prepared in advance" for you to do (Ephesians 2:10). Your vocation is the place God calls you "where your deep gladness and the world's deep hunger meet."[4]

Your work will probably look different in different seasons of your life, and it may or may not involve pay. Whatever job God has called you to—whether it is tending to your home or leading a company—it is not second-class in His kingdom. Resist the temptation to compare yourself with other people, and remember that God's economy is very different from the world's. Societies thrive when disciples of Jesus work in various fields. As Paul wrote, "There are different kinds of working, but in all of them and in everyone it is the same God at work" (1 Corinthians 12:6).

God saved me (Matt) when I was five years old and called me into vocational ministry when I was twelve years old. As a twenty-year-old, I told a mentor that I was in "full-time ministry" because I was a pastor preparing to be a missionary. He wisely replied, "every believer is in 'full-time ministry'—you're in vocational ministry!" God may not be calling you to "vocational" ministry, but He does call you to lifelong ministry, no matter your occupation. My dad Randy worked for IBM (International Business Machines) while also leading Bible studies and mission trips with his church, and my granddad Avery worked for the IMB (International Mission Board) as a missionary. I'm so thankful that as a child I saw godly examples in each arena and felt the freedom to pursue whatever God called me to. Whether you work for IBM or the IMB, you have an important vocation in which to be a disciple of Jesus.

What "full-time ministry" has God given you? How could you use your vocation to accomplish the ministry God has given you?

You read today about Nehemiah, a politician and foreman in the Old Testament who successfully rebuilt the wall around Jerusalem for his Jewish kinspeople. He was successful in his project although enemies tried to sabotage it. They repeatedly invited him to take a break from the project to meet with them so they could kill him. Nehemiah shrewdly replied, "I am carrying on a great project and cannot go down. Why should the work stop while I leave it and go down to you?" (Nehemiah 6:3).

Like Nehemiah did, what is someone or something you need to say no to in order to fully accomplish the mission God has entrusted to you?

Jesus called four fishermen to be His disciples. Jesus repurposed their life vision: "'Come, follow Me . . . and I will send you out to fish for people.' At once they left their nets and followed him" (Mark 1:17-18). You may need to leave your job to reach more people for Christ or leverage your current job more for Christ. Whether or not God is calling you to leave your nets and change jobs, He wants you to be fishing for people, which you'll explore more next week. God sometimes calls people from vocational ministry back into the marketplace to directly reach more people who are far from God.

Pray and ask God if He wants to change anything—minor or major—about your current work. What, if any, changes do you sense God is calling you to make?

In the New Testament, some people in the Thessalonian church wrongly figured they could stop working since Jesus's second coming would happen soon. Paul wrote to them, "The one who is unwilling to work shall not eat" (2 Thessalonians 3:10). He told them to get back to work while still being ready for His return. Of course, for reasons beyond their control, there are times when people may be unemployed.

Believers, however, should never be perpetually lazy, and are instructed to "keep away from every believer who is idle" (2 Thessalonians 3:6). God calls you to do your work with excellence because He is worthy of receiving your best. "Whatever you do, work at it with all your heart, as working for the Lord, not for human masters" (Colossians 3:23).

People tend to categorize life stages into education, then employment, and then retirement. Regardless of your age, however, God wants to do a mighty work through you—just as He's done throughout history. The Bible doesn't set age limits or financial prerequisites or educational requirements on your service in the kingdom.

You won't find much in the Bible about retirement. As much as your health allows, keep ministering to people. Jesus said, "As long as it is day, we must do the works of Him who sent me. Night is coming, when no one can work" (John 9:4). John Piper once challenged a generation of young people with a story about a couple in their fifties who were spending the rest of their lives on their boat, collecting sea shells. He said, "That's a tragedy.. Don't buy it: collecting shells as the last chapter before you stand before the Creator of the universe to give an account of what you did: 'Here it is Lord—my shell collection!'"[5] He contrasted this couple with international missionaries who were actively serving at eighty years old when they died. C.T. Studd's poem sums it up well: "Only one life, 'twill soon be past, Only what's done for Christ will last."[6] You have been called to take your one life and make it matter for the kingdom.

Write Matthew 28:19 below to help you start to memorize it.

Day Three

YOUR TIME, TALENTS, AND TREASURES

Today's passage for your conversation with God: 2 Corinthians 9:6-15

Being a disciple means that you're all in. You give all of yourself to Jesus. Two of the quickest ways to test the quality of disciples is to see how they handle their money and time. In today's passage, Paul was affirming the believers in Corinth who had planned to give money to help Christians who were suffering in Jerusalem. Paul encouraged them—and you as well—to:

- sow generously (v. 6),
- according to your own choice (v. 7),
- cheerfully (v. 7), and
- to trust God to provide for all your needs (v. 8).

Anything you don't share owns you. Your earthly treasures of money, property, and possessions won't last forever and were given to you to be leveraged to bless God and people for eternity. That's why Jesus said, "Don't store up treasures here on earth, where moths eat them and rust destroys them, and where thieves break in and steal. Store your treasures in heaven, where moths and rust cannot destroy, and thieves do not break in and steal. Wherever your treasure is, there the desires of your heart will also be . . . No one can serve two masters . . . You cannot serve God and be enslaved to money" (Matthew 6:19-21,24, NLT).

You can never out-give God. In today's passage, you read that giving brings God's blessings to meet your own needs. When you give, God will also enhance your ability and commitment to generosity. Giving also supplies the needs of people God loves and can prompt people to whom you give to pray for you more regularly. Last but not least, giving brings glory to God.

Our culture fosters consumers, but Christ calls you to be a contributor instead. He wants you to be content with less for yourself so that you can bless others with your excess (1 Timothy 6:6-10). Contentment is more than just trusting God to provide—it is trusting His heart to know exactly what you need in every season. Stewarding your money well includes, but is not limited to, giving a tithe—ten percent of your income—to your church and offerings above that to your church or a Christian organization. Jesus did reference tithing (Matthew 23:23), but His teachings on money focused more on the condition of the heart rather than on specific numbers.

The early church modeled giving above and beyond a tithe (Acts 2:45). If you do not have the margin in your finances to give God at least a tithe, something else you are funding must be outside His will. You can use money and serve God, just don't serve money and use God.

My granddad Avery said, "I have met tithers who were not spiritual disciples, but I have never met a spiritual disciple who did not give to God's work at least ten percent of his or her income."

Are you honoring God by giving Him at least a tithe of your income? If so, what growth have you seen as a result of pursuing this spiritual discipline?

If you do not tithe, what is holding you back?

In addition to money, God has blessed you with spiritual gifts, talents, and practical skills that you can use to help others. Doing so requires another resource: your time. The hardest thing for many Christians to give is their time. You have limited talents, energy, and money, but God blesses you with the same twenty-four hours a day that He gives to everyone else. Discipline, structure, and organization don't come naturally to me, so I've had to work hard to grow in them to get the most out of my time, and you can too.

Jesus did His Father's will perfectly, but it's also amazing that He did nothing else! We or others may have a great idea, but our goal is to do God's perfect will. I feel like I can never accomplish everything on my to-do list, but the truth is I can do everything in a day that God wants me to do. To do so, I can't busy myself with things God doesn't intend for me to do.

What percentage (from 0 percent to 100 percent) of the following resources do you personally give to God and others:

Time ____ **Talents** ____ **Treasures** ____

What adjustments do you need to make to increase one or more of these investments into God's kingdom?

This week, do something outside of your normal routine to give your time, talent, or treasure to someone in need. Use the space below to plan out what you're going to do for whom, or ask the Holy Spirit to move you toward spontaneous generosity. Be prepared to share this experience with your group.

Being on mission with God doesn't mean you never rest—God gives sleep to those He loves (Psalm 127:2). It doesn't mean you can't have a hobby—God wants you to enjoy (1 Timothy 6:17). You can be intentional though, such as including someone in your hobby who you want to invest in. It doesn't mean you can't take a day off—remember how God commanded the Sabbath every week? And it doesn't mean you can't take a vacation. Spending a week away is extremely valuable, as it refreshes your spirit, soul, and body. "Annually Abandon"[8] is the last of our family's four spiritual rhythms.[9] When your heart is set on Jesus, all these things—your rest, hobbies, Sabbath, and vacations—help steward your time, talents, and treasures as you join Him on mission. When you have a clear, God-sized vision and proper priorities, you are compelled to steward your resources more efficiently and wisely.

Review Matthew 28:19, and then write verse 20 below to help you start to memorize it.

See page 279 for resources to more effectively spend your time and energy for God's glory.

Day Four
YOUR PROGRESS

Today's passage for your conversation with God: Acts 20:24-35

I love Acts 20:24 so much that I've memorized it: "I consider my life worth nothing to me; my only aim is to finish the race and complete the task the Lord Jesus has given me—the task of testifying to the good news of God's grace."

Write down the top five goals you would like to see begun and/or completed by the time you cross the finish line of a successful life:

1.

2.

3.

4.

5.

Maybe you wrote down one or more goals along the lines of relationships, spiritual transformation, financial security, physical health, or influence. For example, get married, have kids who follow Jesus closely, retire with a lot of savings at age sixty, live a healthy life until age ninety, or have an accomplished career.

How many of your top five goals are solely focused on you?

How many of them further God's kingdom (such as completing the Great Commission)?

You are called to prioritize God's mission. Maybe you didn't rank that in your top five and perhaps that's because you can't do it alone. You can, however, make disciples of all nations collectively as a member of the church—the largest, most diverse organization of people on earth. Thankfully, the global church empowered by the Holy Spirit will fulfill the Great

Commission. God's mission is a group effort, but you have an individual role to play. Someone who understood this better than most is the apostle Paul.

Aware that he would never see the people of Ephesus again, Paul declared in Acts 20:27 that he had not shrunk back from proclaiming the entire will of God to them. Near the end of his life, he also told Timothy, "I have fought the good fight, I have finished the race, I have kept the faith" (2 Timothy 4:7).

If your life were to end later this year, could you say the same? Why?

What can you do differently, if anything, to ensure that God's highest priorities prepared for you are fulfilled before you die?

We typically overestimate what we can accomplish in the short-term but underestimate what we can do in the long-term. Praise God all things are possible with Him (Matthew 19:26)! Many people's lives are more like a marathon than a sprint, and this diagram illustrates the pathway toward spiritual maturity.[10]

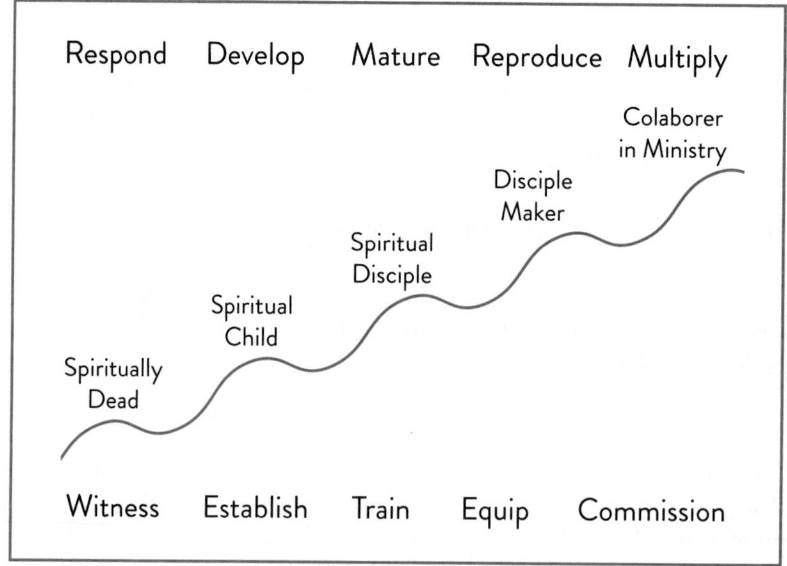

Every person begins as spiritually dead because of his or her sins. Only those who accept Christ's salvation ever progress in spiritual maturity, and in so doing become a spiritual child. You can mature to the last three stages through desire, obedience, faithfulness, and power from the Holy Spirit. You can't skip any of the steps.

The words at the top of the graph (respond, develop, etc.) name the responsibilities for your own growth according to what stage you're at along the path. For example, when you were spiritually dead apart from Christ, your only responsibility was to respond to the gospel through repentance and faith. When you're faithful on the left side for your own growth, your responsibilities on the top line expand to the right side of the illustration. One of the best ways to grow as a disciple is to help other people become disciples.

Prayerfully consider which of the five levels of maturity illustrated above (spiritual child, disciple, etc.) you are currently in and circle that level. What do you want to do or whom do you want to ask for help so that you can mature even further?

As you become more spiritually mature, your responsibilities for other people's spiritual growth progress on the bottom line (witness, establish, etc.) according to which phase the other person is in. For example, if you are a disciple maker, you train people who are spiritual disciples. As you progress to the right, you ought to remain faithful in preceding levels—continually witnessing to spiritually dead people and establishing those who are spiritual children.

Write the name of a few Christians you know personally whom you would like to offer to help grow as a spiritual child, disciple, or disciple maker:

Chapter 2 of 2 Timothy provides a great overview of discipleship. The fruit and ultimate purpose of discipleship is to see people saved and experience God's glory (2:10). The secret of your individual usefulness as Jesus's disciple is to keep yourself pure (vv. 20-21). The finished product of your discipleship is that you are ready for every good work the Master wants to do through you (v. 21). The essence of discipleship is you being a person of good character who can minister to anyone (vv. 24-25). A joyful part of your discipleship is getting to watch God change other people's hearts (vv. 25-26)!

May God grant you continued grace to finish the race and complete the task He has given you.

Use your verse card to review Matthew 28:19-20, and keep practicing it until you've got it memorized.

Day Five

YOUR VISION AND MISSION STATEMENT

Today's passage for your conversation with God: 1 Corinthians 9:22-27

In today's passage, you can see Paul's desire to impact a lot of people—and many types of people—for Christ. He urges you to not just live but to be fully alive; to not just exist but to race like you want to win. This means living with a sense of significance and urgency rather than plodding through life unaware. Paul says you should train and engage like a champion athlete, with intention and laser focus. Unfortunately, many Christians settle for being spectators.

Imagine your last month as if it were a round of boxing. How did you do? Were you active and busy but punching the air? Were you knocked down? Or did you see great victory?

Stephen Covey quipped about our life's direction, "If the ladder is not leaning against the right wall, every step we take just gets us to the wrong place faster."[11]

Millions of people have read Rick Warren's book *The Purpose Driven Life* because so many people struggle to know their purpose. Rick wrote, "The purpose of your life is far greater than your own personal fulfillment, your peace of mind, or even your happiness. It's far greater than your family, your career, or even your wildest dreams and ambitions . . . you must begin with God. You were born by His purpose and for His purpose."[12]

As a follower of Jesus, you are not entitled to pursue whatever mission you want. You are to join in His mission. Your ultimate mission is to glorify God by being a lifelong disciple of the Lord Jesus Christ, making disciples, and joining God's mission to establish His kingdom among all nations.

God has the same general purposes for your life as He desires for every person: that you do things with excellence for God's glory and people's good. However, your fulfillment of these purposes is unique. Crafting your own vision statement and mission statement is a clarifying tool that will help you discern your life's purpose and focus.

Many employers have statements like these for their organizations, but most people cannot articulate similar statements for their own lives. Some people work just to pay the bills and provide for their family without much care for why they have a particular occupation. A vision statement specifies why you are alive, and a mission statement explains what you desire to accomplish. Without these guideposts, life can be drudgery and feel aimless.

My family crystallized a vision statement and mission statement many years ago that still hangs in a prominent place in our home to remind us of our purpose. Our vision statement is, "To daily be intimate with Jesus Christ through loving, obeying, and surrendering to Him." Our mission statement is, "To grow as disciples and make disciples of Jesus Christ of the least-reached people." These commitments influence our major and minor life decisions, our investments, and our daily behaviors.

An acrostic tool that can help you construct your vision statement and mission statement is called S.H.A.P.E.[13] God has uniquely shaped you to complete a special mission subservient to His overarching mission.

Write a few words about yourself that could be used in your own statements next to each of these bullet points:

- **Spiritual Gifts (See Romans 12:3-8. You will learn more about this on page 220.)**

- **Heart (or passion)**

- **Abilities**

- **Personality**

- **Experience**

You may refine it later, but at least write a rough draft now of your personal vision and mission statements below.

Vision Statement (why I am alive):

Mission Statement (what I desire to accomplish):

Reflectively consider these questions to make your statements as executable as possible:

- **Do they honor God in size and scope? Is my vision big enough that I can only accomplish it by depending on the Holy Spirit to do it through me?**

- **Is my vision measurable? How do I know if I'm doing it well?**

- **What is the best strategy for how to fulfill these?**

- **Who will I ask to keep me accountable for living according to these?**

After looking through these questions, revisit your vision and mission statements to see if you would like to revise them.

Using your verse card, try to say Matthew 28:19-20 by memory. Keep working on it until you've got it.

Optional passages for more conversations with God:

Day 6: John 4:27-42
Day 7: 2 Timothy 4:1-8

Week Eleven

BEING HIS WITNESS

That if you confess with your mouth, "Jesus is Lord," and believe in your heart that God raised him from the dead, you will be saved.
ROMANS 10:9

Why are you still here on earth? Certainly God has a purpose for you to be here—otherwise He would have already taken you to heaven. Heaven will have greater praise and worship experiences than you could ever have in this world, more knowledge than your favorite authors and preachers can currently convey, and sweeter, intimate fellowship than you can imagine. Not to mention a new and improved version of you! So why are you still here?

When you get to heaven, you won't have any more opportunity to share the gospel or minister to people. God wants you to use the time you have left on earth to bless other people. The apostle Paul said, "To live is Christ, and to die is gain . . . I am torn between the two: I desire to depart and be with Christ, which is better by far; but it is more necessary for you that I remain in the body" (Philippians 1:21,23-24). In short, you are here to live out and share the gospel.

What is the gospel? The gospel, or "good news," is the way anyone can experience a saving relationship with God. Just telling someone "God loves you" is not the same as sharing the gospel with that person—the gospel has essential components that shouldn't be left out when you share it. For example, if you talk with your neighbor about God but don't mention the sinless life, death, and resurrection of Jesus, you have initiated a good spiritual conversation but not a gospel conversation. The goal of spiritual conversations is that they will lead to gospel conversations.

THE GOSPEL is the good news that God sent His Son Jesus to bear His wrath against people's sin through His substitutionary death on the cross and to show His power over sin and death in the resurrection from the grave. All who turn from their sin and themselves and trust in Jesus alone as Savior and Lord will be reconciled to God forever.[1]

Romans 3:23; 5:8; 6:23; and 10:9 are very helpful when sharing the essence of the gospel. When I share the gospel with people, the main verse I quote is the one you'll memorize this week, Romans 10:9, because it describes how they can be saved.

If you are a disciple, you are a witness. A witness is anyone who has a life-changing experience with Jesus. Although you haven't seen Jesus in bodily form like the first disciples did, you have seen His truth and power in your life. When you received Jesus as your Lord and Savior, you became a new creation and an ambassador for Christ. And after reconciling you to Himself, Christ gave you the ministry of helping others be reconciled as well (2 Corinthians 5:17-20). You are both an ambassador and a witness.

Read the very last words Jesus spoke on earth before His ascension: "But you will receive power when the Holy Spirit comes on you; and you will be my witnesses in Jerusalem, and in all Judea and Samaria, and to the ends of the earth" (Acts 1:8). The final truth Jesus spoke into His disciples' identity is that they were to be His witnesses. This is why it's one of the vital arms of the Disciple's Cross, illustrated here. This week, I pray you will step more fully into your identity as His witness and learn new skills that will help you live it out both near and far.

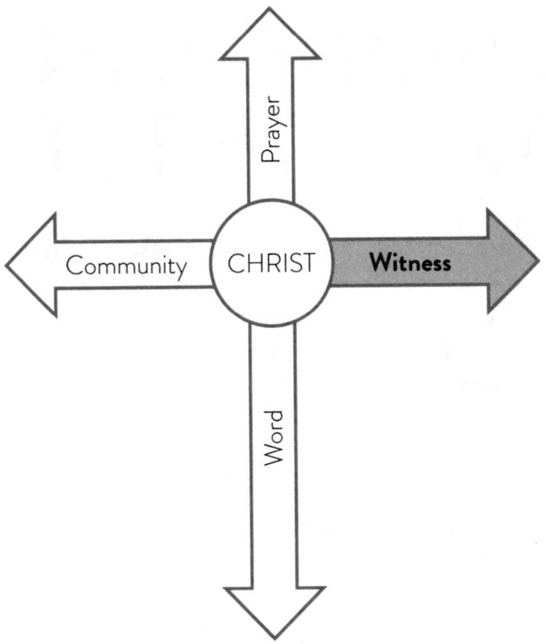

PRAYER

Heavenly Father, I praise You for being the atoning sacrifice for the sins of the whole world. I will tell about Your righteousness and salvation all day long—even though it is more than I can fully comprehend! Thank You for making me a new creation in Christ and Your ambassador to my neighbors and the nations. Give me the desire to be Your witness. Holy Spirit, fill me with Your power so that I will speak Your words to people, telling them how they too can be saved and experience an eternal relationship with You. In Jesus's name, amen.

Day One

BEARING INNER AND OUTER FRUIT

Today's passage for your conversation with God: Ephesians 5:1-21

As Christ's witness, you are to share and show the gospel in both word and deed. You cannot communicate the gospel without words. Your smile alone cannot show people how to place their faith in Christ. Likewise, words of the gospel spoken without love are like a resounding gong or a clanging cymbal (1 Corinthians 13:1-3). Communicating the gospel without Christlike kindness or compassion is hypocrisy and will crush your witness. Jesus desires both your integrity and intentionality. He says, "Let your light shine before others, that they may see your good deeds and glorify your Father in heaven" (Matthew 5:16).

The goal of witnessing is not to see new converts but to see new believers who bear fruit as disciples. A convert wants what you have, but a disciple wants who you are. God calls you and those you lead to Christ to bear fruit in increasing measure (2 Peter 1:5-8).

Salvation has three key phases: justification, sanctification, and glorification.[2] Justification is the once-for-all turning point when God declared you righteous by your faith in the perfect sacrifice of Jesus in your place (Romans 5:1). Your sin's penalty of eternal separation from God has been done away with, you have a new spirit, and you now get to experience eternal life with Him.

Sanctification is the lifelong process of becoming more holy like Christ (Philippians 2:12). You used to be mastered by sin but now you are transitioning to being mastered by righteousness in this life (Romans 6:14-19). Your mind, will, and emotions are a battleground, but you have victory as you surrender to the Holy Spirit's transforming work in you.

Glorification is when your faith becomes sight as you behold God's glory, and receive a new body and a perfect eternity with Him in heaven (Romans 8:17). To sum up these three phases of salvation, you're immediately justified when you accept Christ; you're gradually sanctified for the rest of your earthly life, and you're permanently glorified in heaven.

Today's passage speaks to your sanctification as you live among unbelievers who are yet to be justified. Verse 9 from today's passage reminds you again of what you have previously read in John 15 and Galatians 5—you will bear good fruit. You should bear inner fruit in character and outer fruit in ministry—leading people to faith as described in John 4:35-38. A purer disciple and church are brighter witnesses who attract people seeking life in God. In Ephesians 5:4, Paul urges you to use your tongue not for foul language or inappropriate jokes but for thanking

God and speaking life, love, and truth to people. This is an example of inner fruit. In verse 16, you are called to prioritize bearing fruit with your limited time because the days are evil.

In which areas do you need to repent for being "unfruitful" (Ephesians 5:11)? (Examples include sins, time-wasters, not sharing the gospel, etc.)

Read and meditate on 1 Peter 3:13-16.

In these verses, Peter said that when you have a clear conscience, you can be His witness with compelling confidence. You have been given authority by God to be His witness. You don't have to "earn the right" from someone to share the gospel with him or her. Jesus purchased that right for you with His blood and gave you the right or "authority" to share the gospel with anyone, anytime, anywhere (see Matthew 28:18-20, where the original word translated as *authority* is translated as a *right* in John 1:12). Doing so with respect, you can share the good news with anyone the first time you meet him or her, as the New Testament repeatedly describes.

Jesus initiated a spiritual conversation in His first encounter with a Samaritan woman in John 4. This woman, who had lived a sinful life and had certainly never been discipled, began to believe in Jesus during their conversation and immediately began pointing her townspeople to the Messiah. If she could lead so many people to Christ, so can you—no matter how tainted your past is. Being a disciple does not mean you're perfect; otherwise, none of us could be His witnesses. You don't, however, have a license to be a hypocrite who talks about the gospel but doesn't live it out. Be careful of the other extreme as well—that you don't live so separated from unbelievers that they don't hear the gospel from you.

Reflect on how God has already worked through you as His witness. Who have you led to faith in Christ?

If you had to leave that answer blank, consider trying out this strategy: prayer, care, and share. In my prayer notebook, I have a list of people I've been trying to share the gospel with more. I pray for them by name regularly, asking God to open their hearts to receive Jesus's salvation.

If you have never shared Christ with someone, who has God placed in your life that you can share with?

This foundation of prayer is strengthened by genuinely caring for people. People don't care how much you know about God unless they know how much you care about them. Just because you don't have to "earn the right" to share the gospel doesn't mean you shouldn't build relational equity with unbelievers so that they might be more willing to hear you out as you share with "gentleness and respect" (1 Peter 3:15). People are not projects and shouldn't be treated as such. A lack of authentic care for a person could be your number one roadblock to witnessing to him or her. Ask God to show you something tangible you could do to show your care for each person you are praying for. Consider serving them in some way, writing them a note, inviting them over for a meal, or just asking them how you can pray for them.

Caring paves the way for sharing the gospel. You naturally talk about what you love. You don't need training on how to talk about your family, friends, or pets—nor do you need booklets or tracts to help you convince people why your favorite sports team is the best. Because you love these things so much, you naturally share them out of the overflow of your heart. If you are not sharing the gospel, it may be because your love for God is lacking. Or maybe you love what people think of you more than you love them. If you are hesitant to share because you do not feel prepared, I have good news for you. Later this week you will learn and practice effective ways to share the gospel.

How could you show you care for people who are far from God in your spheres of influence?

Pray now that God increases your love for Him and people so much that you won't be able to help but tell everyone about what you know and experience in Him. Pray that God would lead more people to faith in Christ through your witness.

Cut out the Romans 10:9 verse card at the back of this workbook, and practice saying it a few times: "If you declare with your mouth, 'Jesus is Lord,' and believe in your heart that God raised him from the dead, you will be saved."

Day Two

JESUS: THE ONE AND ONLY WAY

Today's passage for your conversation with God: Acts 4:1-20

Jesus Christ is the one and only way people can be saved from their sins and have eternal life with God. Denial or doubt of this truth washes away the necessity and urgency of evangelism. Many religious leaders, like the ones you read about in today's passage, will tolerate you talking about God in general but will cringe if you agree with what God's Word says about Jesus. How did the first witnesses reply? "Salvation is found in no one else, for there is no other name [besides Jesus] under heaven given to mankind by which we must be saved" (Acts 4:12). They heard Jesus say, "I am *the* way and *the* truth and and *the* life. *No one* comes to the Father *except through me*" (John 14:6, italics mine). The good news is that "God . . . wants all people to be saved and to come to a knowledge of the truth. For, there is one God and one mediator between God and mankind, the man Christ Jesus" (1 Timothy 2:3-5).

Do you think that people can experience salvation without accepting Jesus as their Lord and Savior? Why or why not?

The desire for people to reject Jesus is strong and enticing. Jesus said, "Wide is the gate and broad is the road that leads to destruction, and many enter through it. But small is the gate and narrow the road that leads to life, and only a few find it" (Matthew 7:13-14). Heaven and hell are real places—and all people will spend eternity in one or the other. God is giving mercy to people until the day of judgment comes (2 Corinthians 6:2).

The Bible clearly teaches that everyone has sinned and falls short of God's glory (Romans 3:23). All people are on a trajectory to an eternity in hell unless they turn away from their sins and trust in Christ as their Savior and Lord. Romans 5:8 says God demonstrates His love for us in this: "While we were still sinners, Christ died for us." If Jesus had never come to earth and died on the cross, all people would be eternally separated from God. Romans 6:23

says "the wages of sin is death, but the gift of God is eternal life in Christ Jesus our Lord." No one can boast in their own righteousness, because everyone was once as far from God as those without faith still are. It has been said that sharing the gospel is simply one beggar humbly telling another beggar where to find bread.

When thinking about this topic, a common question is: can people who are far from God be saved without ever hearing of Jesus? It's a natural question to ask, but we must affirm that the Bible says this isn't possible. The belief that all people will be saved reguardless of how they respond to Jesus is universalism and is not supported by Scripture. If people who are far from God can be saved without ever hearing of Jesus, the worst thing you can do for them is obey what Jesus said in Acts 1:8 by being His witness "to the ends of the earth"—because then they are accountable for what they now know. If the worst thing you can do in a situation is to obey Jesus, something is wrong. The Bible says no one—not even "good" people—can be righteous apart from Him (Romans 3:10,23). For this reason, those who never hear of Jesus will experience the same Christless eternity as those who deliberately reject Him. No wonder Jesus calls His disciples to be His witnesses!

Despite the somber reality that those who never hear of Jesus are headed toward eternal separation from Him, God says, "You will seek me and find me when you seek me with all your heart" (Jeremiah 29:13). Our heavenly Father often reveals Jesus to people during their life on earth when they are seeking God. That's exactly what God did for Cornelius—a man who was trying to please God but did not yet know Jesus. God used a witness named Peter to lead Cornelius to salvation through Jesus (see Acts 10). I've met people from Bangladesh and Afghanistan for whom God has done something similar—sometimes through the same means of another believer, and other times through a Christian TV program, the Bible, or a dream or vision. In every case, the message of Jesus must be communicated. Unfortunately, many Christians today do not believe Jesus is the one and only way to be saved.

- Of American Christians, 66% believe there are multiple paths to heaven.[3]
- Of born-again Christians, nearly 70% disagree with the biblical position that Jesus is the only way to God.[4]
- Of people with evangelical beliefs, 51% believe God accepts the worship of all religions, including Christianity, Islam, and Judaism.[5]

When Paul spoke with idolaters, he did not say, "You have many good things in your religion. Keep up the good work." Instead, he proclaimed Jesus and stated, "In the past God overlooked such ignorance, but now he commands all people everywhere to repent" (Acts 17:30).

Do not believe the lie that all religions offer salvation and true transformation. Believing that lie denies Jesus and the Bible as the authoritative truth. If other viable pathways to heaven existed, Jesus should have never come to the earth and suffered. If salvation could have happened any other way, Jesus died needlessly and the cross was in vain! If a doctor told you that at last there was a cure for your deadly illness, would you say, "Why is there only one cure?" Of course not! Let the nations be glad that eternal healing is available through Jesus.

Put a star beside any of the following obstacles that keep you from being a witness who is convinced that Jesus is the only way for people to be saved:

- **Previous ignorance of Scriptures such as the ones mentioned today**
- **Uncertainty, doubt, or having not spent enough time deeply considering this reality**
- **Fear of rejection or confrontation, or being ashamed of the gospel (Romans 1:16)**
- **A lack of love that would otherwise overcome your hesitation to share the gospel**
- **Feeling unequipped to adequately share the gospel**

How might you overcome these obstacles?

If none of these apply to you, spend a few moments thanking the Lord for how He has used you to be His witness.

I pray that you will be confident that Jesus alone can save people from their sin and separation from God and that you will have a sense of urgency in sharing the gospel while you still have time. And if you are met with opposition when you share, borrow a line from the first disciples who said, "We cannot help speaking about what we have seen and heard" (Acts 4:20).

Use your verse card to continue memorizing Romans 10:9.

Day Three
TELLING YOUR STORY

Today's passage for your conversation with God: Acts 22:1-21

Perhaps one of the obstacles you circled yesterday that prevents you from being Jesus's witness is feeling unequipped to adequately share the gospel. Today and tomorrow's lessons will give you the tools to do so. In addition, two optional group sessions during which you can practice using these tools are recommended at the end of this discipleship experience.

Think of a gospel conversation as three stories: their story, your story, and Jesus's story. For the first story, you will simply be a listener. You can ask them, "Would you mind telling me about your spiritual journey?" or "Can you tell me more about your life story?" Listen carefully to their spiritual story not only to show that you care for them but also so you can find parts of their story that will naturally bridge to your story and Jesus's story. After you have heard their story, you can ask, "Do you mind if I tell you my story?"

Paul told his story in today's passage. It contained three parts:

1. His life before Jesus (Acts 22:1-5)
2. How he met Jesus (Acts 22:6-16)
3. How his life changed after knowing Jesus (Acts 22:17-21)

Today you will learn how to tell your own story—also known as your testimony—using these same three parts: your life before Christ, how you accepted Christ for salvation, and how your life has changed since then. The story you will refine today is a simple, fifteen-second testimony. Knowing how to share a quick testimony is important because most people have a short attention span. I encourage you to craft a longer version of your testimony later—one that is around three minutes (as Paul did in Acts 22). It is helpful to know both versions so you can share whichever one best fits the situation.

Your story should reflect that Jesus is the Hero of your life. Your goal is to share how Jesus has changed your life and is still transforming you. Your testimony is powerful no matter its details, because no one can disprove what God has done in your life.

The first part of your fifteen-second testimony uses two words to describe what was broken in your life before you met Christ. The second part uses two words to describe the specific time you turned away from your sins in repentance and trusted in Jesus. The third part uses two words to describe what Jesus has been doing in your life since then. You can see in this diagram that the three symbols at the top represent the three parts of your testimony. Here is an example of what mine looks like:

Here's how I (Matt) tell my story based on the six words I chose: "**There was a time in my life when I was** *guilty* and *ashamed*, **but then Jesus changed my life**. I *turned* away from my sin and *trusted* in Jesus to save me. Ever since, I have been *depending* on God and He has never left me or forsaken me. I am now *confident* of who Jesus is and who I am. **What do you think about my story?**"

Here's how Allison tells her story (her six words are in italics): "**There was a time in my life when I was** *afraid* of many things and I felt *unknown*, **but then Jesus changed my life**. He *saved* me years ago and I have been *following* Him ever since. **Now**, He has given me *peace* that surpasses understanding when I'm still tempted to fear. And now I know I am fully *known* by the God who created me. **Do you have a story like this?**"

Now it's your turn to craft your story. Write down two key words in the lines under each of the three parts of your story below.

Write out your story below based on the six words you chose. Use the bold phrases above to help it flow, and be sure to include a follow-up question at the end. After you have written out your story, practice saying it out loud a few times.

While sharing the absolute truth of the gospel at the head level is important, your story also communicates at the heart level. Many people resist the gospel with their hearts more than their minds. Most people don't primarily resist the gospel because of some doctrine, but rather because of some person in their lives. That person might be a religious or irreligious parent, a hypocritical Christian, or an abusive minister. Or on the flip side, maybe they don't want to lose a relationship with someone who will reject them if they accept Christ. Your testimony can bridge the gap between someone's mind and heart and take them from simply hearing information to seeing transformation.

Prioritize sharing the gospel with people face-to-face, but when that is impossible, you can share a digital version. Plan a time in the next few weeks to record your story by video so you can either post it on social media, as I have done, or post it on YouTube, as Allison has done (see bit.ly/AllisonWillis). Then you can text its link to people as the Holy Spirit leads you. Consider asking someone to keep you accountable for creating this digital version of your testimony.

Use your verse card to continue memorizing Romans 10:9.

If you want to watch videos of gospel conversation trainings with some of the elements I've mentioned, I recommend this series of videos, the first three of which our church created. They were made for our specific local church but their principles apply to believers outside of our context. In the second video you can see each of us leading this training.

- bit.ly/gospeltraining1
- bit.ly/gospeltraining2
- bit.ly/gospeltraining3
- bit.ly/411training

Day Four

TELLING JESUS'S STORY

Today's passage for your conversation with God: 1 Corinthians 15:1-11

Yesterday you learned how to share your story. Today you will learn how to tell Jesus's story, which is the gospel itself. Jesus's death, burial, and resurrection are paramount to the gospel, as you read in today's passage. My favorite tool to use when sharing Jesus's story is The 3 Circles,[6] so it is the tool I will show you today. It looks like this:

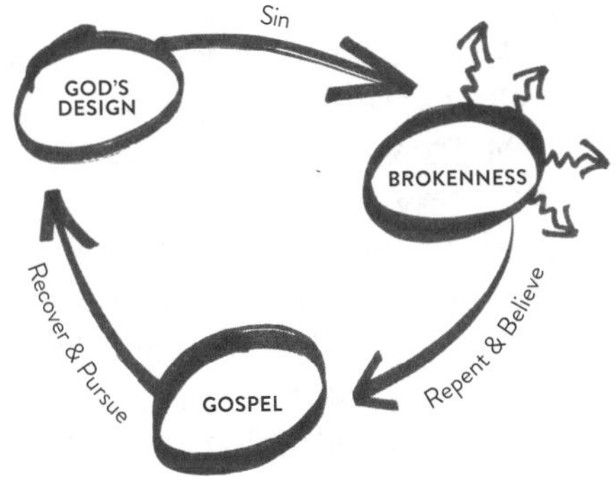

Pause now and watch a video of The 3 Circles in action at bit.ly/Circles3.

It's important to know how to transition from telling your story to sharing Jesus's story. After sharing your story, ask, "Can I share a picture with you that gives me a lot of hope?" The person you are sharing with will probably say yes. You can use a phone app,[7] a booklet, a sticker, or draw it out on a blank piece of paper so that you can leave it with him or her. Here is what you say:

1. Start by drawing a circle and writing *brokenness* in it. Say, "It's obvious that we live in a broken world, right? There are broken families, broken governments, broken systems, and broken individuals, but it didn't always used to be this way."
2. Draw a preceding circle to the left and write *God's design* in it. Say, "In the beginning God created the heavens and the earth. He loves all people. The Bible tells us that God has a design for every single area of our lives and wants what is best for people."
3. Draw an arrow from the *God's design* circle to the *brokenness* circle. Say, "The problem is that every single one of us has departed from God's design because we do things our own way." Write the word *sin* above the arrow. Then say, "The Bible has a word for this,

and the word is *sin*. God's Word says all of us have sinned, and we all fall short of God's design for our lives. Sin is rebellion against God's authority and goodness."

4. Point back to the circle of *brokenness*. Then say, "When we sin against God and depart from His design, we experience brokenness. It feels like shame, regret, or emptiness; it's the feeling of being used, it's loneliness. Brokenness calls our attention to the need to change."
5. Draw squiggly lines out from the *brokenness* circle, representing people's flawed attempts to escape it. Then say, "When we're in brokenness we try to change things and so we sometimes put all of our hope in a relationship, or we try to escape reality through the internet or movies, or we try to numb our pain with substances. The change we need won't come from inside of us. The good news is that God wants to heal the broken places in our lives."
6. Draw a third circle beneath the others and write *gospel* in it. Say, "The Bible has a word for *good news* and the word is *gospel*. Although we couldn't get to heaven, heaven came down to us through Jesus, who is fully God and fully man. He is the only One to ever live without sinning, and He died on the cross for the sins of the world. He was raised from the dead on the third day."
7. Draw an arrow from the *brokenness* circle to the *gospel* circle with the words *repent and believe*. Say, "Repent means to change our mind and direction. It means to turn away from our sins and trust in Christ to save us. When we repent of our sins and believe in Jesus, He forgives our sins and heals the broken places in our lives."
8. Draw an arrow from the *gospel* circle back to the *God's design* circle with the words *recover and pursue*. Say, "We now can recover and pursue God's design for our lives. Our relationship with God is restored, and we will live with Him forever. He also sends us out to tell others how Jesus can heal them too."
9. Finally, ask the person you are sharing with questions such as, "Does what I shared make sense? Where would you put yourself in this story—can you point to it in this picture?"

When I ask people to point to where they would put themselves in The 3 Circles diagram, the most common answer I get is that they're between the brokenness circle and the gospel circle. In that situation, I ask them some variation of these questions: "Where do you want to be? What do you need to do to get there? Do you know any reason you would not be willing to receive God's free gift?" If they seem open, here's a sample dialogue of how to continue:

> *You:* Are you willing to turn from your sin and to place your faith in Christ now?
> *Other person:* Yes.
> *You:* That's so great! The Bible says, "If you declare with your mouth, 'Jesus is Lord,' and believe in your heart that God raised Him from the dead, you will be saved" (Romans 10:9). I invite you to do those two things now. I'll pray an example of a prayer and ask you to repeat each sentence after me since God says to confess with our mouths. In addition, you need to believe in your heart what you're

saying because reciting the prayer alone is not a secret formula to salvation. Okay? Let's pray.

You: (with other person repeating your words)

I admit that I have sinned against you, God. *(Pause to let the other person repeat.)*
Please forgive me of all my sin. *(Pause)*
I repent and believe Jesus died in my place and rose again to life. *(Pause)*
Please give me eternal life because I want to live with You forever. *(Pause)*
In Jesus's name, amen.

It is extremely important to invite people to make a decision about Christ right then. First Peter 3:15 exhorts us, "Always be prepared to give an answer to everyone who asks you to give the reason for the hope that you have." Salvation is more than just a prayer—but praying is an essential part of the journey because it follows Romans 10:9, which is a great verse to quote when you are sharing the gospel with someone.

Try to quote Romans 10:9 now. If you can't, use your verse card to review it.

When you ask people to point to where they are in The 3 Circles, some will say they're in the gospel circle when it seems like they are not saved. In that situation, I ask them follow-up questions, such as "What did you do to get there? When did you do that?"

There will be times when you share The 3 Circles with someone who is truly saved. In those cases, I ask him or her, "Who do you know who needs to hear the gospel presented in this way? Is it possible for you to share it with that person within the coming week? I'd be glad to help you if needed and to pray with you now that God will give you that opportunity."

Today or tomorrow, practice drawing out The 3 Circles on a blank piece of paper while explaining it to a Christian friend as if he or she wasn't a Christian. Practicing it with a Christian friend now will help build your confidence to share it later with someone who is far from God.

Day Five
WHO DO I TELL?

Today's passage for your conversation with God: Romans 10:9-17

The gospel is both God's Word—His truth—and God's work—His power. First Thessalonians 1:5 says, "Our gospel came to you not simply with words but also with power, with the Holy Spirit and deep conviction." God has said and done everything needed for the salvation of anyone who repents and believes in Jesus. That is the good news of Romans 10:13: "Everyone who calls on the name of the Lord will be saved."

Romans 10:14-15 is a reminder of a serious reality: "How, then, can they call on the one they have not believed in? And how can they believe in the one of whom they have not heard? And how can they hear without someone preaching to them? And how can anyone preach unless they are sent?" Sadly, 87% of all non-Christians around the world do not personally know a Christ-follower.[8] God has sent each of us to proclaim the gospel to people—both near and far—in the hope that they will ask God to transform their lives and restore their relationship with Him forever.

Jesus once healed a man who was possessed by many demons. The man wanted to follow Jesus and study the Scriptures with the master teacher. Jesus, however, did not let him but said, "Go home to your own people and tell them how much the Lord has done for you, and how he has had mercy on you" (Mark 5:19). The next verse says the man then went to ten cities telling people how much Jesus had done for him. The best people at sharing the gospel are the ones who have just been saved. Unfortunately, the longer someone has been saved, the more likely he or she is to forget how horrible it was to be spiritually lost—and the more likely that person is to have stopped being friends with people who are far from God.

Who in your sphere of influence is far from God but close to you? Think through your friends—which of them do you still need to share the gospel with? What about your relatives? Sharing the gospel with family members can be difficult—but they'll likely listen to you share the gospel more than they will anyone else. What about your neighbors who are far from God? You are probably the Christian who lives in the closest proximity to them. What about your coworkers? While it may be difficult for you to talk about your faith at work, you could take a coworker out to lunch and share your story and Jesus's story with him or her then.

Intentionally engage and befriend new people too—pray for your server at a restaurant, build friendships through a team or hobby, or go on a mission trip. God has strategically placed you where you are for a purpose. Even if your friends and family never profess faith in Jesus, keep genuinely loving them well just like Jesus does.

Write the names of people who you would like to share the gospel with. Add them to your prayer list so you can begin praying for them regularly.

Plan out when you are going to share the gospel with each of them, and write it down below (for example, "Mike—this Saturday at lunch").

Who will you ask to pray for you and keep you accountable for sharing with these people? Consider also asking them or someone else to go with you to witness (see how Jesus sent witnesses two by two in Luke 10:1-11).

When you share the gospel, those you share with will fit into one of three categories. I like to use the example of a traffic light to describe them as either green lights, yellow lights, or red lights. Green represents go—this is someone who is ready to accept Christ for salvation when you share with him or her. Yellow represents slow—this is someone who shows some interest in what you're saying but isn't ready yet to accept Christ. Red represents stop—this is someone who is strongly resistant to the gospel. For someone like this, Jesus said in Luke 10 that you should wipe the dust off your feet and move on to other people who are more receptive to the gospel. Red lights are what most Christians are afraid of, but the most common response you'll find when you share the gospel are yellow lights.

In Acts 17, you see all three types of responses after the apostle Paul preached in Athens. "When they heard of the resurrection of the dead, some of them sneered" (17:32a)—these are red lights. "But others said, 'We want to hear you again on this subject'" (17:32b)—these are yellow lights. "Some of the people became followers of Paul and believed" (17:34)—these are green lights.

Jude 1:22-23 also addresses all three types of responses. With red lights, Jude said to show them mercy and love but keep a healthy distance from them so as not to argue with those who reject the gospel (v. 23). With yellow lights, he said to "be merciful to those who doubt" (v. 22). With green lights, he said, "save others by snatching them from the fire" (v. 23).

You cannot force people to place their faith in Christ, but look to lead green lights to faith without delay. If they receive Christ, they have been born again and are spiritual babies, so they should not be abandoned. Instead, walk with them, and model spiritual maturity. Consider taking them through the thirteen important steps of obedience listed in week 2 on page 44. Of those, the first steps for them to take would be to get baptized, tell their friends about Jesus, engage in a church, and spend time in the Bible.

For yellow lights, have a follow-up strategy. Imagine that after you share The 3 Circles with Mike, you ask him, "Are you willing to turn from your sin and to place your faith in Christ now?" Let's say Mike replies, "I'm a good person, and I believe God will let good people like me into heaven. I'm not sure if what you're saying is true." You could respond by saying, "If you wanted to get right with God today, I'm glad to help you do that. But if you're not ready today, would you like to study the Bible with me for the next few weeks so we can have more conversations about God?"

Studying the Bible together is an excellent strategy to use with yellow lights. Consider the person's spiritual background when choosing a study, and make sure it is Jesus-centered. Encourage him or her to invite any of his or her friends and family members who he or she thinks might be interested to come along. After a few sessions, invite the person to reconsider placing his or her faith in Christ. If he or she still isn't ready, pray about your next step—whether you should extend the study or simply invite the person to tell you if he or she changes his or her mind in the future. This way, you can invest more of your time sharing the gospel with green lights and then discipling them. You can search for various Discovery Bible Studies online and see an example in the recommended resources list on page 279.

Remember that Romans 10:9 is a great verse to use as His witness! Write it out from memory and then check it for accuracy. If you don't have it down, practice it until you've got it memorized.

Optional passages for more conversations with God:

Day 6: Acts 10:34-48

Day 7: 2 Corinthians 5:11-21

Week Twelve

ALL HIS TOGETHER

And let us consider how we may spur one another on toward
love and good deeds, not giving up meeting together,
as some are in the habit of doing, but encouraging one
another—and all the more as you see the Day approaching.
HEBREWS 10:24-25

Today begins the final stretch of this discipleship experience. Our hope and prayer is that what you have experienced has given you a hunger for more—more intimacy with your Father, more self-awareness, more desire for relationship, and more purpose in your daily life. This week we hope you will gain even more confidence in the God whose glory exceeds your imagination, and in His ability to use you right now in His story.

In the beginning of this journey, you read that God created you by His love and for His love. The fact that you are unconditionally loved by the God who knit you together is the truest thing about you. You are a one-of-a-kind image bearer of Christ.

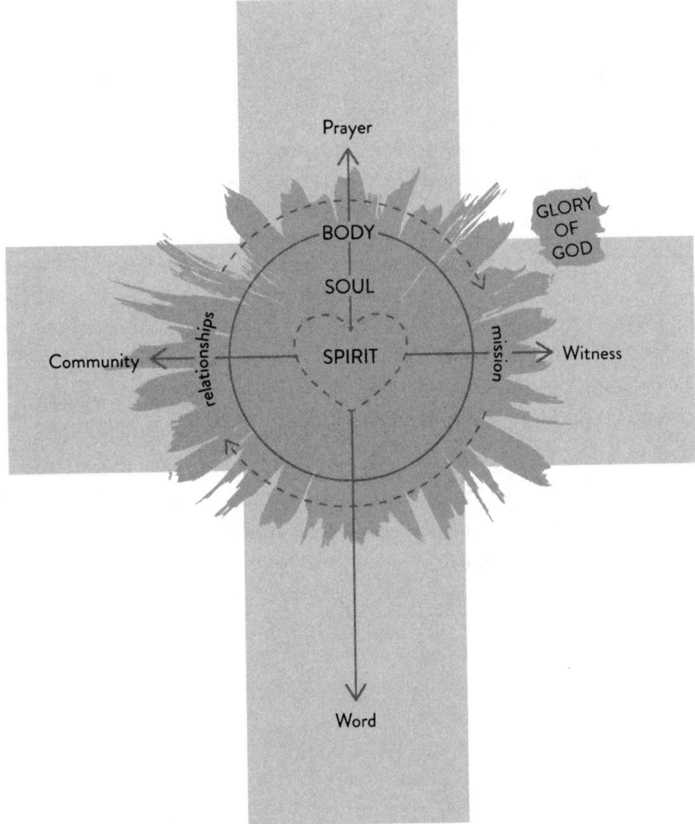

This diagram captures our journey together. The deepest place in you—your spirit—is where God chooses to dwell, as if to beg for your intimacy and trust. Christ in you radiates His glory throughout your entire being (Colossians 1:27). He indwells the essence of you known as your soul—the personality stemming from your mind, will, and emotions. You have all of Him, and His Spirit longs to inhabit even more of you—to live out the fullness of Jesus's life in your very body. He calls your body His temple, and its design pleases Him, displays His glory, and makes you long for eternity.

He designed you for relationship—first with Him, and then with those He has given you. You were not designed to do life on your own but together—with His Spirit inside you and His people around you. His mission, in fact, is to draw all people into these two relationships. And He created you to join Him in doing so. Mission and relationship go together. The verses you will memorize this week attest to it.

Jesus went to the cross for you, and as His disciple, He calls you to take up your own cross and follow Him. He is not asking you to die a physical death, but rather a death to self—and a daily one at that. Knowing you would be prone to flee this death and live for self, He offers Himself as the centerpiece of your spirit. He gives you the stabilizing structures of The Disciple's Cross—His Word, prayer, community, and witness—to keep you surrendered to Him. In anchoring yourself on these disciplines, you will find yourself tethered to Him and growing in His loving presence. This week ties together all you've explored in this discipleship experience and allows you to zoom out to see where His story is headed.

PRAYER

Thank You, Father, for choosing me. For wanting me. For delighting in me. Thank You for enveloping me and inhabiting me. May You have undivided supremacy in my heart and life. May every fiber of my being declare Your worth. May my whole life become a looking up, a crying out from my innermost heart for You to prove Your power and love and to reveal Your glory.[1] In Jesus's name, amen.

Day One
SURRENDER

Today's passage for your conversation with God: Hebrews 12:1-3

Tear out the last verse card in the back of your workbook for Hebrews 10:24-25. Begin memorizing it by saying verse 24 out loud a few times: "And let us consider how we may spur one another on toward love and good deeds."

In week 1, you learned that Christian discipleship is a personal love relationship with Jesus Christ experienced in a lifelong journey of obedience. As you follow Christ, He transforms you to be like Him, He changes your values to His Kingdom values, and He involves you in His mission in your home, church, and world. The more you become like Him, the greater glory you bring Him.

Regarding discipleship, Jesus said this: "those of you who do not give up everything you have cannot be my disciples" (Luke 14:33). Being a disciple of Jesus requires a perpetual surrender to Him. To surrender is to yield to the power, control, or possession of someone else. Surrendering to Jesus means yielding your entire being—your whole self—to Him. It means letting go of your life and placing it in His hands. Second Chronicles 16:9 gives us this insight: "the eyes of the LORD range throughout the earth to strengthen those whose hearts are fully committed to him."

To use an analogy, surrendering is like giving up the title to your car—once you do, it is no longer yours. To surrender to Jesus is to give Him the "title" to your life. You—along with all you own—belong to Him.

The surrender required for discipleship isn't easy. Without proper focus, you are likely to grow weary and lose heart, as you read in today's passage. The author of Hebrews compares discipleship to running a distance race. He encourages you to run with perseverance—aware of those who have gone before you and are cheering you on from the finish line as they bear witness to its glory. He is referring to heroes of the faith, some of whom are mentioned in Hebrews 11, and others who have since joined them.

Our thirteen-year-old daughter Jenna recently asked me a question that caught me by surprise: "Mom, do you see yourself as a hero of the faith?" She prompted me to reflect on those I would bestow that title on, and the word "surrender" fit each one. I also began to ponder the fact that she is looking for such a hero. Would you be a hero of the faith?

"[Throwing] off everything that hinders and the sin that so easily entangles" is the work of surrender (Hebrews 12:1). You are running towards the embrace of Jesus. Anything you choose to hold onto will not only slow you down, but will also get in the way of the embrace you long for. Trying to hug someone when your arms are full is nowhere near as satisfying as a full-on embrace.

What are you carrying as you run the race? (For example, anxiety, selfish ambition, possessions, etc.)

What would surrender look like?

Imagine looking into the eyes of Jesus as you surrender what you are holding, and feel the fullness of His presence and embrace. Consider what He endured for you and experience the victory He possesses and bestows upon you. What was this experience like?

Martin Luther said, "I have held many things in my hands, and I have lost them all; but whatever I have placed in God's hands, that I still possess."[2] Nothing you place in the hands of God is a forever loss.[3]

I wish I could check the "surrender" box and be done with it, but surrender is ongoing. I have found it helpful over the last few years to name the things I am choosing to surrender to Him each morning during my quiet time. But before I give them to Him, I take time to receive what He wants to give to me. I also find it helpful to dialogue with Him every day about each part of my being. I created a tool to help me, and I would like you to try it out today.

End today by praying what is written on the next page and journaling the blanks. If you'd like, you can color in or check off each bullet point as you go.

Note: If you find this tool helpful, you can learn how to create your own custom version for use in your daily quiet times in the appendix on pages 274-75.

SPIRIT

Open my heart to receive and feel these gifts from Your hand anew today:

- ☐ Your strong, gentle embrace
- ☐ Your deep love for me that is grounded in Your goodness, not what I do or don't do
- ☐ Peace and comfort in Your presence
- ☐ Strength from Your power at work in me
- ☐ Other: ____________

I humble myself before You and surrender these to You again today:

- ☐ My agenda for today
- ☐ My family and friends
- ☐ My tomorrows
- ☐ Other: ____________

Heal me in these wounded places:

- ☐ Broken trust in You
- ☐ Unforgiveness of ____________
- ☐ Strongholds (such as shame)
- ☐ Other: ____________

SOUL

Reflecting on Yesterday:

I confess:

What I'm thankful for:

What was tough:

DECLARATIONS FOR TODAY

- ☐ I choose to walk with Your Holy Spirit today;
- ☐ To do what You say, rather than what is comfortable, because I trust You more than myself;
- ☐ To recognize that YOU are God and I am not—therefore I can trust You with today.

BODY

Today, I let go of these anxieties I am carrying, giving them to you:

What I need from You today:

Day Two
YOUR SPIRITUAL GIFTS

Today's passage for your conversation with God: Romans 12:3-8

You were given at least one spiritual gift on the day Jesus saved you. God intentionally assigned your gifts not for your individual enjoyment but for corporate employment to bless other people.[4] Each part of His body exists to serve the whole, and God knows how each part can best be used. Regarding spiritual gifts, the apostle Paul said this: "To each one the manifestation of the Spirit is given for the common good" (1 Corinthians 12:7). When you exercise your spiritual gifts, you are helping the body of Christ carry out God's mission efficiently and effectively.

Spiritual gifts are spiritual abilities given to believers by the Holy Spirit to equip them to carry out God's work in the world. Spiritual gifts are not the same as the natural abilities or talents you were born with, though both gifts and talents are God-given and should be developed and used for the Lord. Spiritual gifts inform what you do rather than who you are. In this way, spiritual gifts differ from spiritual fruit. The fruit of the Spirit described in Galatians 5:22-23 is a group of Christlike qualities that should characterize the lives of all believers. The Holy Spirit produces this fruit inside you. Spiritual gifts, on the other hand, are specifically bestowed upon you so that you can serve on Christ's mission.

Today's passage lists some examples of spiritual gifts, although this list is not exhaustive.[5] In verse 6, the word *gifts* is a translation of the Greek word *charismata*, which means "a favor received without any merit of its own." Just like salvation or any other gift, spiritual gifts cannot be earned. Your spiritual gifts are rooted in God's grace, so there is no basis for insecurity or superiority.

There is no one "magical" way to determine your spiritual gifts, but Spirit-led self-evaluation is a great place to start. You may want to fill out a comprehensive spiritual gifts inventory online by going to lifeway.com/spiritualgifts.

Here is a list of spiritual gifts, grouped according to four categories:[6]

WITNESSING	WORSHIPING	TEACHING	SERVING
Faith	Shepherding	Wisdom	Healing
Evangelism	Exhorting	Knowledge	Giving
Apostleship	Spiritual Discernment	Teaching	Mercy
Miracles	Prophecy	Leadership	Helps

Prayerfully consider each gift. Put a star next to the ones you think you might possess. How are you currently using any of these gifts to serve the body of Christ?

If you aren't currently using your spiritual gifts, pray that God would show you how He wants you to do so.

At the beginning of this discipleship experience you took an inventory to help discern opportunities for your growth. Today, I want you to take this inventory again to help you reflect on how you have progressed during this journey.

Rank the following on a scale of 1 to 4, with "1" being never or disagree; "2" being occasionally or somewhat disagree; "3" being usually or somewhat agree; and "4" being always or fully agree. Write your number next to each statement below.

____ **I not only know but also experience Jesus loving me unconditionally on a daily basis.**

____ **Spending time in God's Word is like eating food—I need it every day to sustain me.**

____ **Communicating with God through prayer comes easily to me and is something I do throughout each day.**

____ **I experience the power of the Holy Spirit as He lives through me on a daily basis.**

____ **I regularly bring to God any thoughts and desires I have that are unpleasing to Him so He can renew my mind with truth.**

____ **When I experience unpleasant emotions, I share them with God and let Him comfort me and reorient me.**

____ **What I consume through my mouth and eyes and how I move and rest my body show honor to God.**

____ **Hallmarks of my closest relationships are love, forgiveness, and healthy communication.**

____ **I regularly and authentically engage with a small group of Christ followers for Bible study, prayer, encouragement, and accountability.**

____ **How I spend my time, talents, and treasures pleases God.**

____ **God has made me His witness, and I regularly engage in this role He has given me.**

____ **I have a deep desire to bring glory to God. I seek to steward my whole life well because I know I am significant in His story.**

Add the totals for each number to get your total score and write it here: ____. Now write your previous total from week 1 on page 27 here: ____. The highest possible score is 48.

Compare your totals to assess growth throughout this discipleship experience while remembering that this is an imperfect tool—your growth as a disciple is more than a number and ongoing. Be encouraged by any forward progress in your intimacy with Jesus and your surrender to Him.

From page 27 (from week 1), identify the areas of growth you circled. How have you grown in these areas these last twelve weeks?

Now, circle the statements that represent the top three remaining areas of growth for you now. Each statement correlates with this material's week where that topic is explored. For example, the sixth statement of this list about emotions corresponds with the sixth week of this study. Ask God how He wants to continue your transformation in these areas, and write any ideas He gives you below.

Check out the resources on pages 277-79 that correspond with the statements you circled. One of those resources is Avery Willis's original *MasterLife* material. *MasterLife Together* is a simplified revision of that resource.

Using your verse card, try to finish memorizing Hebrews 10:24: "And let us consider how we may spur one another on toward love and good deeds."

Day Three
THE TASK REMAINING

Today's passage for your conversation with God: Revelation 5

About sixty years had passed since Jesus had ascended to heaven, and the early church was left wondering when He would return. Many in the church were facing intense persecution, including the apostle John. He had been banished to a hard labor colony on an island in present-day Greece when God gave him a series of visions that he later recorded in the book of Revelation.

The word in the New Testament translated *revelation* also means "unveiling." Revelation pulls back the curtain to reveal Jesus's future triumph over evil and His ultimate reign over all creation. Today's passage is one of my favorite chapters in Revelation. In it, John witnesses the Father sitting on His throne, holding out a scroll—the "title deed" to all He possessed and promised. Only His appointed heir could open it and set in motion the ultimate redemption He began many years ago. A great pause ensued as the angel searched heaven and earth for Him. No wonder John "wept and wept" as He delayed (Revelation 5:4).

But the great pause was not the end as John had feared. Rather, it served to intensify the spotlight upon the One who then emerged—He who is "from above" and "not of this world" (John 8:23). I can only imagine John's response as the Lamb appeared and took the scroll. Crescendoing songs of praise erupted from John and every creature in heaven and on earth. Described in today's passage and again in Revelation 7:9-12, the climax of salvation awaiting us will far exceed any experience we have on this earth.

Jesus Christ is worthy to take the scroll because He was slain to purchase people "from every tribe and language and people and nation" (Revelation 5:9). The Greek word used for *purchase* is the same one used twenty-eight times in the New Testament meaning "to buy such things as food or treasure" (Matthew 13:46; 14:15). Jesus gave His entire being to purchase His people—and you are one of them. And you are not just any one of them but one of the chosen who were made aware of His transaction. As such, you are one of those who have been entrusted with His mission to go and make disciples of "all nations" (Matthew 28:19). It is no coincidence that the same Greek word—*ethnos*, meaning "all peoples"—is used in both the Great Commission and in the great multitude described in Revelation 5:9.

May He not find us to have hidden our precious resources in the ground as many have (Matthew 25:14-29). May we rather steward them and speed Christ's return (2 Peter 3:12)!

Circle the number that represents how you have stewarded the gift of the gospel you've received, up to this point in your life:

1—I have hidden it
2—I have minimally invested it
3—I have invested a lot
4—I have given my life for His gain

Jesus is not delaying His second coming without purpose. The reason Jesus hasn't yet returned is because "He is patient with you, not wanting anyone to perish, but everyone to come to repentance" (2 Peter 3:9). Jesus's sacrifice was sufficient to cover the sins of every person who has ever lived. This includes every single one of the eight billion people alive today. Unfortunately, most of them do not know it.

Some people estimate that just 10% of the world's population are born-again followers of Jesus.[7] More lost people without Christ are alive today than at any other time in history! Every single day, over 155,000 lost people die and enter into an eternity without Christ.[8]

Making disciples of "all peoples" as Jesus mandated involves making disciples in every people group. A people group is "an ethno-linguistic group with a common self-identity that is shared by its various members. For strategic purposes, it is the largest group within which the gospel can spread without encountering barriers of understanding or acceptance."[9] Consider these brutal facts:[10]

- Approximately two billion people alive today have heard little to nothing about Jesus, many having never once heard His name.[11]
- 37% of all living languages have no Scripture translations.
- 40% of the world's population lives in unreached people groups—meaning less than 2% of their population are evangelical Christians.[12]
- Only one out of every thirty missionaries go to unreached people groups.

This is the task that remains for His church who remain on earth. One day—when within every people group there are Christ-following disciples who have formed churches that are evangelizing their entire people—the task will be finished! Until then, the task remaining is yours and mine.

How do these statistics hit you? Which one surprises you most?

The easy-to-reach people groups have already been reached. Movements of God among unreached people groups on the frontline come at a great cost. There are reasons some people are still unreached, including their locations and generational resistance to the gospel. This is why Jesus said, "Blessed are those who are persecuted because of righteousness, for theirs is the kingdom of heaven. Blessed are you when people insult you, persecute you and falsely say all kinds of evil against you because of me. Rejoice and be glad, because great is your reward in heaven" (Matthew 5:10-12).

God is more glorious than anything your suffering threatens to take away. The apostle Peter also wrote to encourage those who suffer: "Dear friends, do not be surprised at the fiery ordeal that has come on you to test you, as though something strange were happening to you. But rejoice inasmuch as you participate in the sufferings of Christ, so that you may be overjoyed when his glory is revealed . . . do not be ashamed, but praise God that you bear that name" (1 Peter 4:12-16).

Are you willing to suffer as those who have gone before you as you take your next step of obedience based on the task remaining? May you and I increasingly pray, give, go, mobilize, welcome, and live with a heart and mind on mission.

As you consider the task remaining, what next step of obedience is God leading you to take?

Review Hebrews 10:24, and begin memorizing verse 25: "Not giving up meeting together, as some are in the habit of doing, but encouraging one another—and all the more as you see the Day approaching."

See page 279 for additional resources related to finishing the task.

Day Four

MULTIPLICATION AND MOVEMENTS

Today's passage for your conversation with God: Romans 15:15-25

This discipleship experience is intended to help you root your life in Christ together with His body. Our culture, however, creates a barrier to this goal. American culture is highly individualistic, which may lead you to ask the question, "What can I do in God's kingdom?" A better question is, "What is it going to take to see God's kingdom fully established?" Part of the answer to that question is a larger multitude of believers actively following Christ. This is why Jesus said, "The harvest is plentiful, but the workers are few" (Luke 10:2).

In today's passage, Paul wrote to the Christians in Rome asking them to financially partner with him in expanding the gospel's reach to new places, such as Spain. He said he had already done everything he could to fully proclaim the gospel from Jerusalem to Illyricum. That statement summarizes the last sixteen chapters of the book of Acts, covering a population of over twenty-five million people in fifteen years![13]

How many more years will it be until there is no place left on earth where Christ has not been named (Romans 15:23)? In AD 100, there was *one* Christian for every 360 people in the world; one thousand years ago, 270 people per Christian; five hundred years ago, eighty-five people per Christian; one hundred years ago, twenty-one people per Christian; and now, seven people per Christian! In AD 100, there were twelve unreached people groups for every congregation of believers. Now there is one unreached people group for every one thousand churches![14] This task is finishable. It is disconcerting that Coca-Cola and cell phone companies have reached more people in less time than Christians have in their spread of the gospel.

The church has been expanding for two thousand years, but could our generation be the last one on earth to have the privilege of fulfilling Christ's Great Commission?

Disciple-making and church-planting movements are multiplying on the frontlines today in very similar ways to what we see in the book of Acts. David Garrison's research shows that in one decade, "literally millions of new believers have entered Christ's kingdom through church planting movements."[15] From one such movement in East Asia, two million people accepted Christ and were baptized in just ten years, leading to the start of 150,000 new churches![16] Another such movement took place among Bhojpuri speakers in North India, where tens of thousands of churches have been planted and millions of new believers have been baptized over the past thirty years.[17]

Paul prayed that the churches he planted would grow not only in width, but also in depth: "Pray that the Lord's message will spread *rapidly* and be *honored* wherever it goes" (2 Thessalonians 3:1, NLT, italics mine). Width and depth both result from faithful disciple-making. Too many Christians are satisfied with mere addition in ministry, but healthy disciples multiply over time. If you reach just one person for Christ each year and disciple him or her—and each year that person and his or her disciples do likewise—one disciple will become two, two will become four, then eight, then sixteen, and so forth. Guess how long would it take to disciple the whole world at that rate? Just thirty-three years![18]

One-on-one discipleship is great, but discipling a small group of people together is even better because that is what Jesus did. There is a limit to how much you can disciple someone in one year's time, but if you disciple ten people together each year—and each year they and their disciples do likewise—together you all will disciple the whole world in ten years! Robert Coleman observed that Jesus's approach demonstrated "it did not matter how small the group was to start with so long as they reproduced and taught their disciples to reproduce . . . it would continue to expand."[19] Jesus didn't focus on programs to reach the multitudes, but rather on disciples whom the multitudes would follow.

The M.A.W.L. approach is helpful in discipleship—first, *model* ministry for your disciples; second, *assist* them as they try it; third, *watch* them do it on their own, debriefing afterwards; and lastly, *leave* them with the responsibility to do it in your absence. Note the difference in roles between a discipler and a disciple: a discipler models, the disciple imitates; a discipler explains, the disciple experiments; a discipler coaches, the disciple applies; a discipler supports, the disciple demonstrates; and a discipler commissions, the disciple represents.[20]

Paul wrote about four generations of disciples when he said, "And the things you have heard me say in the presence of many witnesses entrust to reliable people who will also be qualified to teach others" (2 Timothy 2:2). My grandparents Avery and Shirley lived out this verse. They came from godly ancestors and multiplied godly descendants beyond those they ever met.

Reflect on the number of people whom you have discipled and whom they have discipled. Write the names of the people you have discipled below.

How did you disciple them?

What ministry have those you have discipled pursued?

Ask God to show you who He wants you to disciple in the future and when He wants you to begin. Unless you already have a plan on how to disciple them, consider leading them through *MasterLife Together*. Write your who, when, and how plans for disciple-making below.

Use your verse card to continue memorizing Hebrews 10:24-25.

See page 279 for more resources on multiplication and church planting movements.

Day Five

HIS STORY CONTINUES

Today's passage for your conversation with God: Revelation 21:1-5; 22:1-21

Far from being a mere character in your story, God is the author and narrator of His story—all the world's events for all time revolve around Him. This God of glory chose to write you into His story, and the culmination of what He accomplished over two thousand years ago is just ahead. You are His image-bearer and His image-sharer.

You are living in Bible times! What you read today in Revelation has yet to take place. Satan's current reign on earth will soon come to an end, and until it does or you get to heaven, you have been entrusted with taking back the enemy's territory as you follow Christ. Nothing you do for Jesus is ever wasted. His kingdom, after all, has only one direction—forward!

As the day of Jesus's return approaches, may we continue meeting together as the body of Christ, encouraging one another and serving together with unprecedented commitment.

Try to say Hebrews 10:24-25 by memory.

The One who made the heavens and the earth is seated on the throne and will soon make all things new (Revelation 21:5). There will no longer be any distinction between the secular and the sacred. There will be no more night, no more death, no more mourning or crying or pain, and no more curse. And God's story will continue forever.

Today's passage was written to whet your appetite and to give you hope in your suffering. As Jesus faced the cross, He drew encouragement from the hope of being reunited with His Father in heaven, saying, "I came from the Father and entered the world; now I am leaving the world and going back to the Father" (John 16:28). Much wisdom is found in knowing where you come from, where you are going, and how much those two things matter. Your time on earth is a small part of your eternity—you are "a mist that appears for a little while and then vanishes" (James 4:14). But you matter. Your life is far from accidental or insignificant. You have intrinsic value because you are deeply loved by the God whose glory is unsurpassed.

The glory of God exceeds the limits of human language. The full essence of God put on display is more than can be put into words. If you could see the matchless beauty of His love and the splendor of His holiness, hear the symphony of His magnificent praise, smell the richness of His majesty, taste His infinite goodness, and feel the full weight of His manifold perfections within His intimate embrace, then you would experience His glory.

And one day soon, you will (Revelation 22:7).

The fulfillment of today's passage—the last one in the Bible—may appear to be an end. But then Jesus reminds us, "I am the Alpha and the Omega, the First and the Last, the Beginning and the End" (Revelation 22:13). He is the God "who is, and who was, and who is to come" (Revelation 1:8). "His government and its peace will never end. He will rule with fairness and justice from the throne of his ancestor David for all eternity. The passionate commitment of the LORD of Heaven's Armies will make this happen!" (Isaiah 9:7, NLT). "And he will reign for ever and ever" (Revelation 11:15).

I'd like you to turn back to week 1, day 1 on page 16. Skim back through opening pages that outline His story. Now imagine yourself stepping into its coming chapter:

One day, God will again keep His promise. At just the right time, the Savior Jesus will once again return to reign forever as the Prince of Peace. Majestic celebration will ensue as He takes His followers to live together with Him in heaven where there will be no more brokenness. There will be no end to God's love story because His special love for the people He made will never stop. "For from Him and through Him and for Him are all things. To him be the glory forever! Amen" (Romans 11:36).

Imagine the coming day when you will be with Jesus face to face. How does envisioning that day fill you with joy and inspire you to be faithful in the present?

In light of this discipleship experience and in view of His forever glory, write out a prayer to God who led you to this point.

Our prayer is that this discipleship experience has catalyzed your love for God and given you a passion for joining Him as His story nears climax. We echo these words Paul prayed for the church in Ephesus as with one heart, we pray this blessing over you:

That out of his glorious riches he may strengthen you with power through
his Spirit in your inner being, so that Christ may dwell in your hearts through
faith. And . . . that you, being rooted and established in love, may have
power, together with all the Lord's holy people, to grasp how wide and long
and high and deep is the love of Christ, and to know this love that surpasses
knowledge—that you may be filled to the measure of all the fullness of God.
Now to him who is able to do immeasurably more than all we ask or imagine,
according to His power that is at work within us, to him be glory in the
church and in Christ Jesus throughout all generations, for ever and ever!

EPHESIANS 3:16-21

In Jesus's name, amen. Come, Lord Jesus!

Optional passages for more conversations with God:

Day 6: Matthew 10

Day 7: Revelation 7:9-17

MasterLife Together

LEADER GUIDE

Leader Instructions

Ideally, groups should be between three to twelve people, including leaders. If your existing group is larger than twelve people, we recommend you split into multiple smaller groups and appoint one to two leaders for each group. Weekly group sessions are designed to last about one and a half hours each, although they can be adapted to last anywhere between one to two hours. Group participants should complete the lesson in their workbooks before the group session—except in the introductory session.

The format for group sessions will be the same each week and will include these three parts:

1. **LOOKING BACK** gives your group accountability for memorizing the verse(s) and having conversations with God and gives them the opportunity to share highlights of these conversations with the group.
2. **LOOKING UP** gives your group the opportunity to explore the content of the lesson together by discussing lesson-specific questions and encourages them to share with the group what they have processed in the lesson's exercises.
3. **LOOKING AHEAD** allows your group to process and share how they plan to apply what they have learned and allows you to preview the next lesson together.

You will notice that your role is that of a facilitator rather than a teacher. Allowing your group to process what they are learning out loud together reinforces their learning and connects their hearts to one another.

If at all possible, review the lesson-specific questions (in the Looking Up section) before your group meets. Highlight questions you want to be sure to cover, as you may not have time to discuss all of the questions—especially if you have only an hour allotted for group sessions, have a larger group, or your group is more talkative.

Beginning with session 4, people in your group will take turns facilitating (or co-facilitating) the group sessions. Ideally, everyone in your group will help facilitate a session before this experience ends. The purpose of this is to develop leaders and give people in your group the confidence they need to lead their own *MasterLife Together* group someday. Specific instructions related to this will be given at the end of session 3.

The last part of each group session is to ask, "What prayer needs in your upcoming week can we pray for now?" You can structure this time any way you want, but if you have time, consider having each member of your group write a prayer request on an index card. Collect the cards, and redistribute them randomly. Have a group prayer time where anyone who is comfortable can pray aloud for the request on his or her card. Ask everyone to keep his or her card so he or she can pray over it during the week ahead. One advantage to this format is it creates more time for actual prayer as opposed to simply talking about prayer requests.

Five additional experiential sessions are outlined on pages 262-67 along with reasons for their importance. These recommended group experiences will greatly enhance your group's discipleship experience. You can choose to do any or all of them, and they don't necessarily need to be done in order. Though these sessions are optional, we strongly encourage you to consider leading all of them. Read through them now so you can begin to prayerfully consider extending this discipleship experience.

TIPS FOR LEADERS

Commit to pray. The best way you can serve the members of your group throughout the week is to be praying for them. Also pray specifically for each group session.

Embrace a new perspective. Your group sessions should not be a traditional intellectual pursuit—so don't let your focus be on "covering all the material." Instead, view these sessions as experiences that can be transformational. Let the Holy Spirit lead, and depend on Him to guide the discussion.

Embrace some silence. Don't feel that a moment of silence is a bad thing. People often need time to think about their responses to questions they've just heard or to gain courage to share what God is stirring in their hearts.

Give your own example. If interaction lags—which is normal at the beginning of a new group—be prepared to start the discussion with your own example.

Don't be afraid to call on people. If there are some group members you know better than others, you might call on them first if no one answers after sufficient time has elapsed. As the weeks go on, be sure to give everyone an opportunity to respond even gently asking those that don't naturally respond to contribute by asking, "What do you think?"

Affirm and follow up on responses. Make sure you point out something true or helpful in a response. Don't just move on. Build personal connections with follow-up questions, asking how other people have experienced similar things or how a truth has shaped their understanding of God and the topic you are studying. People are less likely to speak up if they fear you don't actually want to hear their answers or that you're looking for only a certain answer.

Stay connected throughout the week. Participation during the group session is always improved when members spend time connecting with one another away from the sessions. The more people are comfortable with and involved in one another's lives, the more they'll look forward to being together. Explore ways to stay connected with your group. When possible, schedule a meal, a fun activity, and/or a service project for your group during this twelve-week experience.

Intro Group Session

This week will involve group members getting to know each other, and will introduce the material that group members will begin this week. Provide a light snack and a drink if possible for this beginning session. Have chairs in a circle if possible, as this enhances group discussion.

Begin your session with prayer. Explain the importance of members committing to be present for all the group sessions if at all possible. By not showing up, you impact your whole group. You need them, and they need you. Also explain the importance of confidentiality throughout this group discipleship experience—members should keep everything shared in group sessions confidential, unless someone specifically gives permission to share something outside the group. Have your group turn to "Getting Started" on page 8. Read it out loud to your group while they follow along in their workbooks. Make sure they understand that each day they will first read that day's passage and journal their conversation with God before reading the day's lesson. You might show them your notebook with its two columns. Once your group understands the process of this discipleship experience, proceed to the questions below. If you are doing this session with an existing group where members already know each other well, use the "Existing Group" questions instead of the "New Group" ones.

QUESTIONS FOR NEW GROUPS

Provide name tags if possible, and write the following words somewhere within view of your group to remind them what to share: name, family, work, and hobbies.

1. As the group leader, be the first to share your name, family, work, and hobbies. Then share how the Lord led you to this study, and what you hope these next three months will accomplish.
2. Have everyone say his or her name and tell about his or her family, work (or school, stay-at-home, etc.), and hobbies.
3. Would anyone like to share when and why you became a believer?
4. Would anyone like to share why they wanted to be part of this group or a goal you have for these next three months together?

QUESTIONS FOR EXISTING GROUPS

1. What is something you love about this group?
2. What is something that could enhance this group?
3. Share one thing no one in the group knows about you.
4. Would anyone like to share a goal you have for this new discipleship experience?

Close the session by looking ahead to next week. Have your group turn to the introduction to week 1 on page 13. Read it aloud or ask a volunteer to do so as everyone else follows along in their book. A prayer is included at the end of the Introduction. If you would like, you can ask everyone to join in to read the prayer aloud together. Instruct members to complete days 1-5 of week 1 on their own before the next group session. Tell them to bring their journal or notebook to all the group sessions, as they will be sharing some of their conversations with God with the group. Ask if there are any special prayer needs in your group this week, and lead the group in prayer before dismissing them. If you have enough time, consider having each member of your group write down a personal prayer request on an index card. Collect the cards, and redistribute them randomly. Have a group prayer time where anyone who is comfortable can pray aloud for the request on his or her card. Have everyone keep the card he or she got so he or she can pray for that person throughout the coming week.

Note: If your existing group schedule does not allow for this introductory session, you may instruct members to read and complete all of week 1 before meeting for week 1—but make sure they read "Getting Started" pages 8-9 and understand how to journal their conversations with God.

Group Session One

Participants will have completed week 1 in their workbooks before the session.

Note: If your group did not have an introductory session, read "Getting Started" on pages 8-9 aloud to your group as they follow along, and make sure everyone understands how to journal their conversations with God. Tell them to begin bringing their journal or notebook to all the group sessions, as they will be sharing highlights of their conversations with God with the group.

Remind the group to respect members by keeping everything that is shared confidential, and affirm those who are present for their commitment to showing up. Before you begin, briefly explain the three-part format you will be using today and throughout the remaining group sessions:

1. **LOOKING BACK** will include reviewing the verse you memorized and sharing one of your conversations with God.
2. **LOOKING UP** will include discussing the content of the lesson and the questions you answered throughout the week.
3. **LOOKING AHEAD** will include sharing how you plan to apply what you learned and previewing next week's lesson.

Now you are ready to begin! You will start by Looking Back.

LOOKING BACK

- Who would like to open us in prayer, inviting the Holy Spirit to move in our midst?
- Break into smaller groups of two or three—these groups should vary each week. (Allow five to ten minutes.)
- Say this week's Scripture verse(s) to each other from memory.
- Each person should share about a conversationhe or she had with God this week.
- Come back together as a large group. Raise your hand if you journaled your conversations with God this week. Affirm those who did, and ask them to share what the experience was like. Encourage those who aren't journaling their conversations with God to begin this week, as this discipleship experience will not be nearly as impactful for those who aren't doing so. Then ask if anyone would like to share a conversation they had with God with the whole group.

LOOKING UP

QUESTIONS FROM WEEK 1

1. From day 1 on page 17, Have you ever thought about your life in relation to God's bigger story? How is He helping you see this more clearly?
2. From day 2 on page 18, do you see any correlation between the way you view your earthly father and the way you view God as your Father? Describe any similarities and differences.
3. On day 3 you learned the importance of receiving. Which feels more natural to you—giving or receiving—and why? Share examples.
4. From day 3 on page 21, what did God reveal that you needed to receive from Him, and how did it feel to receive it?
5. From day 4 on page 23, share the order in which you prioritize your spirit, soul, and body.
6. From day 4 on page 24, which do you prioritize most—relationships or mission? Being or doing?
7. From day 4 on page 24, describe someone you know whose whole life radiantly shines with the love of God.
8. After taking the inventory from day 5 on pages 26-27, which areas do you most need to grow in?

LOOKING AHEAD

- Break into your smaller groups again. Each person should share his or her main takeaway from this week's lesson. Then he or she should share his or her plan to apply something from this week's lesson to his or her life or how he or she has already.
- Come back together as a large group. Would anyone like to share a main takeaway or an application you had or heard with our whole group? (Omit if needed for time.)
- Preview next week's lesson by sharing its main topic and daily themes, or read the introduction to next week's lesson out loud to your group as they follow along. Remind your group that they will need to read the introduction on their own if you don't read it as a group and complete days 1–5 before the next group session.
- What specific prayer needs in your upcoming week can we pray over now? (If you have enough time, consider having each member of your group write a personal prayer request on an index card. Collect the cards, and redistribute them randomly. Have a group prayer time where anyone who is comfortable can pray aloud for the request on his/her card. Everyone will keep these cards to be praying over for the week ahead.)

Note: Inform your group that a mini composition book or a pocket-sized notebook is recommended for week 3, so they will need it a week from today. Alternatively, you could provide these for your group and make them available at next week's group session, or ask for a volunteer who is willing to do so.

Participants will have completed week 2 in their workbooks before the session. Remind the group to respect members by keeping everything that is shared confidential.

LOOKING BACK

- Who would like to open us in prayer, inviting the Holy Spirit to move in our midst?
- Ask members of the group to start having their Scripture memory cards in hand each week to review with each other. This provides them accountability in establishing this new discipline and ensures accuracy. Remind them they can go to page 284 to find out how to order a holder for the cards but can keep them together with a rubber band until then. Each listening partner should look at the verse while hearing it so that they can kindly let their reciting partner know when they added or missed any words from the verse.
- Break into smaller groups of two or three—these groups should vary each week. (Allow five to ten minutes.)
- Say this week and last week's Scripture verse(s) to each other from memory.
- Each person should share about a conversation he or she had with God this week.
- Come back together as a large group. Ask your group if anyone is having a hard time journaling their conversations with God and troubleshoot these challenges as a group. Remind them that relationships require communication, and their relationship with God is exceedingly important. Share with them these benefits of writing their conversations down: it will help them focus, allow them to have a record of what God is saying to them over time, and etch God's truths deeper on their hearts. Ask if anyone in the group who has been journaling their conversations can attest to any of these benefits or can think of any additional benefits.

LOOKING UP

QUESTIONS FROM WEEK 2

1. Reread aloud what the Barna Group defines as a biblical worldview on page 35 on day 2. Would anyone be willing to share any parts you underlined, and why it is hard for you to believe that specific part(s)? Allow group members to share personal testimonies and/or resources they are aware of that could help strengthen the group members' faith in that particular area.

2. Give each group member a blank piece of paper and ask them to trace their own hand and draw out as much of the Grasping God's Word illustration as they can. They can turn to page 37 on day 3 to complete any parts they can't remember.
3. Which of the six parts of the hand (hear, read, study, memorize, meditate, obey) is your biggest growth area? What will you commit to do this next week to grow in that area?
4. What plans have each of you used to read or listen to the Bible before that you found most helpful (for example, reading the whole Bible in one year, one chapter of Proverbs each day of the month, etc.)?
5. Did any of you try out the sword method described on page 45 on day 5? Let's do it together now, using Hebrews 4:1-16, which some of you may have studied as it was the Scripture for an optional day 7 this week. Let's take it one question at a time. Anyone can answer the first question about God before going to the second question about what we learn about people, and so on. After the exercise, say, "Using this method to study Scriptures in a small group is a great way to gain new insights. Did anyone have as many insights individually as our group came up with collectively?" (Probably not, meaning the small group is valuable.)

LOOKING AHEAD

- Break into your smaller groups again. Each person should share his or her main takeaway from this week's lesson. Then he or she should share his or her plan to apply something from this week's lesson to his or her life or how he or she has already.
- Come back together as a large group. Would anyone like to share a main takeaway or an application you had or heard with our whole group? (Omit if needed for time.)
- Preview next week's lesson by sharing its main topic and daily themes, or read the introduction to next week's lesson out loud to your group as they follow along. Remind your group that they will need to read the introduction on their own if you don't read it as a group and complete days 1-5 before the next group session. Tell your group that a mini composition book or a pocket-sized notebook is recommended on day 5 so they can make plans to have it available by then.
- What specific prayer needs in your upcoming week can we pray over now? If you have time, ask everyone to write down a personal request and have a group prayer time. See page 237 for more details.

Participants will have completed week 3 in their workbooks before the session.

LOOKING BACK

- Who would like to open us in prayer, inviting the Holy Spirit to move in our midst?
- Break into smaller groups of two or three—these groups should vary each week. (Allow five to ten minutes.)
- Say this week's Scripture verse(s) to each other from memory. If time permits, also quote the verses memorized in previous lessons together.
- Each person should share about a conversation he or she had with God this week.
- Come back together as a large group. Continue to encourage your group to journal their conversations with God, and ask if anyone has experienced any progress in doing so this week. Then ask, "Would anyone like to share with our whole group a conversation you had with God or one that you heard from someone else?" (Omit if needed for time.)

LOOKING UP

QUESTIONS FROM WEEK 3

1. Before we get more into our lesson on prayer, I'd like you to raise your hand if you've been journaling through the optional Scripture passages for days 6 and 7 each week. For those who raised their hands, would anyone be willing to share how having these conversations with God has impacted your discipleship experience?
2. Let's turn our attention back to this week's topic. Look on page 50 on day 1 and look at the people and things you have turned to in an effort to meet your deepest needs. Who is willing to share one of your statements with our group?
3. Who would like to share your experience of coming to God as a child, asking Him for something you want—or listening to what He wants from you—from page 59 on day 4? Include what you asked of Him and what He asked of you, if you are willing.
4. This week, we discussed persisting in prayer. Who would be willing to share a testimony of how you or someone you know has persisted in prayer for someone or something as well as any outcomes you have seen?
5. Discuss the following quote (which was not included in this week's lesson) from Andrew Murray: "Our daily life in the world is the test of our communication with God in prayer."[1] If your prayer life this past week was an actual test, what grade would you give yourself: A, B, C, D, or F?

6. Raise your hand if you took the time to pray through your prayer notebook (or list) this week. What setting and/or position did you choose, and what was it like for you?
7. What thoughts and ideas do you have about getting into a more regular rhythm in prayer? How can your group keep you accountable this week?

You will need a bit more time for the next section today, as you will have an extra activity (below) after breaking into your smaller groups.

Break into your smaller groups now. We are going to practice praying for each other out loud. Do not worry about how articulate you are. Talk to God like you would talk to a friend. Each person should share one need you identified (for your body, soul, or spirit) from page 51. Each person should pray aloud for another person in the group, that God would help meet this need.

LOOKING AHEAD

- (Stay in your smaller groups.) Each person should share his or her main takeaway from this week's lesson. Then he or she should share his or her plan to apply something from this week's lesson to his or her life or how he or she has already.
- Come back together as a large group. Would anyone like to share a main takeaway or an application you had or heard with our whole group? (Omit if needed for time.)
- Preview next week's lesson by sharing its main topic and daily themes, or read the introduction to next week's lesson out loud to your group as they follow along. Remind your group that they will need to read the introduction on their own if you don't read it as a group and complete days 1-5 before the next group session.
- What specific prayer needs in your upcoming week can we pray over now? If you have time, ask everyone to write down a personal request and have a group prayer time. See page 237 for more details.

Note: At the end of today's session, ask a leader in your group or another member to facilitate next week's group session instead of you. If there is hesitation to lead, you can pair people up to do so—for example, husband and wife participants could co-lead a session. Ideally, everyone in your group will help facilitate a session. Facilitating a session will give the people in your group the confidence they need to one day lead their own group through MasterLife Together. Assure group members that the only thing they will need to do to prepare is to complete the week's homework, read the short leader's guide and session-specific questions in advance, and pray that the Lord will guide the group session.

1. Andrew Murray, *With Christ in the School of Prayer*, 110.

Group Session Four

Participants will have completed week 4 in their workbooks before the session.

LOOKING BACK

- Who would like to open us in prayer, asking the Holy Spirit to move in our midst?
- Break into smaller groups of two or three—these groups should vary each week. (Allow five to ten minutes.)
- Say this week's Scripture verse(s) to each other from memory. If time permits, also quote the verses memorized in previous lessons together.
- Each person should share about a conversation he or she had with God this week.
- Come back together as a large group. Would anyone like to share with our whole group a conversation you had with God or one you heard from someone else? (Omit if needed for time.)

LOOKING UP

QUESTIONS FROM WEEK 4

1. Before we talk more about this week's emphasized topic of the Holy Spirit, let's take a minute to reflect as we've been journeying together for about a month now through this material. What has this discipleship experience been like for you so far?
2. Let's shift back into this week's lesson. Turn to page 70 on day 1. Describe your experience hearing the Holy Spirit remind you that you are God's son/daughter and that you belong to Him, or describe your experience soaking up your identity in Christ and which parts ministered the most to you.
3. When you thought about the fruit of the Spirit on page 75 on day 3, who came to mind and why?
4. Look on page 75 on day 3. In which settings is it most difficult for you to be filled with the Spirit and why?
5. Look at the last exercise of day 3 on page 76. Share anything you are willing to from your experience with the Holy Spirit.
6. Look at page 78 on day 4. Describe the evidence of the Holy Spirit's power in your life from the time you received Him up to the present. This is part of your testimony.
7. Looking at page 78 on day 4, and share what your life would look like if all of your being was flooded with Him and all His power was used in you.

8. Have your group break up into same-sex pairs so that they will be more comfortable sharing personally. From page 80 on day 5, ask each person to share any strongholds that you are asking the Holy Spirit to give you victory in. Then the other person will pray (aloud) for victory for the person who just shared. Then, it's the other person's turn to do likewise.

LOOKING AHEAD

- Break into your smaller groups again. Each person should share his or her main takeaway from this week's lesson. Then he or she should share his or her plan to apply something from this week's lesson to his or her life or how he or she has already.
- Come back together as a large group. Would anyone like to share a main takeaway or an application you had or heard with our whole group? (Omit if needed for time.)
- Preview next week's lesson by sharing its main topic and daily themes, or read the introduction to next week's lesson out loud to your group as they follow along. Remind your group that they will need to read the introduction on their own if you don't read it as a group and complete days 1-5 before the next group session.
- What special prayer needs in your upcoming week can we pray over now? If you have time, ask everyone to write down a personal request and have a group prayer time. See page 237 for more details.

Note: Enlist another member to facilitate next week's session, or you can ask for anyone to volunteer. Ideally, everyone in your group will help facilitate a session. I recommend you have as many members as possible sign up now to facilitate all the remaining sessions. See the note on page 243 for more information.

Participants will have completed week 5 in their workbooks before the session.

LOOKING BACK

- Who would like to open us in prayer, asking the Holy Spirit to move in our midst?
- Break into smaller groups of two or three—these groups should vary each week. (Allow five to ten minutes.)
- Say this week's Scripture verse(s) to each other from memory. If time permits, also quote the verses memorized in previous lessons together.
- Each person should share about a conversation he or she had with God this week.
- Come back together as a large group. Would anyone like to share with our whole group a conversation you had with God or one that you heard from someone else? (Omit if needed for time.)

LOOKING UP

QUESTIONS FROM WEEK 5

1. Would anyone be willing to share a lie that Satan etched on your heart regarding your identity and how he did so from page 87 on day 1?
2. Let's talk about the following statement from page 90 on day 2: a lie you believe as true will affect your life as if it were true—even though it is a lie. Do you agree with this statement? Would anyone like to share evidence from your own life to illustrate it?
3. Look at the diagram on page 90 on day 2 that shows your beliefs leading to your thoughts, leading to your emotions, leading to your behavior, which reinforces your beliefs. As a group, walk through this cycle based on the belief, "I am unwanted." If possible, write the answers on a whiteboard. Then ask the group, "What are the implications this belief could have on someone's life?" Afterwards, identify the opposite belief, "I am wanted," and identify corresponding thoughts, emotions, and behaviors as a group. Then ask, "What kind of a difference would it make in someone's life to believe what is true rather than Satan's lie?"
4. Is anyone willing to share your own examples of this cycle related to your beliefs about who you are from the exercise on page 91 on day 2? Please share the cycle related to the lie you believed as well as the cycle related to what is true.
5. Is anyone willing to share your own examples of the cycle related to your beliefs about who God is from the exercise on pages 94-95 on day 3? Please share the cycle related to the lie you believed as well as the cycle related to what is true.

6. Would anyone be willing to share a desire they brought before God from page 96 on day 4? How do you think God responded to you sharing that desire with Him?
7. On page 98 on day 4, you read that three of the most foundational human desires are control, comfort, and approval. Is anyone willing to share which of these fleshly desires you battle with most and why?
8. For anyone who is willing, share a destructive thought pattern you identified on page 93 on day 3, or share which tools from day 5 you plan to implement to renew your mind.

Note: Ask someone in your group to pray aloud for that person after he or she shares.

LOOKING AHEAD

- Break into your smaller groups again. Each person should share his or her main takeaway from this week's lesson. Then he or she should share his or her plan to apply something from this week's lesson to his or her life or how he or she has already.
- Come back together as a large group. Would anyone like to share a main takeaway or an application you had or heard with our whole group? (Omit if needed for time.)
- Preview next week's lesson by sharing its main topic and daily themes, or read the introduction to next week's lesson out loud to your group as they follow along. Remind your group that they will need to read the introduction on their own if you don't read it as a group and complete days 1-5 before the next group session.
- What special prayer needs in your upcoming week can we pray over now? If you have time, ask everyone to write down a personal request and have a group prayer time. See page 237 for more details.

Group Session Six

Participants will have completed week 6 in their workbooks before the session.

LOOKING BACK

- Who would like to open us in prayer, asking the Holy Spirit to move in our midst?
- Break into smaller groups of two or three—these groups should vary each week. (Allow five to ten minutes.)
- Say this week's Scripture verse(s) to each other from memory. If time permits, also quote the verses memorized in previous lessons together.
- Each person should share about a conversation he or she had with God this week.
- Come back together as a large group. Would anyone like to share with our whole group a conversation you had with God or one that you heard from someone else? (Omit if needed for time.)

LOOKING UP

QUESTIONS FROM WEEK 6

1. Share your thoughts about Pete Scazzero's quote on page 104 from the introduction: "Emotional health and spiritual maturity are inseparable. It is not possible to be spiritually mature while remaining emotionally immature."
2. What was it like listening to God's heart for you after reflecting on Zephaniah 3:17 on page 106 on day 1?
3. From day 2, how often do your pleasant emotions lead you to worship?
4. How does your previous perception of the breadth and depth of God's emotions compare to what you explored this week?
5. Who is willing to give an example of something you felt this week and its impact throughout your being on page 111 from day 3?
6. On page 111 from day 3, how did you rank your feeling muscles, and do they impact your emotional health?
7. How do you usually cope with unpleasant feelings (for example, stuffing or spewing), and what are long-term implications if you continue to cope in this way?
8. Share your experience using the NEAR tool on pages 116-17 from day 5. How did the Holy Spirit lead you to respond?

LOOKING AHEAD

- Break into your smaller groups again. Each person should share his or her main takeaway from this week's lesson. Then he or she should share his or her plan to apply something from this week's lesson to his or her life or how he or she has already.
- Come back together as a large group. Would anyone like to share a main takeaway or an application you had or heard with our whole group? (Omit if needed for time.)
- Preview next week's lesson by sharing its main topic and daily themes, or read the introduction to next week's lesson out loud to your group as they follow along. Remind your group that they will need to read the introduction on their own if you don't read it as a group and complete days 1-5 before the next group session.
- What special prayer needs in your upcoming week can we pray over now?

Participants will have completed week 7 in their workbooks before the session.

LOOKING BACK

- Who would like to open us in prayer, asking the Holy Spirit to move in our midst?
- Break into smaller groups of two or three—these groups should vary each week. (Allow five to ten minutes.)
- Say this week's Scripture verse(s) to each other from memory. If time permits, also quote the verses memorized in previous lessons together.
- Each person should share about a conversation he or she had with God this week.
- Come back together as a large group. Would anyone like to share with our whole group a conversation you had with God or one that you heard from someone else? (Omit if needed for time.)

LOOKING UP

QUESTIONS FROM WEEK 7

1. What was it like reflecting on the way Jesus gave up His body for you on the cross, on page 123 from day 1?
2. What did the Father reveal to you when you asked Him what it would look like for you to honor Him with your body, on page 125 from day 1?
3. What did God show you about your gender on day 2 on page 127?
4. On page 127 from day 2, would anyone be willing to share what the reality of the curse has been on your own masculinity or femininity?
5. On page 131 from day 3, what are secondary sources of love, pleasure, or security that you tend to lean on rather than Jesus?
6. What does accountability look like in your life, on page 131 from day 3?
7. How did you feel you were doing at meeting your body's needs on page 133 from day 4?
8. Share your experience on page 135 from day 5, when you asked God to help you accept the body He gave you, and you felt His love and acceptance as a good Father.
9. Share your experience on page 136 from day 5 when you pictured yourself in heaven in a new body with Jesus (Romans 8:23). How did you envision worshiping Him with your new body, and how could you apply this vision toward the way you worship Him with your current body?
10. What was it like offering each part of your body to God on page 137 from day 5? Describe the impact of this experience.

LOOKING AHEAD

- Break into your smaller groups again. Each person should share his or her main takeaway from this week's lesson. Then he or she should share his or her plan to apply something from this week's lesson to his or her life or how he or she has already.
- Come back together as a large group. Would anyone like to share a main takeaway or an application you had or heard with our whole group? (Omit if needed for time.)
- Preview next week's lesson by sharing its main topic and daily themes, or read the introduction to next week's lesson out loud to your group as they follow along. Remind your group that they will need to read the Introduction on their own if you don't read it as a group and complete days 1-5 before the next group session.
- What special prayer needs in your upcoming week can we pray over now?

Group Session Eight

Participants will have completed week 8 in their workbooks before the session.

LOOKING BACK

- Who would like to open us in prayer, asking the Holy Spirit to move in our midst?
- Break into smaller groups of two or three—these groups should vary each week. (Allow five to ten minutes.)
- Say this week's Scripture verse(s) to each other from memory. If time permits, also quote the verses memorized in previous lessons together.
- Each person should share about a conversation he or she had with God this week.
- Come back together as a large group. Would anyone like to share with our whole group a conversation you had with God or one that you heard from someone else? (Omit if needed for time.)

LOOKING UP

QUESTIONS FROM WEEK 8

1. Discuss these statements from this week's introduction on page 140: "It is through maintaining your vertical love relationship with God that you are able to maintain your horizontal relationships with other people. Your relationships with other people are like a spiritual barometer—if they are consistently unhealthy, your relationship with God needs a check-up." Do you agree, and if so, why? Is anyone willing to share a testimony of this from your own life?
2. Discuss this statement from day 1 on page 143: "The extent to which you value and love God and subsequently value and love yourself as His image-bearer is the extent to which you are capable of loving God and others well." Do you agree, and if so, why? Is anyone willing to share a testimony of this from your own life?
3. Look at the last exercise on page 143 from day 1 where you thought about the way you treat yourself. Do your thoughts, emotions, and behaviors give evidence that you love yourself the way God desires you to? Share what He revealed to you as you processed this with Him.
4. In the last exercise on day 2 and in the first exercise on day 3, (pp. 146-147), you identified relationships in your life that could use some attention, and you also identified some biblical responses. Would anyone be willing to share any action steps the Lord is leading you to take and your plan to follow through with them? Ask for a volunteer in the group to pray specifically for each person who shares.

5. What was it like picturing yourself as the servant in the Matthew 18 parable on day 4, page 150?
6. Read aloud to your group what forgiveness is not and what it really is, from day 4 on pages 150-51. What stood out to you?
7. From day 5 on page 154, would anyone be willing to share if you tend to overfunction or underfunction in relationships? Ask those who share if they would be willing to give an example of this. As a group, discern one step he or she could take to correct any over- or under-functioning. Then discuss as a group how this would strengthen the relationship.
8. From the last exercise on page 155 from day 5, is anyone willing to share a boundary they need to put in place in a relationship?

LOOKING AHEAD

- Break into your smaller groups again. Each person should share his or her main takeaway from this week's lesson. Then he or she should share his or her plan to apply something from this week's lesson to his or her life or how he or she has already.
- Come back together as a large group. Would anyone like to share a main takeaway or an application you had or heard with our whole group? (Omit if needed for time.)
- Preview next week's lesson by sharing its main topic and daily themes, or read the introduction to next week's lesson out loud to your group as they follow along. Remind your group that they will need to read the introduction on their own if you don't read it as a group and also complete days 1-5 before the next group session.
- What special prayer needs in your upcoming week can we pray over now?

Note: Next week, we recommend your group wash each other's feet during your group time. You will be tempted to skip this experience, but we want to strongly encourage you not to. This experience will be memorable and transformative for your group. You will want to let the group know what to expect so they can prepare accordingly. You will need to provide a bucket of water and a cup or small pitcher for pouring it, a small tub to wash feet in, a bar of soap, and a large towel(s) for drying feet. If you have never done a foot washing for someone else before, practice once before the group session. From our experience, some group members will feel uncomfortable at the idea and others may want to avoid it all together. Despite these hesitancies share with the group beforehand why you feel it is a exercise worth pursuing even though it might make some feel uncomfortable. If people decided to opt out, encourage them to participate as prayerful observers. We believe those who participate will share in a meaningful experience they will never forget.

Group Session Nine

Participants will have completed week 9 in their workbooks before the session.

Special preparation for recommended activity this week: We would strongly encourage your group to wash each other's feet during your group time. To prepare before hand, you will need to provide a bucket of water and a cup or small pitcher for pouring it, a small tub to wash feet in, a bar of soap, and a large towel(s) for drying feet. If you have a large group and are able to provide multiple sets of the above supplies, that is good to do more than one simultaneously. If you choose to include this activity, detailed instructions are given below. If someone wishes to watch rather than participate, that's okay as well. If this is your first time washing someone's feet, practicing once beforehand is helpful.

LOOKING BACK

- Who would like to open us in prayer, asking the Holy Spirit to move in our midst?
- Break into smaller groups of two or three—these groups should vary each week. (Allow five to ten minutes.)
- Say this week's Scripture verse(s) to each other from memory. If time permits, also quote the verses memorized in previous lessons together.
- Each person should share about a conversation he or she had with God this week.
- Come back together as a large group. Would anyone like to share with our whole group a conversation you had with God or one that you heard from someone else? (Omit if needed for time.)

LOOKING UP

FOOTWASHING AND QUESTIONS FROM WEEK 9

1. We have talked a lot about receiving in this discipleship experience, as it is the basis of the gospel. Today we are going to wash each other's feet to remind us what it feels like to receive, to practice honoring the body of Christ, and to obey what Jesus told us to do in John 13:1-17. Read Jesus's example and command in John 13:1-17 before beginning.
2. Follow these instructions for the foot washing experience:
    a. Ask that the group members sit silently throughout the experience, and explain that first they will wash someone's feet, and then that person will pick someone else's feet to wash until everyone's feet have been washed. (If you have multiple sets of supplies, you may have those whose feet have been washed to continue washing others' feet simultaneously). You may play music in the background if you choose.

b. Have group members take off their shoes and socks, and roll up their pant legs a bit if needed. Put their feet in the wash tub.
c. Begin washing someone's feet. Pray out loud for the person as you wash his/her feet.
d. Dry their feet with a towel, and let them put their socks and shoes back on. Now they are ready to wash the next person's feet.

3. If someone wishes to not participate, invite them to prayerfully observe.
4. Debrief afterward: What was it like having someone wash your feet? What was it like washing someone else's feet? What does God want you to take away from this experience?
5. On page 160 from day 1, what was it like for you to envision yourself among the global body of Christ praising Him?
6. On page 161 from day 1, what impact has the Christ-centered community you have experienced in this group made on your life?
7. On page 166 from day 3, would anyone be willing to share a personal testimony of James 5:16—confessing sin to another believer, praying together, and receiving healing? Or of speaking the truth in love?
8. On page 169 from day 4, would anyone be willing to share an action step the Lord is leading you to take in a relationship with another believer?
9. From day 4's example, practice a reflective listening conversation as a group. Ask for someone to volunteer a real-life topic for the conversation. If no one shares an idea, use this topic: I feel like you are not being honest with me. Ask for two volunteers to have the conversation. One volunteer should take the initiative to have the conversation as instructed on page 170. The other person should agree. The leader should set a timer for two minutes, allowing each person to share. After the four-minute conversation, debrief the group by asking the following questions: What things went well in this conversation? How could a conversation like this strengthen a relationship?
10. On page 172 from day 5, which areas of your life could use more boundaries?

LOOKING AHEAD

- Break into your smaller groups again. Each person should share his or her main takeaway from this week's lesson. Then he or she should share his or her plan to apply something from this week's lesson to his or her life or how he or she has already.
- Come back together as a large group. Would anyone like to share a main takeaway or an application you had or heard with our whole group? (Omit if needed for time.)
- Preview next week's lesson by sharing its main topic and daily themes, or read the introduction to next week's lesson out loud to your group as they follow along. Remind your group that they will need to read the introduction on their own if you don't read it as a group and complete days 1-5 before the next group session.
- What specific prayer needs in your upcoming week can we pray over now?

Participants will have completed week 10 in their workbooks before the session.

LOOKING BACK

- Who would like to open us in prayer, asking the Holy Spirit to move in our midst?
- Break into smaller groups of two or three—these groups should vary each week. (Allow five to ten minutes.)
- Say this week's Scripture verse(s) to each other from memory. If time permits, also quote the verses memorized in previous lessons together.
- Each person should share about a conversation he or she had with God this week.
- Come back together as a large group. Would anyone like to share with our whole group a conversation you had with God or one that you heard from someone else? (Omit if needed for time.)

LOOKING UP

QUESTIONS FROM LESSON 10

1. Do you feel paralyzed or energized by such a monumental mission God has given to you? Why?
2. On page 180 from day 1, which of God's seven ways did you circle as most relevant to you now? What do you need to do in response?
3. You read on page 181 from day 2, that every Christian is in full-time, lifelong ministry, no matter your occupation. What do you think about that? How does that change your perspective on your job?
4. On page 182 from day 2, you asked God if He wants to change anything—minor or major—about your current work in life. Who's willing to share what God revealed to them?
5. Discuss the following statement from page 184 from day 3: "Anything you don't share owns you." Do you agree? Why or why not?
6. On page 185 from day 3, what adjustments do you feel you should make to increase the investments of your time, talents, and/or treasures into God's kingdom?
7. You were asked on page 186 from day 3 to do something in addition to your normal routine this week to give additional time, talent, or treasure to someone in need. Who can tell us what you did this past week and how did that experience go?
8. On page 187 from day 4, how many of you rethought or rewrote your top five life goals after you considered the follow-up questions? How so?

9. On page 188 from day 4, you prayerfully considered where you are in your relationship with Christ and circled which of the five levels of spiritual maturity you think you currently are at. Who is willing to share which stage you marked yourself at? What do you want to do to mature even further?
10. On page 191 from day 5, who is willing to share your vision and mission statement? If you haven't finalized it yet, you can share what you have brainstormed so far. I'll read mine first. (Encourage your group to give feedback to each person who shares.)

LOOKING AHEAD

1. Break into your smaller groups again. Each person should share his or her main takeaway from this week's lesson. Then he or she should share his or her plan to apply something from this week's lesson to his or her life or how he or she has already.
2. Come back together as a large group. Would anyone like to share a main takeaway or an application they had or heard with our whole group? (Omit if needed for time.)
3. Preview next week's lesson by sharing its main topic and daily themes.
4. What special prayer needs in your upcoming week can we pray over now?

Note: Read through the recommended "Group Experiences" details and why they're important on pages 262-267. Though these experiential sessions are optional, we strongly encourage you to consider leading all of them because discipleship principles are more easily caught than taught. The first twelve sessions offer incremental growth while these experiential sessions offer potentially exponential growth—multiplication over addition. You will need to decide soon if you will continue meeting beyond week 12 for these experiences. Feel free to discuss these with your group to get their input. If you plan to do them, discuss logistical details in advance with your group so they can plan accordingly.

Participants will have completed week 11 in their workbooks before the session.

Note to group leader: prepare a TV, projector, or larger screen to show The 3 Circles video today.

LOOKING BACK

- Who would like to open us in prayer, asking the Holy Spirit to move in our midst?
- Break into smaller groups of two or three—these groups should vary each week. (Allow five to ten minutes.)
- Say this week's Scripture verse(s) to each other from memory. If time permits, also quote the verses memorized in previous lessons together.
- Each person should share about a conversation he or she had with God this week.
- Come back together as a large group. Would anyone like to share with our whole group a conversation you had with God or one that you heard from someone else? (Omit if needed for time.)

LOOKING UP

QUESTIONS FROM LESSON 11

1. On page 199 from day 1, who have you led to faith in Christ? Share the story if you are willing. Rejoice together for all those God has saved through your group's collective witness.
2. On page 202 from day 2, what are some false beliefs about repentance and faith in Jesus alone being necessary for salvation that you may have agreed with in the past or are struggling with now?
3. On page 203 from day 2, which obstacles keep you from being a witness who is convinced that Jesus is the only way for people to be saved? Why did you circle those obstacles?
4. Share your fifteen-second testimony with the group including the six words on page 205 from day 3. Then ask for volunteers to practice sharing theirs. Remind them that all of you are learning, and the group can help if you get stuck. Alternatively, you can have them get into pairs so that everyone has a chance to share. If you have enough time, people can share why they chose their six words for the structure of their story.

5. Ask, "How many people watched The 3 Circles video on day 4?" Regardless of how many watched it, watch it again together as a group because repetition helps (bit.ly/Circles3).
6. Assign them into pairs to each tell Jesus's story using The 3 Circles so that everyone has a chance to practice.
7. On page 211 from day 5, who would you like to witness to? Have a time of prayer for all the people who your group would like to share with. Pray both for those lost people and for those witnesses in your group that they will have the boldness to share with them.
8. Think about believers with whom you could share the witnessing tools you have learned this week, such as how to tell your story and Jesus's story. Share their names as well as how and when you could share with them.
9. It's recommended that after week 12 we spend two experiential sessions on sharing the gospel. One session would give us more time to practice and get reps with these tools and role play doing the whole thing together. The second session would involve us actually sharing the gospel in pairs with lost people. Would you all like to plan on doing these?

LOOKING AHEAD

1. Break into your smaller groups again. Each person should share his or her main takeaway from this week's lesson. Then he or she should share his or her plan to apply something from this week's lesson to his or her life or how he or she has already.
2. Come back together as a large group. Would anyone like to share a main takeaway or an application they had or heard with our whole group? (Omit if needed for time.)
3. Preview next week's lesson by sharing its main topic and daily themes.
4. What special prayer needs in your upcoming week can we pray over now?

Note: You need to decide if your group will meet beyond week 12 to do the recommended Group Experiences outlined on pages 262-267. If you plan to do so, discuss logistical details in advance with your group so they can plan accordingly.

Participants will have completed week 12 in their workbooks before the session.

LOOKING BACK

- Who would like to open us in prayer, asking the Holy Spirit to move in our midst?
- Break into smaller groups of two or three—these groups should vary each week. (Allow five to ten minutes.)
- Say this week's Scripture verse(s) to each other from memory. If time permits, also quote the verses memorized in previous lessons together.
- Each person should share about a conversation he or she had with God this week.
- Come back together as a large group. Would anyone like to share with our whole group a conversation you had with God or one that you heard from someone else? (Omit if needed for time.)

LOOKING UP

QUESTIONS FROM LESSON 12

1. As a group, draw the diagram in this lesson's introduction, element by element, starting with "spirit." Use a white board or a poster board if possible. Alternatively, each person could draw the diagram on a blank piece of paper. Briefly review the meaning of each element as you add it to the diagram. If needed, you can have someone read paragraphs two through four of this lesson's introduction out loud while someone else draws.
2. From day 1 on page 218, share something you are carrying as you run the race and what surrender would look like.
3. What was it like going through the Quiet Time Tool at the end of day 1? How was it helpful, and does anyone have any takeaways from this experience?
4. From day 2, share your spiritual gifts or those that resonated with you. Share how you are currently using these gifts and/or how you would like to in the future.
5. From the inventory on day 2 on page 221, share your progress as a disciple throughout these last twelve weeks.
6. From day 3 on page 224, share how the Holy Spirit led you to rank yourself regarding using the way you have stewarded the gospel so far.
7. From day 4, on page 228, share your plans for discipling others—the who, how, and when. What help do you need from anyone in our group to make that happen? Ask someone in the group to pray for each person who shares.

8. From day 4 on page 226, share how the statistics impacted you, and which surprised you the most.
9. From day 5 on page 230, share which five words you used to describe your vision of meeting Jesus.

LOOKING AHEAD

- Break into your smaller groups again. Each person should share his or her main takeaway from this week's lesson. Then he or she should share his or her plan to apply something from this week's lesson to his or her life or how he or she has already.
- Come back together as a large group. Would anyone like to share a main takeaway or an application they had or heard with our whole group? (Omit if needed for time.)
- Consider asking particpants to lead their own group by reading or saying the following:
    - I'd like to ask each of you to pray about leading a *MasterLife Together* group in the future. I'm going to send these questions to you and ask that you respond within the next week. I'll ask them now in case any of you know you are interested now and want to talk with me after our group time today:
        - Do you want to lead or colead a *MasterLife Together* group within the next year?
        - If coleading, with whom do you want to colead?
        - Which month do you want to start a new *MasterLife Together* group?
    - Please write a short (one to two sentence) testimony about *MasterLife Together* to encourage others to experience this in the future.
    - I will follow up with each of you to help you prepare for a group, according to your answers.*
- Explain the upcoming group experience(s), if applicable. If your group will not be meeting for these experiences, consider at least planning a celebration sometime in the next few weeks. See pages 267-268 for ideas on this session.
- What special prayer needs in your upcoming week can we pray over now?

**Note: Even if they don't plan to lead or colead a group in the future, encourage them to invite people they know who might be interested in going through MasterLife Together to join future groups—especially those that might form out of your group. If you don't know of any future groups, pass on the names of anyone who is interested to a pastor in your church to see if someone might be willing to lead a group. Try to keep the disciple-making momentum going!*

Recommended Sessions

These additional sessions are designed to enhance your group's application of what they have learned in earlier sessions. The first twelve sessions offer incremental growth while these experiential sessions offer potentially exponential growth—multiplication over addition. These group experiences can be done in one and a half hours, but if you are able, extending the length of these sessions to two to three hours each will be even more beneficial.

SESSION 13: PRAYER RETREAT

The purpose of this session is to experience a longer time with the Lord in focused prayer and to expand how you commune with the Father.

You will need to find a location where everyone can gather as a group but then go off to individual spots, preferably in nature. Ask them each to bring along their Bible and journal and their prayer notebook/list or worship music if desired. If these are on their phone, they should set their phone to "Do Not Disturb" and silence notifications during this time so they can focus on their communication with the Lord.

PART 1: INTRO (15-30 MIN) Before you split up, remind your group of the various ways to pray: praise, thanksgiving, reading Psalms or other Scriptures to the Lord, confession, intercession for the needs of others, listening to the Lord, journaling their prayers, and simply "being still and knowing that He is God." If possible, ask everyone to make a plan for their time in advance, and have them try to incorporate as many different types of prayer as they can—especially ones they have never experienced.

Pray for the group, inviting the Holy Spirit to meet each one and lead their time.

PART 2: INDIVIDUAL PRAYER (1 HOUR OR MORE IF POSSIBLE) Have everyone seek out a spot to meet with the Lord. Tell them what time they need to be back for the debrief.

PART 3: DEBRIEF (15-30 MIN) Regather the group and ask participants to report how the time went for them using the following questions:

1. How was it to have an extended time of prayer?
2. What was new for you?
3. What was the most significant portion of the time for you and why?
4. Is this an experience you would likely repeat?

Close out the retreat by having a group prayer time or praying a blessing over your group.

SESSION 14: PRACTICE SHARING THE GOSPEL

The purpose of this event is to further increase each member's confidence and competence in witnessing and give them an opportunity to practice with other Christians. Although not required, you can recruit volunteers to play the role of lost people with whom your group members practice sharing the gospel.

PART 1: INTRO (15 MIN) Participants should bring their initial testimony they wrote on page 205 in week 11.

As a leader, remind your group of the following important elements when sharing a testimony:

1. Keep it short so that the person listening will not become uncomfortable.
2. Tell what happened to you. It is your story that others want to hear. Do not say "you"; say "I" and "me."
3. Avoid negative remarks. Do not criticize religious groups or a specific church.
4. Ask yourself, *If I were far from God, what would this mean to me?*
5. Eliminate religious words. People who are far from God do not understand religious jargon like Sunday School, walked the aisle, got baptized, and so forth.

Pray together as a group that the Lord will use this time to refine testimonies and build confidence in each person as they share it.

PART 2: PRACTICE (1-HOUR MINIMUM) Break off in pairs. Invite participants to share their testimony with a partner and revise it as needed according to the guidelines. Invite them to practice sharing The 3 Circles from pages 207-208 in week 11 with each other, drawing it while explaining it. Once each participant is confident in sharing both their story and Jesus's story, they should practice telling both of them together with all of the questions and transitional statements suggested in week 11. During the first round(s), the partner can offer advice to help the other person improve at sharing the gospel. During the second round(s), the partner role-plays each of the following types of unbelievers: "green light" (ready to believe), "yellow light" (hesitant), and then a "red light" (resistant). Try to engage with each type of unbeliever by asking to hear their pretend spiritual story and looking for common ground that can bridge naturally to the gospel. With the "green light" person, be sure to practice leading them to place their faith in Christ. In role-playing, the partner should provide an opportunity for them to expand their testimony rather than critique them. After the role playing is completed, the person sharing the gospel should take notes and make revisions, if necessary. Then, you switch roles. The person who was listening to the gospel now practices sharing the gospel with the same partner they heard it from, and the person who had shared now listens and role-plays. Encourage each participant to keep practicing the telling of their story and Jesus's story during this experience and after, until they are ready to do so with an actual unbeliever.

PART 3: DEBRIEF (15-30 MIN)

Come back together as a large group, and ask the following questions:

1. What did you learn from this experience?
2. How did this practice refine your testimony and/or build confidence in you?
3. What would help you share your story and Jesus's story more often?

Pray together for boldness to share and for those He wants you to share with.

SESSION 15: SHARING THE GOSPEL EXPERIENCE

The purpose of this event is to give your group experience sharing the gospel with unbelievers and inviting them to place their faith in Christ. Believers are less likely to share the gospel without another believer locking arms with them and experiencing it together.

PART 1: INTRO (15-30 MIN) Read Luke 10:1-12,16 aloud to your group and begin with a time of prayer for those God has prepared to hear the gospel through you today. Tell them that they will be going out in pairs as the disciples in Luke 10 did to share the gospel with people they probably won't know. Pairing up to witness not only halves the rejection they may face but also doubles the joy when people allow them to share the gospel. Remind them to pray before, throughout, and after this experience of sharing the gospel.

Remind your group why it is important to share the gospel not only with people you know but also with those you don't know. People you already know are more likely to respond positively to the gospel, but some people don't know anyone who is a believer. If a stranger doesn't share with them, they may never hear the gospel!

Each pair should go on a prayer walk and ask the Lord to direct them to those they should engage with the gospel. This might be at a park, a common area at an apartment complex, or a shopping mall (when it's cold or rainy). A public place like these is preferable rather than going door-to-door to people's homes (unless it's your own neighbors).

As the Holy Spirit leads, they should start up a conversation. A good way to do so is to say, "We are followers of Jesus and are wanting to serve our community by praying for people. We would love to pray for you right now if you are willing. How can we pray for you?" If the person is open to prayer, the pair should pray out loud for them. After, they can say, "Thank you for letting us pray for you. It was an honor. One of the reasons I like to pray for people is because there was a time in my life when I was . . . [begin sharing your story]." Then they can ask the person, "Do you have a story like this?" or "Would you mind telling me about your spiritual background?" The pair should listen to the person's story carefully, looking for ways to bridge the gospel. Lastly, one person in the pair should share Jesus's story with the person. (The other person should listen and pray silently. They can also assist if needed!) One person might be able to better answer an unbeliever's question than the other. There are a variety of different evangelism environments and approaches, and some believers are able to share better in some contexts than others.

Prepare them for the four possible responses they will have when they share, as follows:

- If the person is a "red light," they should politely move on. You may say to them what Jesus instructed in this situation, "The kingdom of God has come near to you" (Luke 10:11).
- If the person is a "yellow light," they should exchange contact information and offer to meet again for a Discovery Bible Study.
- If the person is a "green light," they should lead him or her to repent and place his or her faith in Christ for salvation, and they should not abandon this "spiritual newborn." Have them follow up with the person to help them connect to a local church and small group for discipleship.
- If the person says they are already a believer, they should ask if they would like to learn a new way to share Jesus's story, and if they agree, teach them how to share Jesus's story. Then invite that person to join you for the rest of your prayer walk and sharing.

Divide your group into pairs. If you have an uneven number of people, one group can have three people. Tell them what time they will need to meet back up. Ask if there are any questions before groups head out.

PART 2: SHARING THE GOSPEL (45 MIN-1 HOUR OR MORE IF POSSIBLE)

PART 3: DEBRIEF (30 MIN)

Ask your group to share their experiences. Use the following questions to stir up discussion:

1. Describe your experience and who you were able to share with.
2. How did you experience the Holy Spirit at work?
3. In what ways did pairing up for this experience help you?
4. Is this something you would like to do again?

Consider meeting regularly (weekly, monthly, or quarterly) as a group to share the gospel in the community and put the next date on the calendar. Share with your group the following ideas for sharing the gospel individually in the future:

- **Church guests.** Ask your church for the names and contact information of recent guests to your church. When you make contact with them, ask if you can take them out to coffee to get to know them, and answer any questions they may have about your church or about God.
- **Friends.** If you want to share the gospel with someone you already know, invite that person to your home for a meal or snacks or meet at a coffee shop or restaurant. Paying for their food or drink shows you care for them. It also gives you sufficient time to have a gospel conversation. If you have a witnessing partner who your friend has never met, try

to make a natural connection between them. For example, you could say, "Jamey, I want you to meet Becky who has been a friend of mine for years. You two both love the same salad at this restaurant!"

- **Neighbors.** Consider visiting someone who is new to your neighborhood. Bring them cookies and invite them to your church or to an outreach event. You could even create your own outreach event such as a neighborhood block party or a cookout at an apartment complex.
- **Others.** The website blesseveryhome.com and its app helps you to pray better for lost people, learn more about the people in your community, and strategically engage them with the gospel.

Although in-person witnessing is the best, you can also share the gospel online with seekers by volunteering with a ministry such as Need Him Global (needhim.org).

Close the session in prayer. If you have time, have a group prayer time and pray over all the names of those your group shared with today.

SESSION 16: SPIRITUAL GIFTS EXPLORATION

The purpose of this event is to help your group to identify and discuss their spiritual gifts, confirm each other's gifts, and determine settings to try out various gifts.

PART 1: TEACHING ON SPIRITUAL GIFTS (15-30 MIN)

Download and print the Spiritual Gifts assessment freely available at lifeway.com/spiritualgifts for everyone in your group.

Begin with prayer, asking the Lord to give your group discernment and encouragement throughout the session. Read the passages on spiritual gifts: Romans 12:3-8; 1 Corinthians 12–14; and Ephesians 4:11-16. Remind your group of these purposes of spiritual gifts: to bring glory to God; to encourage, build up, and equip the body; and to demonstrate the love of God. Using the handout, briefly review the description of each gift and how it might be used in various settings within the body of Christ as well as outside it. Encourage discussion but limit debate on varied teachings.

PART 2: EXPLORING SPIRITUAL GIFTS (45 MIN-1 HOUR) Ask the participants to prayerfully indicate which gifts they may have seen demonstrated by the power of the Holy Spirit in their lives by putting a check mark on those gifts. They can indicate their level of confidence for the gift by underlining as well as checking for the gifts they feel more strongly about.

Depending on the size of the group, the next portion can be done as a whole group or in smaller groups, with an ideal group size of six or less. Allow each person to share what they have identified and why. Use the following questions to spur sharing:

1. Why did you place your check mark where you did?
2. What has happened in your life that confirms the presence of this gift?
3. How deep is your conviction about this gift?
4. Do your gifts cluster in one area of ministry?

Speaking the truth in love, other members may respond by sharing their observations of that person's gift(s) in operation. They might also identify gifts they have observed that were not included on the member's self-evaluation.

Before moving on to the next person, gather around that person and pray for him or her, asking the Holy Spirit to fill him or her and use him or her mightily through his or her spiritual gifts.

PART 3: ADDITIONAL EXPLORATION (15-30 MIN)

Bring the whole group back together and go through each of the gifts, asking participants to raise their hand for the gifts they possess. Use a white board or poster board to write the initials of each person next to the gifts he or she possess. Identify gift clusters that seem to have a higher concentration within the small group and consider what ways or avenues the Lord may be calling the group to minister together.

Now go back through each gift again, having your group share settings or opportunities in which they have used those gifts or seen others using them. Also discuss how different gifts can be combined for greater effectiveness in the kingdom, and come up with some examples.

Challenge each person to identify one gift they want to be more open to using. End with prayer, asking the Holy Spirit to do whatever He chooses through the gifts He has given to your group to expand Christ's kingdom and build up His church.

CELEBRATION AND COMMISSIONING SESSION

The purpose of this event is to help your group celebrate the completion of this discipleship experience and to commission them for further maturity and ministry.

The leader's guide for session 12 encouraged you to send these questions to each member and ask them to prayerfully send their answers to you before this celebration and commissioning. If possible, follow up with each person in your group before this final session to get their answers to the following questions:

- Do you want to lead or co-lead a *MasterLife Together* group within the next year?

- If co-leading, with whom do you want to co-lead?
- Which month do you want to start a new *MasterLife Together* group?
- Please write one to two sentences of testimonial about *MasterLife Together* to encourage others to attend in the future.

Even if they don't plan to lead or co-lead a group in the future, encourage them to invite people they know who might be interested in going through *MasterLife Together* to join future groups—especially those that might form out of your group. If you don't know of any future groups, pass on the names of anyone who is interested to a pastor in your church to see if someone might be willing to lead a group.

Try to keep the disciple-making momentum going!

Encourage everyone in your group to invite a few family members or friends who might be interested in participating in a future *MasterLife Together* group to this group's celebration and commissioning. If anyone in your group is planning to lead a *MasterLife Together* group in the future, invite your guests who are interested in participating to connect with them before they leave to learn the dates and exchange contact information.

Make it a fun time and include something to eat and drink—consider having a potluck. Ask members to answer these questions either before, during, or after the snack or meal:

- What is the funniest thing that has happened to you during *MasterLife Together*?
- What is the most embarrassing thing that has happened to you during *MasterLife Together*?
- What are you most proud of as a result of *MasterLife Together*?
- What are you most thankful for as a result of *MasterLife Together*?
- How has *MasterLife Together* impacted your life?

Consider giving a small gift to everyone in your group. Close in prayer by laying your hands on each person's shoulders and commissioning him or her to follow the Master wherever He next leads. You may want to include this phrase in your prayer: "I pray that this *MasterLife Together* experience has been a milestone and breakthrough for this person to help him or her find greater destinations of discipleship and experiencing God."

MasterLife Together

APPENDIX

Four Spiritual Rhythms

God designed much of His creation to function rhythmically—think about sunrises and sunsets, seasons, ocean tides, sleep cycles, and your heartbeat. You too will function at your best by establishing rhythms in your life. These four spiritual rhythms will help you increase your intimacy with Christ:

1. **DAILY DIVERT:** This is your daily quiet time. Spending time with God should be the foundation of your day, as it is the best way for you to grow as His disciple. Hallmarks of your quiet time should be listening to God through reading His Word and sharing your heart with Him through prayer. To have an effective quiet time, schedule a regular time for it, choose the best place to be alone with Him at that time, and follow a regular process that works well for you. (See week 2, day 1.)

2. **WEEKLY WITHDRAW:** This is taking one day each week to rest from your work. God calls it the Sabbath, and it is actually one of the Ten Commandments (Exodus 20:8-11). You can choose any day of the week to be your Sabbath, but it is helpful to make it the same day each week when possible. Use the Sabbath to engage in activities that are life-giving to you and to connect more deeply with God and those you love. (See week 9, day 2.)

3. **MONTHLY MOVE-OUT:** This is taking anywhere from a few hours to a full day each month to recenter your life around Jesus. Your monthly move-out can include reflection, journaling, worshiping through music, spending time in nature, or doing anything that recharges you and connects you more deeply to God. Try to schedule these times a year in advance—and fiercely protect them—as they will keep you healthy and safeguard you from burnout. The book *Solo* by Steve Smith is an excellent resource that will help you plan out and maximize your move out. (See week 5, day 5.)

4. **ANNUALLY ABANDON:** This is time away from your normal routine and ideally involves a full week off work in a different location to enjoy an extended time of rest and/or play. Be sure to schedule your annual abandon far in advance so you will have it to look forward to. (See week 10, day 3.)

Come near to God, and He will come near to you.
JAMES 4:8A

NEAR Process

N Name what you feel without judging yourself

E Experience & Express it all to God without holding anything back.

A Ask God to reveal His truth about Himself, about you, and about other people and circumstances involved.

R Respond to the Holy Spirit by doing what He says

Making a Prayer Notebook

Buy a pocket-size notebook or a mini composition book. Consider writing in pencil so that you can more easily update requests in the future.

You will divide your notebook into three sections:

First section—daily requests
Second section—weekly requests
Third section—monthly requests

THE FIRST SECTION is for your daily requests—those people or things closest to your heart. Each person or thing will have its own page. You can list as many or as few requests as you want—but start with one or just a few. I like to write seven requests and then pray for one each day. Both a simple and a more advanced samples are below:

SIMPLE
Joshua
Love for God
Integrity
Work hard at school

ADVANCED
Joshua
M—Love for God
T—Hunger and thirst for the Lord
W—Focused quiet times
TH—Victory over sin
F—Wisdom and vision for his life
S—Perseverance and grit
Su—Godly friendships

Make the last few pages of this section for "Etc."—this is where you can add in temporary requests that come up.

THE SECOND SECTION is for your weekly requests—those people or things you want to pray for once a week. You will have seven pages in this section, one for each day of the week. You can list as many or few requests as you want but start with one or just a few. A sample is below:

SUNDAY
My small group
President
Pastor Will
Shanks (Missionary family in Asia)
Maithili speakers in Eastern Bihar

THE THIRD SECTION is for your monthly requests—those people or things you want to pray for once a month. List as many or as few requests as you want but start with just one per date. Start by writing a circled or underlined *1*, *2*, and *3* vertically on the first page, giving space between each number (see below). On the second page, write *4*, *5*, and *6*; then keep going with three numbers (which represent dates of the month) per page until you get to thirty-one. Put a paper clip on the first page of this third section so you can find it easily. A sample is below:

1
Uncle Cliff and Aunt Krista
Mike and Elyse (neighbors)

2
Persecuted believers in Asia
Coworker Johnnie (atheist)

3
Ukraine
Jag (mailman—Hindu)

To pray through your new prayer notebook, begin on the first page of your first section, and flip through each page, praying for one request on each page. Then turn to the page in the second section that corresponds with what day of the week it is, and pray for all the requests written on that page. Then turn to the page in the third section that corresponds with what date of the month it is, and pray for the requests listed under that date.

At some point, make time to ask the people you pray for daily what you can be praying for them and ask God what He wants you to pray for them. Include these requests in your daily section.

Daily Check-In Tool

First, take some time to answer the following questions, as these will form your tool.

1. **In my current season of life, what are things I need to receive from the Lord each day? (Consider His embrace, His promises, His righteousness, His victory, His character, etc.)**

2. **In my current season of life, what are things I need to surrender to the Lord each day? (Consider your agenda, family, friends, work, money, standards, reputation, etc.)**

3. **In my current season of life, were do I need continued healing? (Consider places of illness or wounding in your body, soul, and spirit.)**

4. **In my current season of life, what are things I need to declare to myself and God each day? (Consider where you need to renew your mind with truth.)**

Now, you will take your answers and write them into the form on the following page. You will use this form as part of your daily quiet time by praying through the top part and filling out the bottom part. Alternatively—though more time-intensive—you can fill out the entire form on a daily basis. Consider photocopying or printing thirty copies at the beginning of each month, hole-punching them, and keeping them in a three-ring binder, like I do. Every month or two, reassess and update the blanks that correspond with the questions above to reflect your current needs.

Today's Date:

SPIRIT

Open my heart to receive and feel these gifts from Your hand anew today (insert your answers from #1):

- ☐ ______________________
- ☐ ______________________
- ☐ ______________________
- ☐ ______________________
- ☐ ______________________
- ☐ ______________________

I humble myself before You and surrender these to You again today (insert your answers from #2):

- ☐ ______________________
- ☐ ______________________
- ☐ ______________________
- ☐ ______________________
- ☐ ______________________
- ☐ ______________________

Heal me in these wounded places today (insert your answers from #3):

- ☐ ______________________
- ☐ ______________________
- ☐ ______________________
- ☐ ______________________
- ☐ ______________________
- ☐ ______________________

SOUL

Declarations for today (insert your answers from #4):

- ☐ I choose to
- ☐ I choose to
- ☐ I choose to

REFLECTING ON YESTERDAY:

I confess:

What I'm thankful for:

What was tough:

TODAY

I let go of these anxieties I am carrying today, giving them to you:

What I need from You today:

With Gratitude

Father God, thank you for entrusting us with Your work and empowering us to do it. Your faithfulness keeps growing our faith. This is all for You!

Granddad and Grandmom, thank you for praying for families of Christ-followers for many generations to come and for passing the baton to us. We feel so honored to steward your legacy of discipleship. We can hear you cheering us on from heaven!

Our parents, Ken and Lou Franklin, and Randy and Denyce Willis, thank you for rooting us in the Lord, loving us unconditionally, and releasing us into His hands.

Our children Joshua, Jenna, and Ethan, you are treasures. We love you deeply. Thank you for maturing us as disciples and for joining us on mission wherever, whenever, and however He leads.

The Willis families Randy, Sherrie, Wade, Krista, and Brett, thank you for believing in and supporting us.

Our prayer team, we are indebted to you for bathing this project in prayer. You did the most important work of all. May the Lord richly bless each one of you for your unseen labor of love. A special thanks to Mom (Lou), Andrew Franklin, Lanie Ehlinger, Mark and Jennifer Gragg, Jan Sharp, Susan Butler, Krista McAtee, June Gordy, Kari Shank, Amy Carlson, and Dawn Clifford.

Randy, Lanie, and Scott and Pam Reed, thank you for your careful eyes and attentive hearts in the editing process. Your investment of time and energy meant the world to us.

Linda Burke, Lanie, Sharon Rivers, Randy, and Scott Butler, thank you for being willing to lead pilot groups. Your feedback was extremely valuable to us.

Pilot group participants, thank you for keeping up with pages and pages of last-minute print-outs and our pathetic drawings so that we could figure out what worked best and what didn't. Thank you for being willing to get messy with us. You have encouraged us more than you know.

Fellow pastors at Calvary Baptist Church, especially Dr. Steven Ackley and Dr. Gary Chapman, thank you for taking time to give us your professional insights—they really helped shape our content and process.

Our first *MasterLife* group to lead together—Scott and Susan Butler, Tommy and Peggy Lott, the Reeds, Lanie, Linda, and Michelle Arias—thank you for trusting us, walking alongside us and loving us so well. You will always be special to us.

Joel Polk, Reid Patton, Jon Rodda, and the entire Lifeway team, thank you for your faith in us and for putting feet to our vision. Working with you has been a joy.

And to those who have believed in us and poured into our lives over the years—Carolyn Nuthman, Aunt Sally Burr, Coach Clay, Curtis and Tricia Bridges, John and Sally Repass, Johnnie Holland, Tonya Zunigha, Nathan and Kari Shank, Stephen and Gwen Smith, Scott and Barb Ready and many more—thank you for shaping who we are. We treasure each of you.

Recommended Resources

LESSON 1

Packer, J. I. *Knowing God.*

LESSON 2

To purchase a kit that includes verse cards and a vinyl holder to use for Scripture memory in the future, search online for "the Topical Memory System and the Navigators" (www.navpress.com/bible-studies/scripture-memory). Alternatively, you can create your own verse cards by cutting cardstock in a rectangle that is 1.75 x 2.55 inches. You can also use normal index cards.

LESSON 3

Morris, Roosevelt, Questions for Prayer and Personal Revival; available at bit.ly/3QZ4w0i
Murray, Andrew. *With Christ in the School of Prayer.*

LESSON 4

SCOPE International. *Be Transformed: Discovering Biblical Solutions to Life's Problems.*

LESSON 5

Moreland, J. P. *Love Your God with All Your Mind: The Role of Reason in the Life of the Soul.*

LESSON 6

Scazzero, Peter. *Emotionally Healthy Spirituality: It's Impossible to Be Spiritually Mature, While Remaining Emotionally Immature.*
Scazzero, Peter. *The Emotionally Healthy Leader: How Transforming Your Inner Life Will Deeply Transform Your Church, Team, and the World.*
Additional *Emotionally Healthy* books, workbooks, and a podcast by Peter Scazzero are also available.

LESSON 7

SEXUALITY

Franklin, Andrew. *Created for Love.*
Comiskey, Andrew. *Strength in Weakness.*
Stringer, Jay. *Unwanted: How Sexual Brokenness Reveals Our Way to Healing.*
Allender, Dan B. *The Wounded Heart: Hope for Adult Victims of Childhood Sexual Abuse.*
Thomas, Gary and Debra Fileta. *Married Sex: A Christian Couple's Guide to Reimagining Your Love Life.*
Powlison, David. *Making All Things New: Restoring Joy to the Sexually Broken.*

FOOD AND EATING

Bible study: *Food Freedom*, www.bodybloved.com.
Courses and support: www.findingbalance.com.
Podcast: Todd, Erin L. *Intuitive Eating for Christian Women.* Podcast audio. www.intuitiveeatingforchristianwomen.com/category/podcast/.
App: Downloadable from www.hellopeacewithfood.com/.

BODY IMAGE

Golbek, Aubrey. *Grace, Food and Everything in Between.*
Morgan, J. Nicole. *Fat and Faithful.*
Mackillop, Alexandra. *Faith, Food, Freedom.*

SCREEN ADDICTION

Reinke, Tony. *12 Ways Your Phone is Changing You.*
Murrow, David. *Drowning in Screen Time.*

LESSON 8

Terkeurst, Lysa. *Forgiving What You Can't Forget.*
Wilson, Jim. "How to be Free from Bitterness." www.storage.cloversites.com/gracecovenantpresbyterianchurch2/documents/Bitterness%20Article.pdf.
Cloud, Dr. Henry and Dr. John Townsend. *Boundaries: When to Say Yes, How to Say No, to Take Control of Your Life.*

LESSON 9

Bonhoeffer, Dietrich. *Life Together: The Classic Exploration of Christian Community.*

LESSON 10

Winter, Ralph D. and Steven C. Hawthorne. *Perspectives on the World Christian Movement: A Reader.*
Check the website perspectives.org to join a class happening near you.
Willis, Avery T., Jr. *MasterLife—Book Set: A Biblical Process for Growing Disciples.*
Willis, Avery T., Jr., and Sherrie Willis Brown. *MasterLife: Developing a Rich Personal Relationship with the Master.*
Willis, Avery T., Jr. *MasterLife Student Edition—Member Book.*
Brown, Sherrie Willis. *I Aim to Be That Man: How God Used the Ordinary Life of Avery Willis Jr.*
Blackaby, Henry T., and Avery T. Willis Jr. *On Mission with God: Living God's Purpose for His Glory.*
Warren, Rick. *The Purpose Driven Life: What on Earth Am I Here For?*

TIME MANAGEMENT

Raynor, Jordan. *Redeeming Your Time: 7 Biblical Principles for Being Purposeful, Present, and Wildly Productive.*
Hyatt, Michael. *Free to Focus: A Total Productivity System to Achieve More by Doing Less.*
Challies, Tim. *Do More Better: A Practical Guide to Productivity.*
Allen, David. *Getting Things Done: The Art of Stress-Free Productivity.*
Swenson, Richard A. *Margin: Restoring Emotional, Physical, Financial, and Time Reserves to Overloaded Lives.*
Earley, Justin Whitmel. *The Common Rule: Habits of Purpose for an Age of Distraction.*
Covey, Stephen R. *The 7 Habits of Highly Effective People.*

LESSON 11

The Bridge to Life illustration is another great tool for sharing Jesus's story, which can be found at www.navlink.org/bridge.
You can see an example of a seven-session *Discovery Bible Study* that Jeff Sundell designed called "The Seven Stories of Hope," which has a leader's guide, at www.ncbaptist.org/wp-content/uploads/stories-of-hope-dbs-1.pdf.
Coleman, Robert. *The Master Plan of Evangelism.*

LESSON 12

www.Imb.org/research/maps.
Peoplegroups.org.
Johnstone, Patrick. *Operation World.*
Johnstone and Wall. *Pray for the World: A New Prayer Resource from Operation World.*
Joshuaproject.net.
Finishingthetask.com.
Shank, Nathan and Kari Shank. "Four Fields of Kingdom Growth." Free PDF available online.

CHURCH PLANTING

Garrison, David. *Church Planting Movements.*
Garrison, David. *A Wind in the House of Islam.*
Smith, Steve with Ying Kai. *T4T: A Discipleship Re-Revolution: The Story Behind the World's Fastest Growing Church Planting Movement and How it Can Happen in Your Community!*

WEEK 1

1. C.S. Lewis, *Mere Christianity* (New York: Touchstone, 1996), 190–191.
2. For an excellent resource on loving others, see Dr. Gary Chapman, *The Five Love Languages* (Chicago: Moody Publishers, 2015).
3. Abraham Kuyper, *A Centennial Reader*, ed. James D. Bratt (Grand Rapids: Eerdmans, 1998), 488.
4. Deitrich Bonhoeffer, *The Cost of Discipleship* (London, UK: SCM Press, 2015), 44.
5. John Piper, *For your joy.* (Minneapolis: Desiring God, 2005).

WEEK 2

1. Andrew Murray, *With Christ in the School of Prayer* (Alachua: Bridge-Logos Publishers, 1999), 169.
2. From Justin Whitmel Earley, *The Common Rule: Habits of Purpose for an Age of Distraction* (Westmont: InterVarsity, 2019).
3. These rhythms are adapted from "Rick & Kay Warren Extended Interview," interview by Kim Lawton, August 11, 2006, Religion & Ethics Newsweekly, www.pbs.org/wnet/religionandethics/2006/09/01/september-1-2006-rick-kay-warren-extended-interview/3647/. See the appendix on page 270 for a full description.
4. Arizona Christian University Cultural Research Center, *American Worldview Inventory 2020: Millennials and Worldview*, September 2020, www.arizonachristian.edu/wp-content/uploads/2020/09/CRC_AWVI2020_Release10_Digital_01_20200922.pdf.
5. "Inaugural CRC Study: Dangerously Low Percentage of Americans Hold Biblical Worldview," Arizona Christian University, last modified March 24, 2020, www.arizonachristian.edu/2020/03/24/inaugural-crc-study-dangerously-low-percentage-of-americans-hold-biblical-worldview/.
6. "Competing Worldviews Influence Today's Christians," Barna Group Inc., last modified May 9, 2017, www.barna.com/research/competing-worldviews-influence-todays-christians/.
7. "Baptist Faith & Message 2000," Southern Baptist Convention, accessed May 12, 2022, bfm.sbc.net/bfm2000/.
8. Wilson Geisler, "Rapidly Advancing Disciples (RAD)" (unpublished manuscript, 2011), PDF file, 9.
9. *Hebrew-Greek Key Word Study Bible (NASB)*, (Chattanooga: AMG, 2008), 1720 on term #1897 and 1784 on term #7878.
10. Billy Graham Training Center at the Cove, *A Comprehensive Guide for Cove Guests*, Program Notes, 39.
11. George Patterson and Richard Scoggins, *Church Multiplication Guide (Revised): The Miracle of Church Reproduction*, (Pasadena: William Carey Library, 2002).
12. I learned of the sword method from Nathan and Kari Shank, "Four Fields of Kingdom Growth" (unpublished manuscript, 2014 version), 66. PDF.

WEEK 3

1. Adapted from Andrew Murray's *With Christ in the School of Prayer*, (Alachua: Bridge-Logos Publishers, 1999), 38.
2. Andrew Murray, *With Christ in the School of Prayer*, 18.
3. Andrew Murray, *With Christ in the School of Prayer*, 211.
4. "Richard Chenevix Trench Quotes," AZ Quotes, accessed May 13, 2022, www.azquotes.com/author/20980-Richard_Chenevix_Trench.

5. Similar to a quote by R.C. Sproul, see "Prayer Changes Things Quotes," Quotlr, accessed May 13, 2022, quotlr.com/quotes-about-prayer-changes-things.
6. From *Be Transformed: Discovering Biblical Solutions to Life's Problems*, (OKC: Scope Ministries International, 2001), 4.23.
7. The New Living Translation capitalizes "I AM."
8. Tim Keller (@timkellernyc), Twitter, October 30, 2018, 5:34 a.m., www.twitter.com/timkellernyc/status/1057203962934452224.
9. Andrew Murray, *With Christ in the School of Prayer*, 20.
10. Kevin Miller, *Come Hell or High Water: Stopping at Nothing to Build the Church*, (Bloomington: LifeRich, 2019).
11. Andrew Murray, *With Christ in the School of Prayer*, 124.

WEEK 4

1. John 14:16,26 AMPC; John 6:63; Romans 15:13; John 16:13-14; 1 Corinthians 2:10-13; Romans 5:1; 1 John 4:8-10; Galatians 5:22; Ephesians 1:17-20,3:16; 1 Corinthians 3:16.
2. L. L. Legters, *The Simplicity of the Spirit-Filled Life*, (Christian Witness, 1954). 51–52.
3. *Be Transformed: Discovering Biblical Solutions to Life's Problems* (OKC: Scope Ministries International, 2001), 5.11.

WEEK 5

1. *Be Transformed: Discovering Biblical Solutions to Life's Problems,* (OKC: Scope Ministries International, 2001), 3.6.
2. "John Newton," Quote Park, accessed May 18, 2022, www.quotepark.com/quotes/1008976-john-newton-i-am-not-what-i-ought-to-be-ah-how-imperfect-an/.
3. Adapted from *Be Transformed: Discovering Biblical Solutions to Life's Problem,* 3.28.
4. Adapted from *Be Transformed: Discovering Biblical Solutions to Life's Problems,* 1.8.
5. *Be Transformed: Discovering Biblical Solutions to Life's Problems*, 1.4.
6. Warren Wiersbe, *The Wiersbe Bible Commentary: Old Testament*, (Colorado Springs: David C Cook, 2007), 826.
7. Warren Wiersbe, *The Wiersbe Bible Commentary: New Testament*, (Colorado Springs: David C Cook, 2007), 653.
8. See the appendix on page 270 for the full list of our spiritual rhythms.

WEEK 6

1. Peter Scazzero, *Emotionally Healthy Spirituality*, (Grand Rapids: Zondervan, 2017), 19.
2. "William James Quotes," Quote fancy, accessed June 28, 2022, www.quotefancy.com/quote/934580/William-James-The-emotions-aren-t-always-immediately-subject-to-reason-but-they-are.
3. Adapted from the REED process in *Be Transformed: Discovering Biblical Solutions to Life's Problems,* (OKC: Scope Ministries International, 2001).

WEEK 7

1. John Paul II, *Theology of the Body*, Feb 20, 1980, www.vatican.va/content/john-paul-ii/en/audiences/1980/documents/hf_jp-ii_aud_19800220.html.

WEEK 8

1. Adapted from Andrew Murray, *Humility: The Journey Toward Holiness*, (Bloomington: Bethany House, 2001).
2. Rick Warren came up with this phrase—see Rick Warren, "What to do when you want to give up," Biblical Leadership (blog), August 26, 2019, www.biblicalleadership.com/blogs/what-to-do-when-you-want-to-give-up/.
3. See the appendix on page 270 for the full list of our spiritual rhythms.
4. Dr. Henry Cloud and Dr. John Townsend, *Boundaries*, (Grand Rapids: Zondervan, 1992), 30.

WEEK 9

1. Philip Yancey and Tim Stafford, *The Student Bible, NIV* (Grand Rapids: Zondervan, 1986), 1029.
2. Mark Buchanan, *The Rest of God: Restoring Your Soul by Restoring Sabbath*, (Nashville: Thomas Nelson, 2008), 88.
3. Dietrich Bonhoeffer, *Life Together: The Classic Exploration of Christian Community*, (New York: HaperOne, 1978).
4. "Three-Thirds Process," T4T Global, accessed June 1, 2022, www.t4tglobal.org/three-thirds-process.
5. C. Northcote Parkinson, *Parkinson's Law: The Pursuit of Progress*, (London, UK: John Murray, 1957).
6. Pete Scazzero, *Emotionally Healthy Discipleship* (Grand Rapids: Zondervan, 2021), 95.

WEEK 10

1. J.D. Greear, "The Myth of Calling," excerpted from *What Are You Going to Do With Your Life?* (B&H Books), *Outreach Magazine*, November 30, 2020, www.outreachmagazine.com/resources/books/discipleship-and-spiritual-growth-books-and-media/61586-the-myth-of-calling.html.
2. This paragraph is adapted from Ralph D. Winter and Steven C. Hawthorne, eds., *Perspectives on the World Christian Movement* (Pasadena: William Carrey Library, 2013), 37 and instructor's guide. Publication info needed.
3. Adapted from *On Mission with God: Living God's Purpose for His Glory*, quoted in Ralph D. Winter and Steven C. Hawthorne, eds., *Perspectives on the World Christian Movement*, 57.
4. Frederick Buechner, *Wishful Thinking*, (New York: HarperOne, 1993), quoted in "Theology 101: How to Understand Your Vocational Calling," Institute for Faith, Work & Economics www.tifwe.org/how-to-understand-your-vocational-calling/.
5. Sarah Eekhoff Zylstra, "How John Piper's Seashells Swept Over a Generation," The Gospel Coalition, March 20, 2017, www.thegospelcoalition.org/article/how-john-pipers-seashells-swept-over-a-generation/.
6. Francesca Tavares, "Only what's done for Christ will last," Christian Today, accessed June 8, 2022, www.christiantoday.com.au/news/only-whats-done-for-christ-will-last.html.
7. "Lecrae - Don't Waste Your Life," l-hit, accessed June 8, 2022, www.l-hit.com/en/83454.
8. Rick Warren came up with this phrase/concept—see Rick Warren, "What to do when you want to give up," *Biblical Leadership* (blog), August 26, 2019, www.biblicalleadership.com/blogs/.
9. The rest of the Four Spiritual Rhythms are found in the Appendix on page 270.
10. Avery Willis, *MasterLife: The Disciple's Mission*, (Nashville: Lifeway, 1997), 123.
11. "Stephen R. Covey," Quote Park, accessed June 8, 2022, www.quotepark.com/quotes/850469-stephen-r-covey-if-the-ladder-is-not-leaning-against-the-right-wal/.
12. Rick Warren, *The Purpose Driven Life*, (Grand Rapids: Zondervan, 2002), 17.
13. Rick Warren, *The Purpose Driven Life*, 236.

WEEK 11

1. International Mission Board, *Foundations*, (Richmond: International Mission Board, 2018), 47, www.imb.org/wp-content/uploads/2019/04/IMB-FOUNDATIONSMAG-English-v1.2.pdf.
2. "Understanding justification, sanctification, and glorification," Life97.9, Northwestern Media, July 6, 2018, www.life979.com/2018/07/understanding-justification-sanctification-glorification/.
3. Pew Research Center, *U.S. Public Becoming Less Religious*, "Chapter 1: Importance of Religion and Religious Beliefs," November 3, 2015, www.pewresearch.org/religion/2015/11/03/chapter-1-importance-of-religion-and-religious-beliefs/#paths-to-eternal-life.
4. Steve Cable, "Probe Religious Views Study 2020: Do Christians Believe in Christ as the Only Savior of the World?", Probe Ministries, last modified November 26, 2021, www.probe.org/probe-religious-views-study-2020-do-christians-believe-in-christ-as-the-only-savior-of-the-world/.

5. "What Do Americans Believe About God?", Lifeway Research, Lifeway Christian Resources, October 26, 2018, www.research.lifeway.com/2018/10/26/what-do-americans-believe-about-god.
6. 3 Circles is an evangelistic tool developed by Pastor Jimmy Scroggins and the staff at Family Church in West Palm Beach, FL which is stewarded by the North American Mission Board (NAMB) of the Southern Baptist Convention. For more infomation see www.namb.net/evangelism/3circles/ or lifeway.com/lifeonmission
7. *Life on Mission*, v. 3.0.0 (North American Mission Board, 2022), iPhone and iPad.
8. "Status of World Evangelization 2022," Joshua Project, Frontier Ventures, April 2022, www.joshuaproject.net/assets/media/handouts/status-of-world-evangelization.pdf—World Christian Encyclopedia.

WEEK 12

1. Adapted from Andrew Murray, *With Christ in the School of Prayer*, (Bloomington: Bethany House, 2001), 268.
2. J.H. Merle D'Aubigne, *History of the Great Reformation of the Sixteenth Century in Germany, Switzerland, etc.*, trans. H. White, vol. 4 (New York: RobertCarter, 1846), 183.
3. Lysa Teurkerst, *Forgiving What You Can't Forget*, (Nashville: Thomas Nelson, 2020), 81–82.
4. *The Wiersbe Bible Commentary*, (Colorado Springs: David C Cook, 2007), 485.
5. Spiritual gifts are also listed in 1 Corinthians 12:8-10,28-30; and Ephesians 4:11.
6. Adapted from *Discovering Your Spiritual Gifts*, Member's Booklet/Individual Study Guide, (Convention Press, 1989), quoted in Avery Willis, *MasterLife: The Disciple's Mission*, (Nashville: Lifeway, 1997), 142.
7. "Clarifying the Remaining Mission Task," Joshua Project, Frontier Ventures, accessed June 7, 2022, www.joshuaproject.net/assets/media/handouts/clarifying-the-remaining-task.pdf.
8. Paul Chitwood, "Why the mission remains essential work," International Mission Board, May 20, 2020, www.imb.org/2020/05/20/mission-remains-essential-work/.
9. People Groups, International Mission Board, SBC, last modified June 6, 2022, www.peoplegroups.org.
10. "Clarifying the Remaining Mission Task," Joshua Project, Fronter Ventures, 2018, www.perspectivesonmission.com/resources/Session10_ClarifyingTheRemainingTask.pdf.
11. "Status of World Evangelization 2022," Joshua Project, Frontier Ventures, April 2022, www.joshuaproject.net/assets/media/handouts/status-of-world-evangelization.pdf—World Christian Encyclopedia.
12. To research further, go to imb.org/research/maps or peoplegroups.org for the global status of Evangelical Christianity.
13. Nathan and Kari Shank, *Four Fields of Kingdom Growth*, (self-pub., 2014,) 143, 4-Fields-Nathan-Shank-Final-2014.pdf.
14. "The Amazing Countdown," Frontier Ventures, September-October 2009, www.joshuaproject.net/assets/media/articles/amazing-countdown-facts.pdf.
15. David Garrison, "Church Planting Movements: The Next Wave?", *International Journal of Frontier Missions*, Fall 2004, www.perspectivesonmission.com/resources/Session10_Garrison_ChurchPlantingMovements_Intro.pdf.
16. Ying and Grace Kai, foreword to *Ying and Grace Kai's Training for Trainers: The Movement That Changed the World*, (Monument: WIGTake Resources, 2016).
17. Victor John, foreword to *Bhojpuri Breakthrough: A Movement that Keeps Multiplying*, (Monument: WIGTake Resources, 2019).
18. Avery Willis, *MasterLife: The Disciple's Mission*, (Nashville: Lifeway, 1997), 86.
19. Robert Coleman, *The Master Plan of Evangelism*, (Ada: Baker Books, 2006), 99, 102.
20. Avery Willis, *MasterLife: The Disciple's Mission*, 82.

Scripture Memory Tool

I hope that you will continue memorizing God's Word after going through *MasterLife Together*. Here are some best practices I recommend to help you do this effectively long-term:

1. SMALLER CARDS Start using smaller cards of cardstock thickness so that you can easily review them, store them, and transport them. If you would like to purchase cards, you can search online for "Topical Memory System and The Navigators" for some preprinted cards. If you make your own cards, cut them at 2.55 (L) x 1.75 (H) inches.

2. CARD HOLDER If you memorize verses regularly, a card holder keeps those from the past two months in the same place. Available verse card holders accommodate the smaller cards. A packet or holder for your cards helps them to be portable, for multitaskers and travelers. Place your newest verse card in your clear outside pouch of the packet for quick review until you memorize a new card. If your holder has two flaps, you can put the newer verse cards that you need to review daily in one flap and the older ones that you need to review for that day of the week in the second flap. You can buy verse card holders and similar resources at navpress.com/bible-studies/scripture-memory.

3. FILE BOX The last resource you need for long-term review of memorized verses is a file box with seven tabs—one for each day of the week. After reviewing a card daily for two months, file it in your box in order from Genesis to Revelation and review it weekly. For example, if you have seven older verses memorized, you would review one on each day of the week in addition to your newest cards. If you memorize hundreds of verses, then you can gradually review your verses in a two to four week rotation to keep from getting overwhelmed. You can find these boxes online by searching for "Scripture card box" or "Scripture memory box." Or you can use a business card box or checkbook box to hold your older verses.

HERE ARE SOME FINAL TIPS

1. Be consistent with how often you memorize a new verse—for example, every Thursday.
2. Be consistent with which Bible translation you memorize verses in, though you can make exceptions.
3. Flip the card over the top rather than sideways which makes it quicker to review many verses. This requires that the verse is upside down from the reference on the other side.

Mark 12:30

Romans 12:1

Luke 9:23-24

Mark 12:31

John 15:7

John 13:34-35

Ephesians 5:18b (NLT)

Matthew 28:19-20

Romans 12:2

Romans 10:9

James 4:8

Hebrews 10:24-25

Come near to God and he will come near to you.

And let us consider how we may spur one another on toward love and good deeds, not giving up meeting together, as some are in the habit of doing, but encouraging one another—and all the more as you see the day approaching.

Do not conform to the pattern of this world, but be transformed by the renewing of your mind. Then you will be able to test and approve what God's will is—his good, pleasing and perfect will.

That if you confess with your mouth, "Jesus is Lord," and believe in your heart that God raised him from the dead, you will be saved.

Be filled with the Holy Spirit.

"Therefore go and make disciples of all nations, baptizing them in the name of the Father and of the Son and of the Holy Spirit, and teaching them to obey everything I have commanded you. And surely I am with you always, to the very end of the age."

"If you remain in me and my words remain in you, ask whatever you wish, and it will be done for you."

"A new command I give you: Love one another. As I have loved you, so you must love one another. By this everyone will know that you are my disciples, if you love one another."

Then he said to them all, "Whoever wants to be my disciple must deny themselves and take up their cross daily and follow me. For whoever wants to save their life will lose it, but whoever loses their life for me will save it."

"The second is this: 'Love your neighbor as yourself.' There is no commandment greater than these."

"Love the Lord your God with all your heart and with all your soul and with all your mind and with all your strength."

Therefore, I urge you, brothers and sisters, in view of God's mercy, to offer your bodies as a living sacrifice, holy and pleasing to God—this is your true and proper worship.

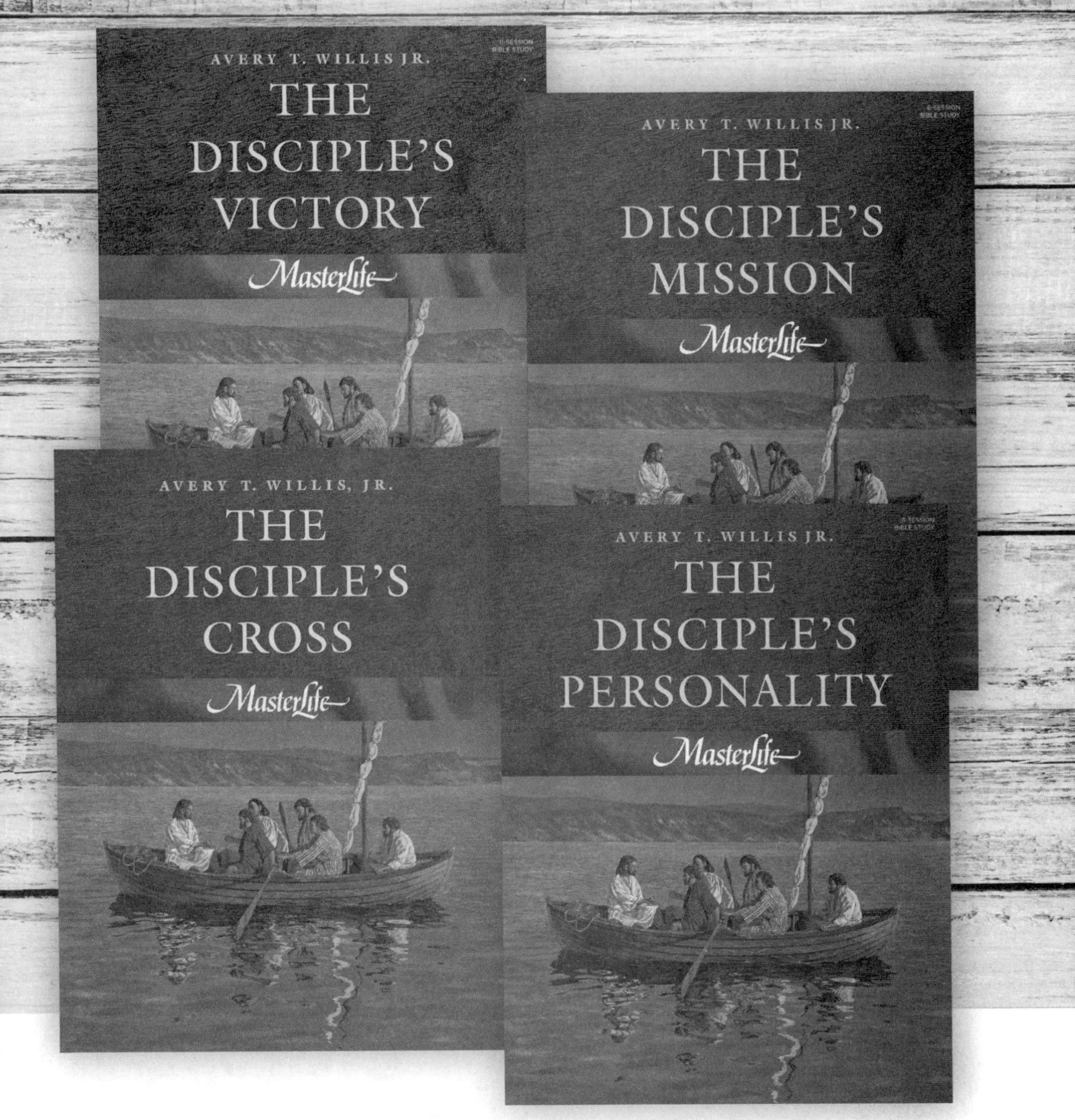
AVERY T. WILLIS JR.
THE DISCIPLE'S VICTORY
MasterLife
AVERY T. WILLIS JR.
THE DISCIPLE'S MISSION
MasterLife
AVERY T. WILLIS, JR.
THE DISCIPLE'S CROSS
MasterLife
AVERY T. WILLIS JR.
THE DISCIPLE'S PERSONALITY
MasterLife

Follow Jesus holistically as a committed disciple.

The exercises assigned throughout the week in this resource are often experiential and require participants to be vulnerable and reflect on every realm of their being—listening as the Holy Spirit reveals personal applications that will be shared in group sessions.

We encourage you to embrace this process, as it will add to the authenticity and accountability within your group. Through *MasterLife Together* you'll:

- Learn what it means to follow Jesus with your whole being—body, soul, and spirit.
- Develop a habit of being in God's Word, hearing from Him, and growing in intimacy.
- Experience the truths of God in a fresh way.
- Participate fully in the mission of Christ.

Are you ready to follow Jesus wholeheartedly?

Avery Willis's *MasterLife* has helped thousands of Christians progress in prayer, personal purity, living in the Word, witnessing, and other key disciplines of the faith. This updated study incorporates key components from the original version but is written for a new generation of believers. Simple yet comprehensive, this resource offers five daily exercises to be done individually each week, enhanced by the authenticity and accountability of a small group. *MasterLife Together* is a discipleship experience meant to help both new Christians and experienced believers follow Jesus with all that they have and all that they are.

Lifeway

lifeway.com/masterlifetogether

RELIGION / Biblical Studies / Bible Study Guides